John W. Root

JOHN WELLBORN ROOT

A STUDY OF HIS LIFE AND WORK

BY

HARRIET MONROE

WITH ETCHINGS AND DRAWINGS
BY CHARLES F. W. MIELATZ AND
FAC-SIMILES OF DESIGNS
BY MR. ROOT

THE PRAIRIE SCHOOL PRESS
Park Forest, Illinois

Library of Congress Catalog Card Number 66-29040
Printed in the United States of America

The first edition of *John Wellborn Root* was published in 1896 by *Houghton, Mifflin & Company.* The publishers are grateful to *Houghton Mifflin Company* for permission to reprint the text of the original book. The present edition is a facsimile of that first edition with new material added. New material includes the entire "Introduction" and a revised paragraph at the top of page 281 in Appendix B.

TO

MARGARET, JOHN WELLBORN, AND MARY LOUISE

THE CHILDREN OF JOHN WELLBORN ROOT

THE AUTHOR DEDICATES

THIS BOOK

NOTE.

The author desires to express her most grateful acknowledgments to the President and Directors of the World's Columbian Exposition, and especially the members of its Grounds and Buildings Committee; to Mr. Daniel Hudson Burnham; to Mr. Frederick Law Olmsted and Mr. John C. Olmsted; to the editors of the New York "Tribune;" and to the many other individuals who have permitted her to quote their utterances or writings, or have extended other courtesies expressive of sympathy with this work.

The plan of the work, which confines the architectural review chiefly to one chapter, has made it impossible to place the drawings in direct relation to the text. They are distributed therefore through the book approximately in chronological order. Large commercial buildings prove stubborn subjects for illustration in little. The stern Monadnock, for example, so resists every effort to reduce its proportions effectively that in these pages no drawing of it has been attempted.

An Introduction

by Reyner Banham

The last clear sight that Harriet Monroe affords us of her brother-in-law, John Wellborn Root, in a professional architectural situation is one that must endear him to every architect (or other professional man who has ever suffered from mealy-mouthed clients) – it is the justly-celebrated story of the interview (shortly before Root's death) between the architect and the prospective client who could not bring himself to be impolite:

> 'Well then, Mr. Root' – it was difficult for so polite a gentleman to confess his trouble – 'I like most of your buildings immensely, but – I do not like the Montauk block.'
>
> Root put his hand on his critic's shoulder and shocked him black and blue by exclaiming, 'My dear Mr. X, who in H--- does?'

This story is significant and revealing of more than Root's self-deprecating humor. It is, for instance, a pleasure to respect Miss Monroe's genteelism for 'Hell' and her most un-*Time-Inc.* reticence about the name of the polite gentleman, in honour of the pioneering quality of this biography which is, among other things, one of the first accounts of a business career to be written by a Victorian lady. For many present-day readers, this aspect of the book may loom larger than the fact that it is also one of the very earliest full-dress biographies of an American architect ever to be published – van Rensselaer's *Henry Hobson Richardson and his Work* is its only substantial predecessor, having appeared eight years earlier, in 1888. With our hindsight of Miss Monroe's later achievement as a poet, and her fame as the founder of *Poetry* magazine, we might expect her to over-write the creative-genius aspects of Root's career, but instead of producing a sort of prototype for that worst of all architectural pseudo-biographies, *The Fountainhead,* she manages – by the standards of her time and place – to fly remarkably straight and level.

Carl Condit has called her 'excessively adulatory,' but it must be remembered that she was not composing a doctoral dissertation a hundred year's after the events she describes: her book was published within five years of its subject's death, and Root was a person to whom she was so deeply committed that she contrived to work a reference to him into the Columbian Ode she was commissioned to compose for the Exposition of 1893. The fact that she stuck out for, and got, a thousand bucks for that Ode, and then stung a New York newspaper (the *World*) for damages to the tune of five grand for leaking the text ahead of publication date, suggests that of all lady poets of the nineteenth century, she may have been the best equipped by temperament to describe sympathetically, and in some depth, a professional's life among men of business in a Chicago with a very distinctive and masculine commercial ethos, a Chicago still, in many ways, raw and pragmatical and even piratical in its dealings.

In some ways, but not in every way, Chicago was also a city with a cultural tradition, and if we are less surprised at Miss Monroe's success in detailing Root's cultural ambience than at her bold stab at describing his business relationships, it is important to note how closely these two aspects of his work and world are related. In the general histories of America as a civilization, the importance of Chicago as a cultural focus is too often overlooked. To re-read Miss Monroe's *Root* is to be forcibly reminded, by the accumulation of small eye-witness details, that the city which arose after the fire of 1871 was not only money-mad and building-crazy, but could also support an architect who wrote music-criticism for the local press, music worth writing about, and a body of musical discourse that Root thought worth contributing to. Come to think of it, what other American city of the period would cough up a thousand dollars for an Ode?

In other words, the life – and therefore the work – of John Wellborn Root might never have taken place in Chicago had the city been the cultural slum that later tradition by un-checked hearsay insists on remembering. The legend of the Capone epoch dies hard, but Root's Chicago was not the kill-or-be-killed business jungle that Hollywood and Leftist literature have bruited about the world. It may well have been the siren call of business that summoned him to Chicago, but it seems extremely doubtful that the creative personality presented by Miss Monroe's account of Root could have survived long except in the relatively gentlemanly cultural milieu that she depicts around him. Or is this, too, a conventional genteelism? I think not – Victorian attempts to play up culture almost invariably involve an attempt to play down business and reveal a snobbish disapproval of 'Trade'. This she does not do. Even though she seems better equipped (in terms of stock of words) to discuss culture than business, the impression one gains is that she discusses neither except when they strike her as throwing a revealing light on her subject – indeed, her triumph is to integrate Root the man of business with Root the man of art, and to show or imply how both supported something which she cannot describe – Root the man of architecture.

It is dangerous, I know, to read between a dead author's lines, but I developed a growing suspicion that Harriet Monroe knew she was licked when it came to accounting for the way buildings got designed. She is no slouch at retelling a design-anecdote when it is to hand and relevant (a notable instance is the account of the design of the Monadnock block, of which more later) but she can hardly be described as a penetrating analyst of architectural design, nor a revealing illuminator of the workings of the architectural mind. This ought to be a crippling weakness in an architectural writer – though Miss Monroe was writing more than just architectural history – but it becomes, in the end, the third great strength of the book. To say this is not to play paradoxes, but to pay tribute to the authoress's constructive modesty. Knowing that she was licked, or out of her depth, she had the wit to let Root speak for himself, and her book is therefore an irreplaceable treasury of observations, aphorisms, essays, stray papers, philosophisings and technical disquisitions by Root himself. Much of this material has since become inaccessible in varying degrees, and we are permanently in Miss Monroe's debt for collecting and preserving for posterity a literary record that might otherwise have been forgotten.

So her biography of John Wellborn Root is a rope of

three strands: one, her account of the man of business; two, her account of the cultured Chicagoan, and three, an anthological autobiography of the architect. The three pull together, but the separate strands can be unpicked. One might prefer a more unified, more holistic vision of the man, but it is difficult to complain. Root — something of a Rationalist and ever the reasonable man — is less damaged by historical subdivision than more obdurate, rhetorical and monolithic architectural personalities might be — Louis Sullivan, for instance, and Frank Lloyd Wright even more so. Furthermore, it leaves open the possibility for later scholarship to strengthen the strands one by one, as information becomes available or criticism grows more profound.

Thus, it would be possible to build on to the Monroe *Root* without unbalancing a carefully integrated work of literary art, whereas it would take a very brave man to attempt any equivalent extensions to Sullivan's *Autobiography of an Idea* (which may be why his reputation has not yet undergone the re-appraisal it so urgently needs). But Root can indeed be so re-appraised, because Miss Monroe's book can be expanded in each of its main components. I doubt if there is much to be added to her personal narrative of the man of culture — though we English, as I have suggested elsewhere, would like to know more about Root's two years of schooling in Liverpool, and his possible acquaintance with Peter Ellis, the outstanding Liverpool office-block architect of that epoch, whose masterly Oriel Chambers was building in Root's Liverpool years, and may have fathered some of the better aspects of the Rookery.

On the business side we already have perspectives of extraordinary value opened up by Carl Condit's publication of the correspondence between Peter Brooks, the Boston financier of that Montauk block polite Mr. X. disliked, and Owen Aldis, his agent in Chicago. From this we can see that whatever originalities were proposed by Burnham and Root could be matched, and appreciated by their best clients, that the drive to rationalize the design of office buildings (rather than merely cheapen their construction) came from both sides of the drawing board, so to speak. And the Brooks correspondence also shows that the Monadnock block was a financier's triumph as well as the architects', and that the responsibility for its final form is to be laid somewhat at the feet of both.

And that final form of the 'stern Monadnock' as Miss Monroe calls it, points to the area of study where our knowledge of Root's architectural mind could best be extended. The key anecdote, related on p141, tantalizingly suggests that it was designed in a mood that may have included both a sardonic jest and an experimental enquiry, something like running the design up the proverbial flagpole and seeing if anybody saluted it. What posterity has been saluting with ever greater conviction for nearly seventy-five years, is strikingly at variance with practically every other building produced by Burnham and Root in its heroic and elementary simplicity. Yet that simplicity lacks any suspicion of the equivocations of jest, the uncertainties of experiment – and one might expect both in a design so far out of step with the rest of its author's work, and the rest of the School of which it forms a geographical and temporal part.

But is it architecturally a part of the Chicago School? Whatever its business rationale and structural rationalism, the architecture of the Chicago School was decoratively eclectic, and the legend of its noble simplicity is – from

Hermann Muthesius to Colin Rowe — a myth devised by Europeans for the correction of their own architecture, but subsequently visited by them on the architecture of Chicago as well (though no-one confronted with the recent work of Mies van der Rohe should find this a cause for complaint). But, as an historical guide, this myth is dangerous: it rests upon too small a part of the Chicago School's output. That is to say, it rests upon the Marshall Field Store, by non-Chicagoan H. H. Richardson; upon the Monadnock and the Reliance Building, both untypical of their periods in the Burnham office; upon the Carson, Pirie and Scott store, almost equally untypical of the work of Sullivan; upon three or four stunningly crude buildings by William LeBaron Jenney; and upon the best period of Holabird and Roche.

This, of course, is in itself a body of work that could shame any other city at that period, but it is less than half the worthwhile buildings of Chicago's golden period, the contribution to it of the dominant Adler/Sullivan and Burnham/Root partnerships was small — and much of it was built after Root's death in 1891. The living Chicago school that Root helped to animate was almost as prodigal of decoration as other comparable local schools of the Eighties and Nineties, and although he could be as sceptical verbally about the value of decoration as European Rationalists of the order of Auguste Choisy, Root continued — like most other Rationalizing theorists — to decorate his buildings. Most of them would be infinitely the poorer without their ornament — the Rookery for instance, both outside and in — because they were conceived from the beginning as decorated structures, even when that decoration was applied to masonry dressings that were in no way essential to the structure or performance of the building.

Yet the stern Monadnock would be no richer even for the addition of Louis Sullivan's notoriously superficial decorative arabesques to the surface of its structurally essential brickwork. It is a building of a different order to anything else produced in Chicago up to that time, conceived under a very special set of circumstances which included Root's absence from the office during the period when Owen Aldis was applying maximum client pressure in favour of radical simplification. Taking all this together, there emerges an extremely interesting point for speculation. Two related points, rather: how might Root have developed as an architect, firstly, had he not died before the Monadnock was completed, and secondly, had he been more continuously subjected to pressure from men like Brooks and Aldis?

Would he have gone on growing in masterly simplicity — the record of Holabird and Roche's work in the nineties and first years of the present century suggests that the Exposition did not make such a tendency impossible, in spite of the pious legends spread to account for the decline of Sullivan's work. But would a person as deeply committed to the Exposition as Root, so deeply involved with its basic stylistic committments — would such a person have wanted a more simple style? Or, against this, could more men like Aldis have forced him to hold to a simpler style? Suppose Chicago had been more like the tougher and less cultured place that tradition mis-remembers, would it have caused him to produce starkly rationalized monuments to business earlier in his career? It certainly appears that Chicago's respect for culture included a toleration of that eclectic decoration which constituted proof of a cultured approach to architectural design in the closing years of the last century — how else are we to account for the splurge of academic decorative art which covered the eclectic buildings of the Exposition? It may well be, therefore, that the cultural ambience depicted by Harriet Monroe permitted Root a degree of Victorian decorative self-indulgence that a less gentlemanly ambience might have persuaded him to forego for good.

This is only speculation; the kind of speculation that is encouraged by the evidence that the Monadnock affords of Root's superior understanding of the meaning of the Marshall Field store — superior that is to Adler and Sullivan's purely decorative imitation of Richardson's rustic arcading on the Auditorium building. Root, one feels, understood the lesson behind Richardson's structural forms, and carried its meaning a stage further forward. But it is also the kind of speculation that seems the more worthwhile in the light of Miss Monroe's full and rich presentation of the world in which Root moved, and his responses to it. She tempts us to historical speculation, and to suspect she had taken to heart a striking observation on the use of historical evidence that Root had uttered and which she herself quotes on p68, thus:

> It is, of course, very easy to say what men of other times did, but it is not easy to tell whether our conceptions of these men and their surroundings are true to the life, or are pictures painted by ourselves and without models. No building or architect of this or any other time can be a conclusive precedent until we get a stenographic report of the interviews which were held between the architect and his client, and even this is incomplete without a photograph of both.

Our concern in reading her book is not with historical precedents, but with historical understanding; but Harriet Monroe's devoted and sympathetic account of her brother-in-law comes very close to being an historian's or biographer's response to this ideal specification.

Reyner Banham

We have sympathized with sorrow, — you and I and all of us. But which of us has the rarer gift of sympathy with joy? And so who will listen while I try to tell the story of a joyous life? It may be that I cannot tell it. My heart fails here at the outset of the journey, when I remember the swift grace of this man's walk through life, and resolve to stumble on where he trod with lightness. The flowers whose seeds he scattered lavishly by the wayside may wither in my hands, and my garland prove but a poor tribute. And though I could pluck and wreathe them at sunrise, and give them to immortality with the morning dews still fresh upon them, yet even then must I acknowledge that these were but the bounty of a rich nature, and that the best was never given to the world. For certain men of genius live more for life than for art, and often fate indulges this secret preference of the soul by the tribute of scant opportunity and early death. Of such men, when they are gone, it is almost futile to speak the truth. The essence of their lives is as subtle as perfume; it passes like the song of a bird. Perhaps it would be better that none should attempt to preserve it; that we should intrust it to the magnanimity of Nature, as we intrust the mysteries of color and sound, sure that, though light yield to darkness and music to silence, the glory of them will wake again and endure through innumerable changes forever.

But this man of genius was lavish of his joy. Not yet may it fade into the infinite and the eternal, like that of flowers, and children, and women's faces, and days of June. To-day or to-morrow the world will make demand of those who knew him concerning the soul whose word, half uttered, was yet so eloquent. And so I, who knew him well, will turn back over the years of our intercourse, reproaching at every step the pitiful weakness of memory, longing for some magic lamp to illumine the path once bright.

CONTENTS

LIST OF ILLUSTRATIONS

JOHN WELLBORN ROOT

LIFE OF JOHN WELLBORN ROOT

I

ANCESTRY AND CHILDHOOD

MANY varying qualities of race and character were united in John Wellborn Root, who was born in the little town of Lumpkin, Georgia, January 10th, 1850, the first child of Sidney Root and Mary Clark, his young Southern wife. Sidney Root is descended from good New England stock. His relatives — sturdy, honest, simple-hearted Puritans — still plow and sow and reap in northern Vermont and western Massachusetts, along the beautiful valley of the Connecticut. The Roots are supposed to be of French origin, Huguenots expelled from France and taking refuge in England, whence, a few generations later, so many of them emigrated to the colonies that the name is now rare in Great Britain and unknown in the parish of Badby, where the refugees originally settled. The American Roots have been tall, athletic men, loving an active out-of-door life, independent and fearless, hospitable, liberal, never tainted with parsimony, finding it easier to make money than to keep it. The family history shows them observant and quick-witted but rarely studious, good talkers, keenly humorous even to sarcasm, lovers of music, in which they often attained great skill, and somewhat more energetically devout than their neighbors, their strong religious faith manifesting itself rather in good works than in meditation and spiritual communion.

Sidney Root inherited many of the family traits, but proved more imaginative than the business tendencies of his race allowed. In early youth he shocked his parents by expressing a desire to study architecture, and his father thereupon did his part toward knocking this lawless impulse out of the boy's head by apprenticing him to a jeweler. He was scarcely twenty when a roving disposition carried him South. The town of Lumpkin, where he settled and opened a dry-goods shop late in the forties, was a typical Georgia village of the time, a scanty collection of wooden shops and dwellings, deriving its life from the plantations surrounding it. Notwithstanding the Southern prejudice against trade, and the growing prejudice against Yankees, Sidney Root gradually found a welcome in the attractive homes of the neighboring country, and promptly fell in love with the sixteen-year-old daughter of Judge Clark. She was a pretty girl, small and slight, sweet as a peach-blossom, and with something of its delicate perfume surrounding the innocent beneficence of her life. She was one of many children born to James Clark by Permelia Wellborn, his second wife. Her parents had lived together sympathetically in spite of contrasting traits of character. Judge Clark being extremely taciturn and his wife unconquerably loquacious, the peace of the family was preserved by the Judge's power of placidly accepting the stream of her talk as a soothing background for his meditations, with which it never interfered. Permelia administered her husband's plantations, entertained largely, and cared for a large family and many slaves with unfailing ability and kindness, thus giving her husband time for his devotions and meditations. For no one could penetrate the intense reserve of this Southern jurist, a reserve which grew upon him with years, and left him in his later life absolutely cut off from human sympathy. For years he wrote voluminously, wrote all the time, but no one ever unlocked his iron secret or received from his lips one word of the strange long tale he entrusted to ink and paper for the precarious chance of immortality. And, at last, with heroic consistency he destroyed that chance. Shutting his heart still deeper in its dark chamber of reserve, he burned the manuscripts which might have enlightened or bored the world with the record of a lonely soul. But he was a man of singular force and originality of judgment. In the thrilling days of secession, when Southern patriotism flamed into fever, he was the only prominent man in Atlanta who persistently opposed the war, and predicted the ultimate triumph of the North. And many other incidents of his career proved his exceptional firmness of will and sanity of intellect. He was an able jurist, and the brother and father of lawyers and judges who have practiced before the bar of Georgia, and presided with honor and ability over her district and supreme courts. A somewhat prim and unimaginative race, the Clarks have still a delicate old-world charm and dignity. Their prejudices are even now colonial, their culture smacks of Addison, they read Pope reverently, and quote Latin in their speeches, and dislike to give up even for an hour the well-ordered stateliness of their simple life, with its gentle rectitude of purpose and its assurance of deference, for any contact with the expansive, progressive, iconoclastic forces of the modern world.

But if Judge Clark was taciturn, and his people close bound by formulæ, his loquacious wife came from a more eloquent race, a race of extremists who followed enthusiasm as the law of life, and exalted passion into mysticism. Of such was her brother John Wellborn, whose name was given to the hero of this memoir. Until middle life he walked the ways of this world even as other men, practicing law, going to Congress — in days when election to this post counted much in honor — and living with fastidious daintiness, unwedded but widely loved. When past forty the course of his life was revolutionized by a profound religious experience. He accepted literally the most rigid commandments of Jesus; gave all his property to the church, discharged his valet, and conquered his luxurious tastes, accepting utter poverty with all its consequenses. And for the remaining seven years of his life he wandered about the country preaching to the poor.

It was into this serious race of thinkers and devotees that Sidney Root brought his Northern energy, his latent love of beauty and the arts, his swift imagination, keen sense of humor and facile tongue. The alert young stranger easily captivated the sweet little loyal-hearted Southern girl, and married her in their youth, when the bride was seventeen and the bridegroom twenty-five. Mary Root was a creature of exquisite gentleness, simple, modest, religious; with a soft voice and winning manner, and all womanly tact and discretion. She had no humor, but she was not strenuous; through swift contrasts of fortune she moved always with serenity and grace. Sympathetic and widely charitable, she won the hearts of rich and poor alike as naturally as a flower wins bees. And no one knew the extent of her beneficent influence until the tributes of love and sorrow came pouring in after her death, from friends and strangers, from persons of every condition. Thus North and South, the new and the old ideas, met when these two were married in the little Baptist church one sunny, flowery April morning. The story of their early housekeeping is too simple to demand the telling — an idyl which moved serenely through a daily round of happy incident. When the promise of a new life came to sweeten their marriage, the young husband at once laid definite plans for the character of the son he hoped for, and inspired his wife with his own desire. He must be artistic, this boy of the new era; he must love music, and poetry, and pictures, and all the countless manifestations of beauty. He must be an architect, and practice the fine profession which his father had longed to study. He must do great things for the loveliness of God's world. The young dreamers never tired of forecasting their unborn son's career, the wife catching her husband's enthusiasm and glowing with the hope of giving to the world a man of a type which she had never known and which her race could never have understood.

And at last the son was born and the little life commenced which was to fulfill or disappoint their desire. The child, thus dedicated to art, the young mother consecrated also to the faith by giving him the name of her saintly uncle; and John Wellborn Root became a living, growing entity in the mighty world. A very important entity his parents found him, full of lusty life, untiring in its demands, and guiltless of any taint of weakness from the day of his birth.

As the years passed the young parents found almost as much reason to fear as to hope for their son's career. He was precocious in developing artistic accomplishments, and he learned easily, but all the parental pleadings and punishments could not conquer his laziness or keep him from playing tricks whenever he saw the chance of a laugh. Being sent out one day to cut the grass, he was found lying on his stomach snipping the blades with shears. When his father invited company and served a fine ripe watermelon, the knife cut into an empty rind, and the young culprit who had dexterously abstracted the contents was found chuckling in a corner. And punishment added zest to his pleasure instead of marring it. He had a strong preference for

Hall, House of Augustus H. Byram

managing his life in his own way, and though his methods were not in the least violent, no one ever succeeded in assisting or retarding much a development which was as unconscious, as guiltless of subjective care and planning, as that of a tree.

Mary Root used to say that her son could sing before

he could talk, and that he never made a discord with the toy violin which was given to him at the mature age of two years. His sister recalls his delight in drawing; her earliest recollection shows her sitting for her portrait at the age of three to an artist of seven. Mr. Root decided early that his son should become an architect, so when the family moved to Atlanta a small room in the new house was set apart as a studio, and there John devoted a portion of every day to drawing. Even then he did not like to copy, preferring original subjects. He made a pack of cards, in which the face cards were portraits of various children, the queen of hearts being the reigning belle of the neighborhood.

A piano was purchased when the boy was twelve. Though the instrument was new to him, he sat down and played several airs with apparently no effort, seeming to have intuitively a good touch. Until he was ten he studied at home, and was then well enough advanced to enter classes of boys several years older than he, and lead them with ease, especially in arithmetic. The only punishment he ever suffered at this school was for drawing caricatures of his teacher. He was a strong, perfectly healthy boy, large for his age and absolutely fearless. He would climb the highest trees, and sway with the breeze in the topmost boughs. At thirteen his father made him carry a sworn statement of his age, to prevent his being drafted by conscription officers, who thought him three years older.

Sidney Root became active in the service of the Southern Confederacy, and invested his capital in blockade runners, swift steamers built on the Clyde to elude the Federal guard at Confederate ports and bring merchandise to the beleaguered States. Although one third of the cruisers fell to the enemy, the profits of the successful runs made a large fortune for the investor before the close of the war. Mr. Root was in the confidence of the authorities at Richmond, and was intrusted by President Davis with special missions to one or two foreign courts. While he was absent on one of these embassies occurred the siege of Atlanta, and it was long before he could learn the fate of his family and home.

The idea of war was robbed of its glamour for Southern children at that time. During the siege the soldier was a very bedraggled person, by no means on dress parade. Little people were kept in cellars, for shells flew too often and too near. One day John Root pried open one of these destructive demons and found it stuffed with harmless sawdust instead of powder and scrap. Broken shells were children's playthings, and the two great armies playing their mighty game through that hot July made pretty fireworks on the mountain by night and dim smoky lines by day. The dreadful drama grew so familiar that people forgot it and even the boys learned to keep out of range or to tempt danger, as boys will, careless of the present and fearful only of the Yankee monsters who might burn the city soon and massacre its inhabitants. For the negroes filled young minds with imaginary terrors, and pictured General Sherman as the giant of a fairy tale. I have often heard John tell of the entrance into the city of "Old Tecumseh," the ruthless conqueror about whose head the boy, in spite of fourteen years of wisdom, vaguely expected to find traces of this lurid halo of horror. But neither the glory nor the terror of war lodged in this grim, battered warrior, unwashed, unshaven, shabbily clad from soft hat to dusty top boots, who raised the Stars and Stripes over Atlanta and marched on to the sea.

The invading army took possession of the town, and the residences of the Clarks and the Roots sheltered Federal generals in unwonted comfort. All non-combatants were ordered to leave the city within twenty-four hours, and homes of rich and poor, white and black, were emptied into the wasted fields. At the order, the little wife of Sidney Root valiantly gathered her children and a handful of valuables together, and departed into the wilderness. It was an exciting story as she told it, always without trace of bitterness, a story of hardship and hunger, for travel was difficult and provisions scarce in that impoverished war-ridden country; not a long story, however, for she soon reached one of the Clark plantations, and brought the incredible and disastrous news to her relatives.

Weeks passed before she returned to her home, after the departure of the Northern troops. As John could do little studying in these turbulent times, Mr. Robert T. Wilson, an old friend and business associate of Sidney Root, offered to take the boy with him to England, whither he was about to sail on one of the blockade-runners, which he partly owned. John and another boy reached safely the port of Wilmington, N. C., whence the slippery gray cruisers sailed, but fortunately too late to take the boat they were booked for, which was captured on the way out by the Union ships. Soon after, however, on a foggy night, Mr. Wilson and the two lads boarded another. Swiftly and silently the unlit steamer, gray as the fog which wrapped her, stole out of the harbor and into the invisible sea. No voice was lifted, no signal rung, as the brave ship steered past the armed sentinels of the North and toward the hospitable ocean. A few vague shots were fired at her in vain as she slipped between the national outposts. She made a good run to Liverpool, and the young travelers were received into the household of the English partner of Sidney Root, whence John writes to his sister of his journey, under date of November 17th, 1864.

"I am here in Liverpool at last, after being on the ocean 18 days. We came through the blockade without having but three shots fired at us, and arrived in Bermuda after 2 1-2 days passage. How you would have relished and appreciated the beautiful bay, crowded by stately ships and graceful steamers, and above all the beautiful village of St. George, almost buried in the lap of the bright green hills, whose fortress-capped summits bristled with heavy cannon. Very many soldiers with bright scarlet coats and black pants strutted through the streets, and looked as neat and prim as Confederate soldiers are dirty and ragged. We sailed in a steamship called the Mileta, a large boat over 250 feet long and about 30 feet broad, or over twice as long and nearly as broad as Father's store was in Atlanta. You can't imagine how blue the sea nor how white and beautiful the gulls looked. After being over 15 days on the way we arrived safely in Liverpool. From the place where we anchored we could see the long line of shipping (over 7 miles in length) and the almost numberless ships that steamed or sailed through the bay. Some were being dragged through the water by curious-looking little boats called 'Tuggs.' The wharfs are built of solid granite and surrounded by tall warehouses.

"As we steamed up the bay I noticed a large buoy, on the top of which was a bell, continually ringing, so as to let the sailors know where the shallow water is. The shores are lined with light-houses wherever the water is not deep enough for navigation, or wherever there are rocks on which a ship would probably be wrecked. Liverpool is a place with about 400,000 inhabitants, the streets are lined with handsome buildings and thronged with people. Cabs and drays rattle along the street. The sun does not shine as brightly, and the climate is not as fine as that of the south, but the atmosphere is smoky and damp. Mr. Beach lives in a large house, and it is elegantly furnished. I wish very much that you, with Mother, Father, and Brother, could be here."

A very proper letter, with its touches of schoolboy primness and grandiloquence, with its noble respect for commas, and its evidence, through the youngness of it, of a keen observant eye and a mind in love with color and sunlight. He was put to school in Claremont, near Liverpool, where

House of Sidney A. Kent

the bent of his mind toward architecture and music was fostered by special courses. Already his teachers feared for his facility. One of them, a distinguished organist of Liverpool, told him he would never make a good musician because he had too ready an ear — so the boy wrote home, adding, "in drawing and singing I have been as successful as my most flattering hopes would have foretold." Now, as always, beauty was the chief thing in the world for him; his heart thrilled to the appeal of the arts. He wrote compositions, not on this or that dry, familiar subject — the perfunctory themes which schoolboys usually select, but dedicated to "Poetry," or some other manifestation of the divine harmony, all glowing and fervent with his delight in it. "Few persons exist, and but few deserve to exist," writes this young enthusiast, "who have not in their souls that which echoes each strain of Nature's music, and thrills with delight in the perusal of each line of Nature's poetry, — poetry written on every leaf, and on every enchanting landscape. There is a certain class of men whom I must exclude from this large number: these are Hard-fact men, — dry, disagreeable, and as harsh and grating as a file; to whom all poetry is but the manifestation of lunacy out of confinement. Poor wretches! worn and dusty with the travel of the world, yet refusing the draught of invigorating nectar, which springs from every mossy bank and every mountain-side!

"I know that the world is real" — and the young philosopher makes a solemn face and tries to turn from the flowers along the wayside to the stones on the road. "He who would win in the great human race must devote himself with unflinching determination to his task. Yet it is not the race of a day which he must run, nor is it a course which calls for grasping ambition and unyielding selfishness. He who would win the highest prize must quaff deeply of the cup which gives new life, and read each page of the great folio in which Nature has written her majestic poetry.

"Need I attempt to define this poetry of the heart?" (Now we hear tender rhapsodies.) "Who has not felt its influence unmistakably? Oh, silver Moon, who shall say how many a love-lorn lad has watched thee and felt thy magic power until his heart has overflowed with romance and sentiment! Who shall say how many a sonnet to Carissima's eyes or Delecta's many charms may not be attributed to thy power! And twinkling stars, through which the glory of heaven shines, how much of earth's misery do you not see lightened and removed under your nightly vigils!"

And then he quotes poetry to prove his point, and continues: "What is all the written poetry which floods the world, but faint transcriptions from this great book? The appreciation of all that poets have written, as the expression of their own imagination, depends on the similarity which exists between their thoughts and our own. What could be more stupid and uninteresting than Tennyson's 'Brook,' if we had not heard the low thrilling murmur of some mountain rill? What more unintelligible than some tale of love or constancy, except as we have felt some twinge at the heart, or know something of what constancy means?"

The lad's rhapsody concludes with the inevitable moral. "Let each one of us strive to unite to high lofty aims this love of Nature and this appreciation of the revelations she makes to us, and our life cannot fail to be in itself an unwritten poem, with passages as sublime as any Homer wrote."

A youthful confession of faith, but sincere and ardent, and one which, after all, the course of his after life interpreted and proved. The arts were all his familiars; from boyhood he wrote verses, played, sang and drew with intuitive ease; and later he found that modeling came within his scope. His drawing, from the first, was architectural; conventionalized design, rather than pictorial realism, was the instinct of his talent. And a strong taste for mathematics emphasized and gave balance to this bias toward architecture, the most rigorous and geometrical of the arts.

The boy remained nearly two years in the English school,

holding his own as easily in athletics as in scholarship. In May, 1866, he writes: "I have grown a great deal. Last midsummer I weighed 141 pounds, and now I suppose I weigh much more. I am about the strongest boy in school, where I have a large number of friends and no enemies." Again he records winning the first prize "for the 100 yard heat and the high jump — the latter 5 feet 2 inches in height." He did his share of pommelling in defense of his boyish honor, especially when an English boy or two dared call him Yankee, a title which his Southern education made odious. In June, 1866, at the age of sixteen, he passed the examinations for Oxford University with the degree of A. A., but never matriculated there, as, soon after, to his exuberant delight, he was recalled home.

The war was over now, and Sidney Root had removed his family to New York, where he was living sumptuously, making unlucky investments, and beginning to lose his large fortune more rapidly than he had won it. John was sent to the University of the City of New York, entering the class of '69 as a sophomore in September, 1866, selecting the engineering course. Here, as elsewhere, he stood easily near the head without exerting himself, and conquered all hearts with which he came in contact. He was appointed Junior Orator and Commencement Orator, took the first Butler Eucleian Essay prize, and was made vice-president of the Eucleian Society. One of his class-mates, Mr. Robert W. Haskins, testified after Root's death to the charm of his young personality.

"Every student felt the glow of his bright, genial spirit," he wrote in the *Delta Upsilon Quarterly*, "while to an inner circle was given a friendship peculiar, original, potent in itself. He was so loyal and just, alike in service and affection to professors and students that, in the accidents of college life, if Root tripped, not more deftly could the son of Jupiter string the remnants of the stolen oxen to the tortoise and charm away Apollo's ire, than he adjust the impulsive word or act" so that one loved him the more. Mr. Haskins refers to his cleverness in the class-room, always

Dining Room, House of Sidney A. Kent

"giving the impression that his work was pleasure," and to his gift for music, continuing: "An incident will illustrate the tact with which he could use this talent, and at the same time give us the secret of his power in maturer years. His sympathy, naturally, had been with his Southern home through the war then so recently over. He never discussed the subject, but one evening, seated at the chapel organ after prayers, singing over college songs, a pause in the proposals led him to choose for himself. His hands passed easily over the keys in search of an old familiar theme. Suddenly it was found, a smile lit his face, and turning to the writer, who stood by his side, he broke into 'Dixie,' the song of his motherland. We were hushed, touched, thrilled by the soul that rose like a lark from its nest. We did not speak when the song ended, but we knew ever after that there were two hearts of equal love that suffered in the lost cause. Thus he could conquer prejudice, disarm opponents, and draw us alike into fraternity and justice."

It was "the youth of Narcissus," the opening of a character ardent, sensitive and reserved, and ignorant of its own strength. As sympathetic and intuitive as a woman, he was easily adored by men and women alike. There was something in him which excited emotion and forbade indifference; and already people threw themselves upon him, made him the confidant of their secrets. Many others besides this class-mate are keenly touched by the remembrance of this awakening grace, which developed afterwards into a subtle power, and whose secret was always forgetfulness of self and intuition of others. It was a youth all joy and sweetness, which achieved without effort and had long dreamtimes left over — times for dawdling and drifting, and experimenting with life and the arts. He was no egotist, he was not devoured by ambition, he was content to let whatever talent he had develop in its own way at the touch of circumstance. Meantime, his artistic faculty delighted in doing what was nearest to his hand, either turning a rhyme in praise of beauty, improvising soft airs at twilight, composing a song, working out some fair design, or enacting Romeo like a mediæval lover. While life was as charming as a garden in summer, no amount of admonition could persuade him to knock at the iron doors of fate and hammer out his career before necessity and temperament called him to his work. He loved to spend long idle summers in the country among his father's rustic relatives, where there were woody hills to roam over, the Connecticut to swim in, and wonderful gold and purple mists to delight in. Summers of good honest play these were, with no work more serious than a little hoeing or haying, and no longing for any other kind. When in town, he was, according to his sister, a "great home boy," easily satisfied with their music or his drawing, in spite of a certain zest for society, and a fanciful devotion to a succession of pretty girls. His talent for doing as he liked was the most conspicuous of his gifts at this time, though what he liked was always amiable and generous enough; and he resisted a good deal of advice to be more strenuous. We who remember the astonishing fecundity of his last ten years may smile at those friends of his youth who used to shake their heads and fear for his future in spite of the streak of genius they acknowledged in him. But their doubts were not unreasonable. Probably there was grave danger of dilettanteism to a mind so variously gifted; and doubtless his father's rapid descent from wealth to poverty at this time supplied just the stimulus necessary to turn the boy from his happy pursuit of all the arts to a definite study of one.

II

EARLY TRAINING AND STRUGGLES

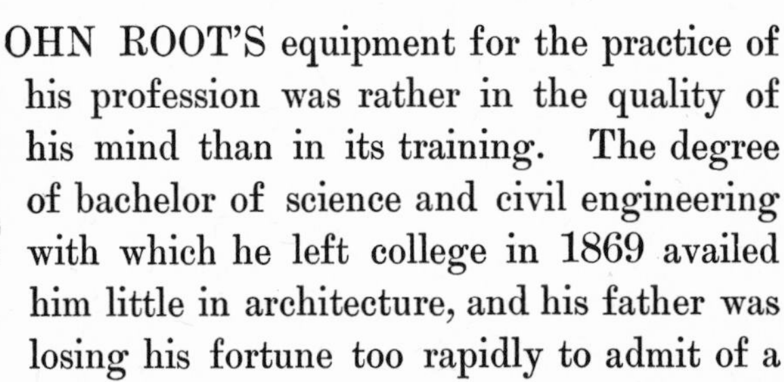

JOHN ROOT'S equipment for the practice of his profession was rather in the quality of his mind than in its training. The degree of bachelor of science and civil engineering with which he left college in 1869 availed him little in architecture, and his father was losing his fortune too rapidly to admit of a course at the Beaux Arts, or a year of study and travel. But his professional education was not so slight as it seemed, because of the quickness of his mind, its sureness of grasp. A hint was worth as much to him as a whole sermon to others. The recollections of Mr. Walter C. Root, of Kansas City, emphasize this point, and show the drift of his life at this time:

"From my earliest recollections of my brother," he writes, "I have always been impressed, almost to awe, with his wonderful facility. When at college, he never seemed to study, yet he was among the first three or four always in his class — graduated second, I think, to a slow-going grub. Music he never 'studied' in the usual way. When he took lessons on the piano, the teachers were always in hot water because the exercises would not be done, and the reading would be slighted. John would pick out the melody, learn it almost instantly, discard the music and play it forever afterward with delightful ease and abandon. He got what he wanted out of music, and apparently always with the greatest ease. When I say he did not study, I mean that he did not 'grind'; he saw through things so quickly that it seemed like intuition. Observers were tempted to think him shallow, until some test of depth would show that John knew, and often to the discomfort and mortification of some rash person who had dared to measure strength.

"At home in New York, John was in college and in many things besides. During several years we always had a lot of drawing-boards in our bed-room on which were done all kinds of work: elaborate drawings of cathedrals (from his mind), palaces (in Spain), grand bridges, triumphal arches (money no object), water-color sketches for the girls, caricatures (of a sort more humorous than artistic, for he never drew the figure well), and all manner of studies for things practical and visionary, sublime and trivial, were to be found in our chamber. In watching the progress of these works I had great delight. At one time we had a brief season of card-playing, principally because father did not approve. John would be working on a drawing, would leave the board and all paraphernalia laid out, while he and I would play a few games of 'seven-up.' If father happened to appear, the cards would be quickly disposed of under the bedclothes, and all the drawing arrangements served as an excellent excuse for light. John would be drawing vigorously and I was supposed to be watching." (Of all the conventional diversions, in later years, cards bored him the most.)

"The first design for a building actually constructed, which John ever made, to my knowledge, was for a Baptist church for the negroes of Atlanta. Father, always a great friend of the negroes, had been to Atlanta, and found an old colored minister, a friend of his, making efforts to build a new church. He promised the negroes that John would make the plans gratis. The conditions being not at all attractive, the limitations rigid, the subject was not inspiring, and there was much grumbling in our chamber during the progress of the work. This was while John was at college.

" For two years or so before we moved from New York John made a little money by playing the organ at the Fifth Avenue Baptist Church, and I pumped of extra occasions. I rather enjoyed it because I was expected to go to church generally, and in the organ-loft I had perfect freedom, could read or go to sleep if I wanted to. Pumping the organ, I felt that I was doing something in the production of the music, and was helping brother make it. I think John was something of an autocrat in our family at that time, though always kind and generous. Certainly we younger children paid great heed to any word spoken by him. For myself, I was always, from my earliest recollection to the end of his life, more afraid of the occasional sarcastic shot (richly deserved always) which I would get on rare occasions, than of any other reproof or correction I ever received. At this time and so long as our united family life lasted, John was the life of the house — he played constantly the piano, directed Florence in her musical studies, accompanied her songs on the piano, read aloud to the assembled family many an evening, and was as interesting and entertaining at home as he was in society. Dickens was in the height of his popularity in those days. Several of Dickens's books John read aloud to us around the sitting-room table. I remember very well lying on the floor and listening to Pickwick, Copperfield, Dombey, and the rest, read with the keenest appreciation of humor and pathos, the author so clearly and quickly comprehended by the reader that

I was enabled to understand, laugh uproariously, and at the 'soft' passages, turn over on the rug to keep from making too public the fact that I was crying.

"An elaborate set of drawings gotten up in our room

Hall, House of A. A. Sprague

was a competitive design for some public building located in a Western city. Father believed John could do anything, and, with a layman's knowledge of such things, thought the chances of winning were good. The competition was one of the old-fashioned (they still obtain) 'fool' kind. John was very young, and without office experience. At any rate, we worked out the drawings; I stretched the paper and looked on, and John did the drawing. We did not 'get a place.' In a vague sort of way, I remember some of these old studies and designs; they were very different from the sort of thing a student would do in a technical school. In the New York University, I think John was taught some engineering, mechanical draughting, use of instruments, etc., but nothing of architecture or design; so that from the beginning he worked out himself his ideas of design, influenced of course by many persons and conditions. I have an old book which John gave me when I first went to Chicago, which shows marks of considerable use; one of the old-fashioned works on architecture, combining a history of the art, details, and descriptions of the styles and orders, and a disquisition on modern work with many original designs by the author, Le Fèvre. This book father bought in his youth when he had architectural ambitions. In a perfunctory way, in the designs for the castles, palaces, and cathedrals 'we' made, I think John used the classical orders. Going into Mr. Renwick's office, his natural taste for the romantic styles was stimulated. Renwick built cathedrals all over the country — everything was a cathedral; he was one of two or three lod New York architects who were the introducers and exponents of the Gothic revival in this country. The experience in Renwick's office was as a student for one year without salary. Next came the experience of looking for a 'job' as draughtsman, which he finally found in Mr. Snooks' office. A very much 'cut and dried' classic style was indulged in in this office, and I believe the year's work there was not valuable except as giving experience in office routine and practice. Whatever was learned in the art was picked up by John's inquiring mind outside the office."

The young man's New York career was cut short by the Chicago Fire, a calamity which cleared a promising field for architects. Two weeks after it occurred, he wrote to his friends in Atlanta of his "state of indecision." "Chicago wants me," he confessed, "Washington is seriously in need of my services, and when these conflicting claims are loudest, there comes a call from Chattanooga 'Come and help us.'" But Chicago conquered. Mr. P. B. Wight, who had seen some of his sketches before removing thither, wrote, offering him employment. Accordingly he started West, with three hundred dollars and a portfolio of experimental designs as his capital, and in his heart confidence enough to banish care. One of the drawings was an elevation for Reed's Temple of Music, Mr. Reed being a relative of the Roots, — a design much simplified, for reasons of economy, when the building was erected. Another was a set of studies in brown ink for a Romanesque cathedral, which is still remembered by good judges as an interesting piece of work.

He found Chicago a lively but uncouth fledgling, lifting her voice in triumph before the pin-feathers of her resurrection had begun to grow. But there was energy in her, and she was using it all, and the young immigrant took his place among those who were trying to reduce her chaos to order. He entered the office of Carter, Drake and Wight, who, like all other established firms, were very busy with the rebuilding. A few days afterward a young Chicagoan named Daniel Hudson Burnham joined the force of draughtsmen. "I remember how John looked," says Mr. Burnham in describing the incident, "as he stood before a large drawing-board with his sleeves rolled up to his elbows.

From the first he pleased me; the strength of his muscles, the babyish whiteness of his skin, his frank smile and manner appealed to me, and we became great cronies." Mr. Burnham was a trifle taller and heavier than Root, almost as blonde and slender and supple. Root's skin had that transparent pink-and-white which often goes with reddish hair, and his eyes were of a rare color — dark violet-blue, a color that is bluer than blue. His eyes always betrayed him; to the last they told the secret of his mood. His instinctive shyness was conquered in a measure by the other's open-hearted fervor, and the comradeship of a score of years began. Mr. Burnham was a few years the elder, an enthusiast full of high but still unformed ideals, who had drifted about for some time in search of himself and his métier, and had finally agreed to his father's choice of architecture as his profession, though the artistic instinct in him found readier expression in arts less severe, less conventionalized. The two young men talked lightly of the coming time when the conditions might justify them in forming a partnership. It came sooner than they expected. In the winter of 1873 suburban real estate was "booming" all around Chicago. A number of Mr. Burnham's friends — young speculators who thought themselves capitalists — agreed to push a certain suburb. A new town was to be laid out, dwellings erected, an academy, a railway-station, shops, and other buildings planned. The ambitious projectors wished to get out of the rut of base architecture, and, with exalted confidence in youthful talent, promised their friends the work on a basis of five per cent. commissions. On the strength of this alluring prospect, and of six or eight other jobs which Mr. Burnham had somehow gathered up, the young draughtsmen gave up their posts in the spring, and formed the partnership of Burnham and Root, the elder man taking precedence in the title of the new firm.

This partnership continued, as it began, to be one of sympathy rather than interest. During twenty years it was never interrupted by a single moment of harshness or suspicion, and the work of each man became constantly more necessary to the other. To it both brought important qualities. Root, as we know, had his gift for architectural design — that happy union of invention and facility which made him afterwards an original force in his profession. But genius avails little without persistence and opportunity, and Mr. Burnham was the plasmic influence which he needed at this time. Root, as we have seen, lacked personal ambition. To the end of his days he dreamed largely of the achievements of his race, anticipating imaginatively its upward development; but considered his own career of little importance. Mr. Burnham, on the contrary, resolved from the first that the new firm should lead the profession, and never flinched from his purpose through the years of waiting. He was always noting or making opportunities, evolving large projects, which the younger man smiled at, but — fulfilled. He had initiative, strength of will, and a certain splendor of enthusiasm which captured men and held them, while his partner was amply content to sit in the inner office, aloof from the boresome talkers, and do his work.

Thus Mr. Burnham's influence during these formative years saved Root from dilettanteism, held him to a definite purpose, and helped to keep him confident in spite of the tardiness of fortune. For no sooner had the young men put the new firm-name on an office door and bought a supply of furniture and stationery, than the financial panic of the summer of '73 destroyed their unbuilt city and all their present prospects with it. The only returns they ever received from all their plans and hopes of this promising suburb, were two suits of clothes of unwonted splendor, paid them by one of the collapsed capitalists to whom a tailor owed some money. It was too late to retreat, however. They must face the situation, which was: office rent, board and clothes for Root, and merely clothes for his partner, who could board at home. Neither of them ever took their financial discomfort seriously; to both the situation was temporary and amusing, though it lasted three or four years. "The true key to the problem," writes Root, "is oat-meal and milk. By this I don't mean grub it all the time. I mean eat it when you don't know what else to eat, so to speak; fill up the chinks and crannies with it. Indeed you can utterly fill up yourself by eating a handful of it raw and then drinking water until it swells. It then presents a problem analogous to that the conjurers give you when they show a little-necked bottle with a huge brass ball filling the inside; and you wonder how on earth it got there."

Root was never thrifty, even when most impecunious. Money always slipped through his fingers; of all commodities it was the least worth struggling for or saving. But though he was often closely cornered at this time, he contrived, without drawing upon his relatives, to keep out of debt and to be recklessly lavish now and then. I remember a story of one of these indulgences. A friend was to be married when the poor young architect was particularly hard up. A wedding gift must be provided; so he sought out a pawn-shop, walked around the block two or three times, finally plucked up his courage, plunged in, and pawned his watch for twenty dollars. Mr. Burnham made great eyes of wonder when he saw among the presents an etching bearing his partner's card. To increase their slender income, the partners, one at a time, gave half a day for a year or so to work in other offices. And Root played the organ again, this time in the First Presbyterian Church. A story is told of his mischievously making a voluntary one Sunday morning of "Shoo-fly," giving the negro-minstrel air with such solemn slowness and so many variations that no one noticed the indecorum.

In some of his letters we find sad evidence of his state of mind and pocket. Even before the partnership he writes to his mother: —

"It is truly astonishing how often a man with the consciousness of but one nickel about his person will turn over

Railway Station, Kewanee, Ill.

in his mind whether he shall expend that nickel or not; and how attractive becomes under such circumstances the delight of walking in preference to taking a carriage. Another peculiarity of my dealings with the world is the extreme snobbishness I affect in availing myself of every occasion to put on a spike-tail coat, the cause being the unpleasant glossiness and varnished appearance of other coats I have the honor to own.

"In regard to the shirts, after due mathematical calculation I have concluded that my collar is $14\frac{1}{2}$ inches long and that my sleeve is $21\frac{1}{2}$ inches outside and 21 inches inside. When I get the shirts, I shall certainly feel like wearing them on the outside."

Again, after a few months of independence, he confesses to his sister: —

"Personally I am *strapped*. For two weeks I have run on a purely impecunious basis. My cash tied up in a 'busted' bank, and my mind strangely prejudiced against going into debt, is it small wonder I should have become such a stranger to greenbacks — in fact scarcely a bowing acquaintance? However, I am happily single, so I compare my plight with what it would be if I were double; and my spirits rise immediately. Indeed, it is impossible to *lay out* an old bachelor of moderate wants for any length of time. A bachelor I am, I expect for good. Not a conventional, crusty one, but a contented, easy-tempered bach of the sort to tell preposterous fairy stories to my nephews and nieces."

Another letter to his sister, dated April 29th, 1875, shows more seriously his submission to his lot: —

"It is always most difficult for us to be philosophical about our own affairs, and very easy to be so about others. And yet we both know that the condition of life in which we are is assuredly the best for us, that any other would be for our hurt. In my own case, I know that if I had been as successful in business as I expected to be when I started, I should have gone to the dickens as fast as my legs would carry me. Now I feel so doubtful of myself that I should very much dislike to be tried with much money. So I can see why I am kept back and thwarted in many schemes that have so fair a promise. There must be in this way some excellent reason for the condition in which we find ourselves."

In these days Burnham and Root had an office in Washington Street, where they managed to keep up buoyant spirits in spite of the dull times. Dr. William Woodyatt, an oculist and aurist, who carried a rare capacity to an early grave a few years later, had his name on the door just below them. "We used to hear Woodyatt running up the stair," says Mr. Burnham, "and dashing into our office. Once there, he would be so stiff and look so indifferent and severe that we would know he had a new patient, and ask him who the great man was. And when we got a client we would dash down stairs and knock at his private door with the news."

This was not very often in the early years. "From the first we fought for five per cent.," Root used to say. "But Chicago at that time had scarcely heard of the regular rates — there was a go-as-you-please relation between architect and client; so that our demand struck people as extravagant. Many a time some prosperous proprietor would come in and talk over a house in the most promising way, only to retreat in terror when we, with much stiffening of backs and gritting of teeth, demanded five per cent. of the cost." Architecture had scarcely risen to the dignity of a profession in the West at that time. The typical architect was usually a graduated house-builder, unencumbered with book-learning or the training of the schools. All details were taken ready-made from joiner and stone-cutter, and upon these still lay the evil influence of the mid-century epoch — that blight of Louis Philippe which clogged all art with heaviness and robbed man's works of grace. Every man of taste had to struggle against crude conditions; he must have the bravery of a pioneer and the ardor of a revolutionist. Burnham & Root had almost to make a place for their profession, a profession which, although it involves the life and happiness of the entire community, though it makes or destroys the beauty of cities, still has no standing before the law. A letter dated March 17th, 1873, shows from what a low estate a great art had to arise in the embryo metropolis. He writes: —

"Everything in business is exceedingly dull here. I, of course, am busy enough, tinkering at one thing and another. But the scarcity of money in financial circles, together with the difficulty in renting, owing to the large number of buildings put up last year, makes everybody hesitate about building. The excitement of the present is the competition for the new Court House. In this place alone more than sixty architects are competing, and in other towns there are perhaps as many more. I have a friend here, a buoyant green architect, who has sent in some exceedingly dubious plans, the chief feature of which is a tremendous dome that could not be built on this soil by any kind of hocus-pocus. He's as confident of getting the first premium, and as trustful in the supreme honesty and integrity of the committee as can be imagined. No doubts of anyone else can shake his confidence. When one reflects that he has no influence of any sort, and that his drawings are so badly made that he himself owns to their unattractiveness, his faith is really refreshing. Most probably, some one of these old numskulls here — the fossils — will bribe his plans in and we shall be afflicted with several million dollars' worth of ugliness. As the frost begins to thaw out the bad building of last year begins to crop out. A very costly building of one of the old men is literally falling down of sheer bad construction; another one opposite our office was for several days in such a condition that no one would walk on the same side of the street. There are half a dozen costly buildings in this neighborhood held up by jack-screws, all because of the inefficience of the architects, who appear daily in the newspapers with cards that talk nonsense about 'bad stone,' 'frost in the walls,' and what not. Some of these fine days the people here will wake up to know, if not what good building is, certainly what it is not."

This letter has proved sadly prophetic. The "several million dollars' worth of hideousness" erected soon after as a Court House, already proves an incubus, and the problem now agitating the public and the newspapers is how to get rid of it.

The first entry in the account-books of the young firm is dated July 5th, 1873, when Mr. Burnham spent $146.26 for office rent, furniture and stationery, and the impecunious Root invested $3.15 for tacks, a tack-hammer, a sponge, "two glasses at 10 cents," and a bottle of mucilage. After this heavy outlay neither receipts nor expenditures gave much trouble to the amateur book-keeper. The sole employé was Harry, the janitor, whose wages — two dollars a week — were a severe strain upon the resources of the firm. The first entry on the other side is a fee of $100, from C. Mason & Co. in November, and the next month "F. A. Riddle's dwelling on Ashland Avenue" proved still more lucrative. After a year of the partnership the firm's books were made up and balanced — a precedent always followed annually thereafter, and we find the following entries: —

Amount of business actually done by firm . . .	$973 25
Amount of expenses of firm	608 48
Amount of profits	364 77
Burnham's share	182 38½
Root's share	182 38½

But Root's expenses had been the heavier, so that he commenced the second year in arrears to the firm, or, "as business stands," indebted to Burnham in the sum of $103.24. Under these entries we find the following endorsement, signed by both partners — the only form of contract ever drawn between them: —

"We hereby certify that the statements of the year's business and its results contained on pages 26 and 27 of this book are correct, attest our hands and seals this 13th day of July, 1874."

The improvement in business after the first year was by no means rapid. It was only during the fourth that the net profits of the firm reached $2000.

In January, 1876, he wrote home: — "I don't fancy we shall ever make a large fortune, indeed I don't care to. A very few thousand dollars a year from professional practice, coming steadily and as a matter of course, is my beau-ideal of pecuniary felicity."

Even during these hard times he contrived to send money to his family. "For a good many years there were crises in our finances," writes Mr. Walter C. Root, "in which John was most free and liberal with help; and as soon as his success began he shared with us all most generously. In those days, I had a minute idea of the value of money, growing more minute as I got harder up. John's idea was expanding as his fortune improved. The Centennial year came and the Philadelphia show. I was sixteen and dead broke — to get to the Centennial seemed about as difficult as to discover the north pole. John had not seen us since Florence's wedding. He came on, grasped the situation, and offered to take me to the show. I think the smile of the Cheshire cat was gloomy compared with my countenance when I received this offer. I had been living in a narrow routine, and living hard. I went to Philadelphia about as I would to Europe. John, I suspect, would not have made the trip so modestly if he had not been forced to share with me. I had a new suit of store clothes to start with, which enabled me to shine with the country girls during the succeeding summer. At Philadelphia, we fell in with a bureau, which steered us to a room of decent and cleanly aspect. Waking about five, I remember that John made many 'quips' and 'cranks' about the flies, about the beauties of the tight board shutter for ventilation during the heated season, and about other features of Philadelphia architecture. The next night they turned another man into our room who snored horribly. John, remembering his organ practice, described to me all the different stops which this man could command in his snore, as well as the movements, musically speaking. We had walked thirty and odd miles and had stuck our noses into all manner of places. We were desperately tired after our first full day and evening, and I believe that, as the night and the snore wore on, the joke about the organ was superseded by remarks of a more forcible, if less jocular nature.

Entrance, Insurance Exchange

"John made notes of the Centennial as a matter of duty. Our legs were good and he kept our spirits as high as the temperature. I very well remember that this trip was to me an initiation into some sort of acquaintance with art. We plowed through the art galleries and John discoursed to me about the pictures, and gave me short lectures on decorative art from time to time. I do not believe there was the general information about such matters which there is now, and I found myself like one of the pupils in Goldsmith's 'Deserted Village' in my wonder at my tutor's knowledge.

"After our visit to Philadelphia, John went with us to Sunderland, Massachusetts, where we spent a delightful month with our relatives. John and I played out-door games, rowed on the river, and went swimming together. Floating on the river, he talked with me in a most fascinating way about many subjects — idealization in art, natural selection in nature, architecture in its artistic and practical phases. Frequently, afternoons, we secured admission to the village church; and to an audience of our party and some of the young ladies from town summering in Sunderland, John played the organ; I blew as of old. The old church rang as never before, and the organ developed tones it had never dreamed of. This month in the country rests in my memory as one of the pleasantest I ever spent — we were so free from care, and so eager in our enjoyment of the quaint quiet surroundings."

In November of this Centennial year Root wrote: — "Our business continues so dull that I have deliberately given myself up to a course of daylight reading. Perhaps it is a 'providence' that we thus have time to cultivate our minds, inasmuch as it saves us from doing much crude work that in after times we should be ashamed of. This compulsory idleness does n't depress me very much, though it is tedious; for the ultimate success of a professional man is so dependent on his knowledge and industry, that when one has the requisite industry and is acquiring the knowledge, he feels he can, if necessary, wait. This winter will be one of universal and strenuous economy, so I shall be quite in fashion, which you know is a good deal."

During these years both partners studied carefully historic architecture. The Gothic was still in vogue, and they called themselves Gothicists, and made countless drawings of moldings and other details. They would make each other guess the period of details published in architectural publications, until at last they could place them within ten years in the nation to which they belonged. The Sherman residence, the firm's first important work, expresses these Gothic sympathies. Other styles also were drawn and redrawn, so that these idle years were by no means wasted.

A little later we find the record of Root's first speculation,— an unlucky precedent which he followed too often for his own good, for though he could theorize admirably about money-matters, he never had the money-making instinct. He tells the story to his sister: —

"You have not heard of the great wheat corner, have you? No, you have n't, because I did n't write to either you or mother about it. Indeed I am anxious mother should not know, since it would needlessly worry her. You see I owned a house — that is, it was partly paid for. Seeing that the winter would be very dull, and that it would be inconvenient to meet the next payment on it, I sold it for $1400. This was $200 more than I had originally paid. About this time came gloomy letters from New York of father's condition. So I thought I could just as well have five thousand as fourteen hundred dollars by a little wheat 'deal.' All the boys were making money. Wheat was certainly going up; 'the boys'—I among them—knew that Russia was going to war. This would close up the Dardanelles, block the Russian crop and put wheat way up. As Sellers says, 'There was millions in it!' So in I went. For some time I had a capital run of luck. Everything was beautiful. At last came the news of impending hostilities in Turkey! All of us bought heavily—all we could 'carry.' I meant to sell out at night, fearing pacific rumors next day and a consequent drop after the first great rise; and so I ordered my brokers—but they thought they knew best and did n't sell. The consequence was that the next day wheat did fall, and I with it. Indeed my fall was completer than wheat's, for I did not get up again. I have no doubt this entire business is another instance of Russia's perfidy. That she should promise the boys to go to war—or as much as promise it—and then not do it, is mean beyond words. Of course, it is barely possible that Russia failed to understand the boys' intentions, and so could n't carry out her part of the contract, but I doubt it. It looks to me like a deliberate breach of faith by a semi-barbarian nation that should be excluded from the intercourse of civilized peoples. Hereafter, I shall put no trust in princes, but devote my attention to architecture. Very likely I have purchased $1400 worth of worldly experience C. O. D."

It was not until '78 or '79 that the tide began to turn. About this time an unexpected honor was thrust upon him, as he records in a letter to his father:—

"As I intimated, we have been very hard worked at the office with new business. This year is a very promising one. I was offered the other day the place of Superintendent of the Government Building here—salary $3000. I don't know why I was singled out, except that I was politically unobjectionable to all parties. The honor I declined with numerous thanks, and the deputation of first citizens, who had been telegraphing back and forth between here and Washington, gracefully descended the staircase. They had

Entrance, House of E. E. Ayer

assured me in the most positive way that the matter was arranged, and there was no sort of doubt about my getting the place if I would have it, and seemed mystified that I should decline. But to have accepted would have taken me away from my own legitimate business, would have identified me with politics. And more than this: I happen to know of so many irregular and dishonest things about the work here, that I should have lost utterly my self-respect to have taken the place and condoned the dishonesty; while, if I had exposed it, I could not have kept the place six weeks. My friends all seem to think I did right."

Another object-lesson in the present method of erecting public buildings. The Custom House here referred to is now (1896) being demolished, Congress having appropriated millions for its destruction and the erection of another.

Burnham and Root had now reached the beginning of their professional career. From this time there was no lack of work, and gradually the demand upon the firm became so great as to tax even Root's facility. The young men had won their place, and if Mr. Burnham's ambition was not yet satisfied, his partner was content to fulfill the present demand and await results. It was at this time that he wrote: —

"I am never completely happy except when I have something to do every day that employs me fully, and am able to get completely rid of worry. Of all things under Heaven deliver me from a condition in which I am oppressed by embarrassments I can't help or remove. My ideal life is that spent in a business which is at the same time pleasure, and with a very reasonable income derived from it. Such a position I hope some day to occupy." But he confesses: "Like Moses, I have certainly spent lots of time in getting 'a good ready.' What the result will be no one can predict. It should be something astounding."

Again, in a letter to his mother, written in May, 1878, he elaborates these views of life: —

"I cannot but regard your move South with pleasure. I can enter into father's feelings on the subject; they are necessarily strong. It seems to him almost like a dishonor. His high spirit revolts at it, and I can well understand how

MAIN ENTRANCE TO THE ROOKERY

it looks like the end to him. But I think no one can overestimate the value to you all of a life removed from the enormous strain incident on waiting for something to turn up. To me any life would be preferable to one of simple

Fireplace, House of Charles Counselman

waiting. Continued disappointment seems to warp us, almost, from true views of life. For how secondary, after all, is any pecuniary success, to that happy living from day to day, which builds up in us a cheerful, reposeful, obedient state.

"I confess it looks to me as if the lovely qualities of men oftener come out under prosperity than adversity. Ease and wealth seem to expand and make genial the dispositions of most men, while want and poverty harden and contract them. But back of all this seeming is a Divine Immortality all seeing and all wise. This thought continually suggests itself to me, not as religion but philosophy. Each of us has a part to do in his own life-work; this part is his own character — his state of affirmation or negation towards the best of all things about him and above him. Our life is not so much what we *do* as what we *are*. The doing, as regards ourselves, is a means, not an end. So that if we view the matter truly, the effort is everything; its result is beyond us and should be outside of our thought. Material prosperity and the position we hold among our fellows affect all the accidentals of life, but life itself — the true man within us — is a mere matter of daily endeavor. In my own case I try to avoid as much as possible all thought or care of results. If I do what is set for me well, if I neglect no opportunity of making the most of the present moment, I have done all the best can do. Beyond this hangs an impenetrable veil which conceals the widening circles of our act's influence; this veil God alone can lift.

"You will very likely think of me as degenerated into a poor preacher, talking over trite commonplaces. But to me it seems that we all (certainly I) keep this view of life too much a matter of sentiment, while it should be a daily 'working view' of it."

III

YOUTHFUL EMOTIONS AND IDEALS

BUT through these years of waiting the young architect was studying life as well as art. Or, rather, he was absorbing it through manifold experience, for never was man born more tractable, more supple, more ready to accept impressions and adjust himself to new demands. He had theories, but they did not bind him. If fate mocked them, as she usually does, he was quite ready to take the lesson with a smile, and destroy them or make them over. And he not only held himself open to experience — he invited it. At this time he was a favorite in five or six of the innumerable coteries into which society was divided in the straggling town, and any of them would have been surprised to hear that he affiliated with any other. There was the "swell" set, established in south-side mansions, which had not yet grown too proud of its splendors to welcome a presentable young man of talent, especially one with a gift for talk. There was the Unity Church set, a crowd of young men and women on the north-side, who liked to give private theatricals and "butterfly balls," and other fanciful entertainments for this or that good cause, to the glory of which John Root was necessary as chief actor or stage-manager. Then through his partner and Dr. Woodyatt, he became intimate in a circle of Swedenborgians on the west-side, persons whose joyous spirituality of life interested him deeply in the religious theories from which it sprang, and permanently colored his religious thought. And he was a citizen of Bohemia — a musical and theatrical Bohemia it was in those days, with letters represented by journalism, and the graphic arts by a few young postulants. We have in his letters mere traces of these various social interests. He writes of his dismay on New Year's morning at the imperative duty of making one hundred and fifty calls. He tells of an alluring invitation which he had to decline because "business is business" — an invitation to go to the Yellowstone with General Sheridan and have "a beautiful trip among the Indians." He describes the Chicago début of Miss Mary Anderson, who seemed an inspired creature in those girlish days, but whose art soon lost in power what it gained in grace. Another year and she had won her triumph — the great audiences, the clamorous applause. But she won it too easily or found it worthless, for the fire went out. Root writes of her superb beauty, her rich voice, her fine intuitions: —

"I wish you could have seen her Juliet. Her own crudeness and girlish lack of art made the Juliet a thing to be remembered. Her whole soul is wrapped up in Romeo, but she lacks all the tricks by which an old experienced woman of the world shows her love. The great passion is a new revelation to her, in presence of which she is almost awed. She submits to Romeo's caresses awkwardly and with manifest lack of practice, but not of fire."

He loved the lake, with its opportunity for aquatic sports. One summer he writes: "Several of us have amused ourselves by going out sailing every day. During the intensely hot weather we leave the pier at about five o'clock, and sail out into the Lake two or three miles; then 'lay to' and jump overboard. After paddling around for an hour or two, two of us take a line, drop astern, and let the boat tow us. You never saw such fun. The boat sets all sail and goes whizzing ahead of the wind, while we have as much as we can do to hang on. Now we are up on the crest of the wave, now jerked out into the air and dropped down into the hollow. The water is white with foam, and the sense of pleasure caused by the rapid rush of the water as you go through is altogether extraordinary."

Through his friends in journalism Root had the run of the theatres, and sometimes he became a journalist himself to review concerts or operas for the Chicago *Tribune*. He commends his good luck in these opportunities for music. "Apropos of music," he writes early in 1877, "there is a funny case of spiritualism here — a Miss Y. She is a big healthy-looking young woman with some facility of execution, who sits at the piano, turns her eyes wrong side out and plays inspired sonatas by Beethoven, Mozart, and the other great masters. The number of persons imposed on is amazing. One of an audience assembled in a drawing-room to hear her play will say 'Play a piece.' 'On what subject?' 'Oh, autumn.' Imagine the result — the falling of leaves, the pensive half-chorales and the rest. It was with a look of unqualified disgust that she met my mild request to play a chaconne by Bach, and when she had fooled around for ten minutes on a 'mixtry' of sounds as like a chaconne as is a funeral march, she turned triumphantly around with 'What next?' 'An arabesque by Schumann,' I said, and that fetched her. She caved; acceding instead to a petition from a weak-eyed young man for 'the brook.' What brings these magnificent improvisatores down is to set them on some precise musical form. They can run on forever at descriptive music."

It was not given to our hero to rove over the world, to

have leisure and a full pocket to help him to the command of fate. But in spite of repressive circumstance the spirit of adventure lived in him, and from the beginning to the end he managed to possess his world. " He was the sweetest, most loyal and lovable young creature in those days," says Mrs. Henry D. Lloyd, who was one of the first to recognize him, and for whose father, the late William Bross, he designed his second house; "and the most sparkling, iridescent, radiant thing in the world. One would exhaust the adjectives of light in describing him — he seemed like flame for brilliancy and color and swiftness. When he and Mr. Burnham were together I used always to think of some big strong tree with the lightning playing around it. He did not seem to belong to this world exactly. But in spite of the enthusiasm people felt for him — and he always touched intimately those who understood him at all — he impressed me as being very lonely. He gave himself freely, up to a certain point; but beyond that he was extremely shy and reserved."

There is a Stevensonian flavor about some of the tales of him, as though Prince Florizel of Bohemia were young again, and staking his treasures in the great game of life. One incident is typical, which occurred when croquet was the fashion, and young Root had become skillful in driving the balls. Rambling past a fair lawn where two young girls were playing, he heard one of them say " Oh, if I could only hit it ! " as she glanced wistfully at a ball far across the field. In an instant our knight was over the fence and bowing before the damsel. Taking her mallet with an offer to hit it for her, he made the stroke, restored the mallet with another lift of the hat, and was off before the astonished little maid had a chance even to laugh. A bit of impudence, doubtless, but masterful impudence — a quality which only success can justify. This trait — the boldness which is not too bold — was perhaps an element of his intuitive sympathy with men and women alike. A stronger element was his artistic self-abnegation — the mirror-like quality of his mind, in which people confessed themselves without the sense of misapprehension or loss. This faculty, rare among men, makes those endowed with it especially attractive to women, and many were his experimental adventures

First Design for St. Gabriel's Church

from the age of six on through many a callow year — adventures through which he carried sentiment in one hand and humor in the other. We have a few confessions of these youthful heart-throbs. When scarcely of age he writes to his sister from Chicago: —

"I have just come back from a jaunt across the lake, the immediate occasion of which was business, the result pleasure. Of all moonlight nights Sunday night was loveliest.

The lake was asleep, scarcely breathing, and the soft air just filling the phantom sails of the numerous craft in sight made one hold one's breath lest the spell should vanish. My destination was Fruitport, a very lovely half country-town, half watering-place, on a beautiful sheet of water. I never had the pleasure of so many introductions in one day by so many persons I did n't know. I think I am getting very irresistible to the women, for half a dozen chaps asked my name and then presented me to their girls — or, perhaps they hailed a newcomer as one who would take the girls out fishing, thus relieving them of a duty become irksome by its frequency. Anyhow, the newcomer did it and had a stupendously jolly time. Particularly coming back, when, by the same heavenly luck, I was introduced to a lovely Hebe and abandoned to the moonlight and my lucky stars, neither of which deserted me. Nor did Hebe, till one o'clock, at which time the moon set in the water, beaming encouragement to the last, but strongly intimating by her retiring that it was well our bed-time. So with long sighs and leaden hearts Hebe and I bade our fond adieux — I to dream of Hebe, Hebe to dream of —." And here there is a break in the dream.

In those days he had theories about women, as well as about most other things in heaven and earth. He had not yet learned that nothing is so dangerous as a theory of either life or art to one who intends to live the one and practice the other. And so with many a vernal ardor our susceptible hero pursued the quest of his ideal — that more or less wooden embodiment of the feminine virtues which most young men enshrine before their imaginations and expect flesh-and-blood women to live up to. John Root's ideal was not as inflexible a deity as one often encounters in the minds of men. She improved as he grew older, and gradually became obliging enough to resign her post of honor in his heart in favor of something more human. But years passed before he arrived at this full knowledge of himself and of the characters of women, years of vain searching and mistaken imaginings — the pathetic struggle of sensitive unripe youth for that perfect sympathy which is the completion of life, and which many lose their chance of by immature entanglements. Now a far-away blonde, dear to his childhood, attracts his roving memories into a flirtation by correspondence. Again it is a stately dark-haired beauty whom he clothes with all the graces of his ideal, one whose sweet, monotonous temperament is as alien to him as a rooted pine to the rolling sea. To a man not born ready-made, who holds mind and heart open for all teaching, there are many stages in the evolution of wisdom. Experience has a more congenial task with such a man than with one strong in egotism and fixed in will: finding him pliant, she treats him gently and rewards him richly, developing his latent desire up to the consummate moment and then fulfilling it with lavish grace. Perhaps this is the secret of perfect poise — to meet life with open arms instead of a weapon, no matter how threatening it looks.

One autumn afternoon, late in the seventies, John Root passed two young girls on the street, and was so attracted by the wilding look in the dark eyes of one of them that he contrived to cut across a corner and pass them again. The dark girl was Mary Louise Walker, her auburn-haired friend was Dora Louise Monroe; and both were destined to influence his life. The two were but a year or two from boarding-school with its engrossing girlish friendships, and the intimacy between them grew ever closer. At this time Minnie Walker was drinking deep of the cup of her short life. Alert, brilliant, keenly intellectual, she won friends by her eager loyalty; and enemies, possibly, by her sharp wit. Fate had showered favors upon her, made her a ruler in her kingdom, and bowed many hearts to her imperious will. She was magnetic, dominant, willful, and yet with a certain wild fresh sweetness.

John Root was introduced soon afterward to Miss Walker, and the acquaintance soon developed into an engagement. But the girl had hardly given her promise before death became her lover's rival, wooing her insidiously, softly, with icy breath and chilling touch. And so, during the months of her betrothal to an earthly suitor she was resisting fiercely another call, expending herself in denials of the higher claim.

It was at this time that I first met John Root, on coming home from boarding-school in the summer of 1879. I remember noticing his athletic supple slenderness, the swift expressiveness of his face, his white skin flushing easily, his emotional violet eyes, and his oddly shaped hands, long in the palm and so short in the fingers that one wondered by what muscular magic they could control the piano. He used to play a great deal, rambling along over the wide range of his musical memories, or improvising with charming directness, for to him music was a more natural utterance than speech. I delighted also in his talk, with a certain awe at the readiness, the wit, the exhaustless variety of it. At that time his success was just beginning, and people were gradually accrediting with power a man whom many had scorned lightly for the unbusiness-like and unavailable character of the many talents they could not deny him.

As the months passed, Miss Walker grew constantly weaker, and the pathos of her fate clamored against the feeling which had always been strong in him, that whatever is is best. Her lungs refused to give service and her voice sank to a whisper, but she held herself erect as sternly as Emily Brontë against the fierce strokes of her malady. In spite of it, she was married at the appointed time, in the appointed way; and her indomitable spirit flashed up for the last time when she greeted her friends brilliantly as a bride. And after six weeks, six weeks of joy and suffering, of passionate denial of her hapless fate and useless struggle against it, she was dead.

Every soul, however serene and well poised, has its periods of imperfect adjustment. Belief in the righteousness of fate is never so secure that a loss like this will not shake it. Yet in a nature fundamentally religious such terms of eclipse yield inevitably to the light, which comes all the more brightly for memories of darkness. John Root was intensely conscious of spiritual values, vividly aware of the world beyond sense, against which all the phenomena of matter and mind are but shifting snows on the shore of an infinite ocean. We find among his papers an essay, written when he was about twenty-six, and doubtless utterly forgotten, which indicates the trend of his thought on this subject, and shows how early he began to define the supernatural in terms of science; or, rather, to insist that religious truth is not supernatural, but in the highest degree natural.

This essay was written as one of a course of lectures given by various laymen, — Messrs. C. C. Bonney, Woodyatt, Burnham, and others — in a little Swedenborgian church on the West Side — the only one of the course which touched a religious topic. It expressed the feeling of a small coterie of young men whose thought wandered fearlessly between the extremes of faith and materialism. Dr. Woodyatt, by instinct and training, was the scientist among

House in Astor Street

these friends. An original and daring investigator, he never shirked an issue, or declined to follow what he felt to be the truth. Prof. Tyndall had but recently declared that, inasmuch as the primitive cell of animal and vegetable organisms is indistinguishable from that of mineral formation, he was led to the conclusion that in matter might reside "the whole promise and potency of the universe." To this famous utterance the young physician said an emphatic no; however indistinguishable, the one kind of cells would unite to crystallize and the other to live, and no power could combine them otherwise. He, Root, Mr. Burnham, and sometimes others, discussed with high enthusiasm the countless issues between faith and science, and Root's lecture gives the results of these investigations upon his own mind.

I shall give an abstract of this youthful confession of faith, in the hope of showing, first, his delight in science, and the eagerness of his mind to interpret scientific discoveries spiritually; second, the naturally religious drift of of his imagination, his keen sense of the infinite, of God in nature and life. In wandering from the narrow orthodoxy of his Baptist forefathers, the extravagance of youth never carried him away from the great religious ideal of Christendom, and to the end of his life his sense of the enveloping mystery grew ever stronger, and of the relative importance of our little lives and labors ever weaker. There was a strain of mysticism in his blood which contended with his frank acceptance of material conditions — a strain which had sent his uncle John Wellborn into the wilderness, and which made him aware, alert and modern though he was, of mediæval sympathies with monks and visionaries. His instinct held close to religious truth as the spiritual triumph of the race, but his sound and sane rationality interpreted this truth by all the modern lights. "The mind instinctively demands," he reasons, "some theory capable of explaining and harmonizing the great processes of nature," and "within this century the question has assumed new force, because of the wonderful discoveries made by men of science. . . . As to the object of modern scientific labor, let us at once acknowledge that it is truth — truth in its purest attainable form. Never in the history of the world has a body of men approached great questions so fully dispossessed of all preconceptions as now. They advance no theory until wide classes of collated facts have plainly indicated it, and yet as to the stress to be placed upon it they proceed with marvelous caution, each new fact being made to test the theory until it stands vindicated or condemned.

"Pushing forward in this way, cautious, conscientious, bold men of science at last reach a point where science becomes useless — that *ultima thule* where life and no-life meet. At this point, where knowledge passes into speculation, they begin somewhat to disagree among themselves. One class says of all the great darkness: 'I know nothing, I can know nothing. Here all tests fail; here my outstretched fingers grasp but the void.' The other class is bolder. It affirms that in the long progress of natural discovery but two things have ever been found, matter and force; both indestructible, both transmutable; that everywhere that matter is found, force is found. Arguing from these data, the materialist says: 'If matter and force be indestructible they must have existed forever. If they are always found united and are not to be dissevered they are parts of one whole. Therefore all that we know leads us to suppose that in matter resides all the promise and potency of the universe.'

"From their standpoint this position is logical and forms one of the two tenable theories of nature. . . . It is complete in all but one respect: in its formation is left out one great factor — identity. This factor cannot be disposed of by any process of reason; it forms the necessary third in the equation, of which the two other elements are matter and force. . . . Its independence and self-existence cannot be banished, any more than matter can be banished. The evidence in all the three cases is identical for the maintenance of type; and the evidence is inherent in identity for the preservation of absolute self. The great mistake of materialists is this: they observe, compare, catalogue, generalize, theorize — all processes of the mind; but the theory they deduce from these processes is such that the mind itself must be classed as an offshoot of the material conditions it has been concerned with — surely a most ungrateful treatment of a faithful servant! So absurd is this conclusion that great schools of philosophy have taken precisely the opposite view, claiming that all natural phenomena are but forms of mental operation — a theory evidently entitled to as much respect as the former, for all that can be advanced in support of one can with equal pertinency be said of the other. Nor is it possible to give the place of honor to force alone, for precisely the same reason.

"We are now compelled to recognize this fact: that above this great triad of matter, force, and identity must be some one infinite principle, permeating all of them, modifying them; that the principle manifests itself in this threefold manner and has inherent qualities common to all. This being true, it must have infinite energy, eternally conserved; it must possess in higher degree all the marvelous attributes of matter; it must have all the intelligence and affections of the mind; and above these it must, as the creator and curator of these infinite interests, be omniscient, omnipresent, omnipotent. This is God.

"All that we see about us, all the forces that play upon us, we ourselves are a part of him. Yet not all alike, for consciousness insists upon the preservation of its identity, and this identity means freedom. Thus we see that of the great primal force — the Creator, the Divine — there are three manifestations — matter, force, identity; that in certain essential respects they are analogous; that as far as matter and force reach, upon their respective planes, identity reaches upon the same planes; that after identity has attained to the full realization of matter and force, certain attributes remain to it alone, which single it out as different in essential conditions from the others. For, while matter is different from force, neither has inherent power to deviate from certain pre-established laws; but in the ego resides a power different from the attributes of matter and force in type and essential quality. This is so evident that the remotest denial of it begins as a logical sequence in attainting the value of all evidence derived from identity by denying its freedom of action; and ends, by logic of equal force, in doubt of every phenomenon of nature that this Identity has been called to estimate. Recognizing this higher quality of identity we are at once struck by its kinship to the great Creator. In Him must reside freedom complete and untrammeled. Over all His creatures He must wield autocratic power. Yet here again comes that insistence even against Him of this identity which cannot brook restraint from Him and live. In this essential quality, this union of freedom and life, this sequence of slavery and death, lies a phenomenon of a great extra-natural world. This world of the spirit is parallel with matter and force, but not of them. It expresses itself through certain combinations of them, but it can never be transmuted into them. For this reason it is not so much one of a triad of phenomena as an intermediate phenomenon, between matter and force, as existing in external Nature on the one hand and the great creative force on the other. The plane of its existence is that great world of moral and intellectual forces which is complete within itself and demands nothing of visible nature except the vehicles of its expression. In this higher world identity touches identity apart from all material conditions, and within it existence is absolute and entire. Within this higher sphere dwell identities totally dissevered from matter as we understand it. In the process of self-evolution the creative force has pursued on a great plane a course parallel with that which we see about us everywhere in nature. The first differentiation from Him is the world of spirit, of identity, of conscious freedom; the second degree is the world of nature about us, lower than the other and dominated by inviolable laws. But as the great Creator permeates all of both worlds, so that world first removed from Him permeates all of the material world beneath it. These two realms are parallel with each other; one lies above the other as the ether does above the earth; and as all light and heat from the sun reach the earth through the circumambient ether, so all the forces of the Divine reach the plane of material conditions through the circumambient ether of the moral world."

Entrance Hall in Astor Street House

The writer then proceeds to test these theories by history and life, tracing the manifestations of the creative principle through perfect law, and asserting the parallelism between the account in Genesis, which "treats the facts of creation subjectively," and that presented by science, which treats them objectively. As the great epic of life is evolved, he finds at every step evidence of limitless power and infinite prescience, everywhere a perfect adjustment to divine law. In his conception primitive men — "the Adam and Eve of tradition," were children of nature, to whom she spoke face to face in "elemental intercourse" — a simple race, differentiated from the beasts by the unprecedented attribute of mind. This new faculty, developing and continually asking why, "wove about them a tissue of philosophies which ultimately shut them out from the early and simple communion with nature, when 'God spake with them' in the garden. Man was now beginning the long struggle for truth through the medium of his senses. Every phenomenon he met was by his senses tested and catalogued on their direct evidence. Applying this material, sensual test to all things within reach, he built for himself systems of religion which were only those sensuals intensified. . . . From this great flood of false philosophy, into which the whole race was swiftly sunk, only a small remnant, the Noahs of tradition, holding blindly to something higher, escaped. From these the great tradition was transmitted to the Abrahamic age, which began the long process of education by which, through artificial laws, a race of barbarians was made into the great Hebraic nation, the conservators of the most wonderful book the world has ever seen. Here began for humanity the reign of law against chaos."

But only a few illumined souls appreciated the beautiful symbolism under the Mosaic code. With the majority of the Jews obedience was literal and formal, and at last the very system which had uplifted them became the instrument of increase of crime. "For when men drag down to minister to wrong and injustice the very laws which had once taught them virtue and humanity, the depth of all possible degradation has been reached — not of necessity in outward morals, but in ossification of the mind, in induration of the heart." At this crisis, in a world of rotten morals and dead religions, when it had become impossible for man to regain his spiritual communion through processes of the mind, came to him, as the only possible redemption, the Immanuel, the God-with-us. "All those virtues which man in his eagerness to acquire knowledge had lost, all those spiritual ideals he had but dimly seen in dreams, were embodied on the plane of his daily life. Alone in all the world a divinely human, a humanly divine voice spoke the words 'Blessed are the poor in spirit,' and with these words began the new era of life."

The writer refuses to discuss "the precise measure of Christ's divinity," for, "whether he was incarnate God or not, this is true: that when the loftiest human mind groups into one personality all human virtues and no human vices; when he conceives of these virtues as ideally perfect, without a spot or flaw, he has reached as far as he ever can

Main Hall in Astor Street House

toward a definite conception of God, and this is Christ. Beyond this ideal personality lies an infinite and to us therefore formless Force, which we call God. But we cannot by any effort of the mind think of this Force as related to us, except in terms of human experience." By Christ's reconciliation of "the highest good with material conditions, by this ideal spirituality in human form, was brought back to the lately dead world all that it had lost. The difference lay in this: that originally man had seen the eternal goodness without himself; now he could see the eternal goodness within himself. Man, free to take his own course, had chosen the cultivation of his senses. Christ at last brings back to him those qualities, without which the perfect cultivation of the senses is valueless. In this perfect form is realized all of the divine he can ever know. . . .

"Christ is a philosophy, but Christ is also a force. Through him acts the great primal Force, bringing into existence philosophies long since dead. Moral truth does not spread like intellectual truth. Its course is more subtle, more remote. Through wide intervals, through unknown channels does this new incarnation exercise its force, till peoples to whom the person of the Immanuel is unknown have found in their old and dead philosophies new and vital truth, made new and vitalized when it had been dead by the new inflow of the divine into a human organism. Here could be seen, reflected in a human face, the divine thought toward man, just as man's thought toward his fellow-man is seen. In this personality is reinstated the communion lost by Adam. He met the great Creator in his natural laws; we may meet the great Creator in the spiritual laws and life of the man Christ."

This essay, though written in early manhood, chiefly for the purpose, probably, of formulating his religious thought — of determining where he stood with reference to matters of high moment, yet expresses, in spite of its crudities, the general drift of his religious feeling through life. This feeling, it will be noted, was colored by the teachings of Swedenborg; as was also his sure faith in a future state, which looked forward to the next world as a great opportunity for progressive development, approaching ever nearer to the divine perfection. His mind never doubted the truths that lie beyond sense, and his life held many of those strange clairvoyant intuitions which remind most of us, however rarely, of that chaotic borderland between sense and spirit, whither science has not yet followed the human soul.

IV

HIS IDEAS OF MODERN ARCHITECTURE

THE young partners were pioneers of what was almost a new profession in the West. The mighty energies of a young metropolis had been conquering the wilderness; in hewing a great monument out of granite, the fathers of the city had used heavy iron tools, and had not yet reached the finer stages of cutting and polishing. At first they built without the aid of architecture. Then self-graduated builders began to hang out their signs as architects and win important commissions; and many of these lingered on into the new era, retaining the confidence and patronage of business men not yet awakened to possibilities of beauty in building. Gradually educated men began to appear from the East, capable designers of the type of buildings then in vogue, but rarely attempting to free themselves from the models of a debased period. Thus the young firm brought into the contending energies of an ardent civic life the first suggestion of another motive, of a modern and revolutionary spirit of beauty. They were obliged to fight strenuously, not only for their own place, but for that of their profession as well; from the beginning they strove to establish it in the respect of men, and to assert its rightful relation to the community. In many offices slip-shod methods of work prevailed, degenerating among the disreputable hangers-on of the profession into methods positively dishonest; and all these irregularities were exaggerated by the pressure and haste which followed the Fire. An irregular scale of prices; an indefinite code governing relations between architect, client, and contractor, carelessness in planning and constructing — against these and many other unbusiness-like inexactitudes the young men fought a hard battle for years. By maintaining a scrupulous code of professional honor, by requiring a uniform percentage on the cost of buildings, by exactness in estimates and care in superintendence, by a scrupulous regard for the rights of clients and of rival architects, they won the respect of a community trained to precision in matters of business and welcoming it with joy in matters of art.

From the artistic side they had still more to do in awakening the community to the possibilities of their profession. The blight of mid-century heaviness lingered long in America, destroying beauty and vitiating taste. In Chicago it could not be escaped — the city was not old enough to show examples of eighteenth and early nineteenth-century refinement. Heavy mouldings and cornices, mansard roofs, jig-saw carvings and galvanized iron ornaments, meaningless accumulations of cut stone — these were the dishes offered to a public appetite vaguely demanding better things but unable to get them.

In resisting such conditions, the men of the new school had to teach themselves by experience as well as the public. The problems they confronted were new. If architecture was to give a vital answer to the demands of modern life, it must not merely repeat the formulæ of the past — it must use its ancient language, the accumulated wealth of many centuries, to tell a new story. By their sympathy with their own time, their adaptability to its needs, the artistic success of the young designers would be measured. More than any other art is architecture dependent upon its public. Its dreams cannot be written in words or notes, or set forth in color on a bit of canvas, to wait for the judgment of time. It requires the costliest materials for its expression, and hence its history is a series of necessary concessions to those who must pay for these materials. Young men, especially, must conform their ideals to the present problem, and by conquering that, win the chance of a higher range.

I have given little idea of Root's temperament if I have failed to indicate its fluidity, its adaptability. He had no scorn of the place or the hour in which his lot was cast; on the contrary, the vigorous modernity of the Western life appealed to his imagination as a strong artistic motive, as much entitled to respect as any motive of the hallowed past. In his opinion, the art which is to vitalize this age must not be at war with science and commercialism; it must sympathize with them. "The one quality in all art which the genius of this age insists upon is accuracy; any other crime may be pardoned but that of untruth" — so he writes in one of the numerous fugitive papers which were demanded of him by societies of architects or laymen, and from which I shall quote largely in showing the motives of his work. "American students," he insists, "have at least this advantage, that while they have no great national art history, they certainly have no ignoble history; for all that has been done up to the present counts for nothing. They are therefore free; free in a deep and significant sense. Artists in other countries may have the advantage of a greater art momentum, but we, approaching their traditions from without, and reinforced by what is now conceded to be a great national spirit, have the advantage of

THE ROOKERY, CHICAGO

clearer vision and judgment." The artist should keep his mind open to "all those influences which lie most closely about him, with which he is most familiar because of daily association. Remote and unfamiliar aspects of nature or types of men or conditions of life cannot be felt with earnestness deep enough to fully permeate the work produced under their influence. In all the world's history it has been true and it must always remain true that art produced solely under foreign inspiration has been worthless."

And so, more specifically, with architecture. "To rightly estimate an essentially modern building, therefore, it must not be viewed solely from an archæological standpoint. 'Periods' and 'styles' are all well enough, but you may be sure that whenever in the world there was a period or style of architecture worth preserving, its inner spirit was so closely fitted to the age wherein it flourished, that the style could not be fully preserved, either by people who immediately succeeded it, or by us after many years. It is exactly as if his majesty's tailor had made for Louis XIV. a coat so beautiful and well-fitting that for ourselves we must at all risks get that particular coat and hang it on our own shoulders. Our architecture if it is good will fit us — every part of us, shoulder-blades and all.

"So varied are the phases of modern civilization that no architect can afford to neglect the study of every style of architecture, whether that which crowned the Acropolis with the temple of Pallas Athene, or that which erected the teocalli at Palenque. But he can never succeed in erecting for our complex purposes a house which is a perfect specimen of a given style, unless his client is willing to undergo some physical discomfort to further this end. The object of all this study must therefore be to acquire from former times the spirit in which his predecessors worked; not to copy what they did. Whenever architects get to be finical about the purity of their style, you may know that you have a period of architectural decadence. Purity of style is for us a means, not an end; it is an integument, not a structure. Where architects faithfully follow out the logic

Vestibule, Rookery Office Building

of a predetermined theory of their buildings, they have purity of style."

In a lecture written for an architectural journal, and entitled "A Few Practical Hints on Design," he shows so clearly the attitude of his mind toward the client and the problem, that I shall quote it almost entire. These hints "relate, first, to conditions environing the architect; second to methods of preparing his mind for his attack upon his design; third, to the actual solution of the problem."

After clearing the ground he continues: "As a man of the century the typical client wants knowledge more than anything else, and what he needs when off the track is only information to put him right. To combat his whims with whims equally unreasoning, to fight his groundless notions of style with our groundless notions, to make him cease laying down absurd law by ourselves laying down law equally as questionable — all this is the height of folly. Ours is no more a position of unassailable virtue than his. With what thin disguise of recently acquired saintliness do we protest that a thing is bad to-day which yesterday we ceased doing and to-morrow will do again! Fashion becomes our only fortress. We fight our battles behind bulwarks made of stays and ruffs, laces and ribbons, baggy and tight trousers, snuff-boxes and smelling-salts, 'Queen Anne' gables, and 'Neo-jacobean' bays and 'Romanesque' turrets; battlements behind which we risk our professional lives to-day, and which, to-morrow, we blow into oblivion with a sneer. For our own self-respect, for the dignity of our own position, for the sake of an architecture which shall have within it some vital germ, let us come out from our petticoat fortress and fight our battles in open field. In science and literature, in art, is heard, loudly calling, the voice of reason. For any branch of human knowledge or imagination or aspiration to shut itself from this cry is death.

"In his relations with his clients the architect must take a position as reasonable as that which he occupies to his design and to himself. In the present catholic condition of art there seems to be no reason for violent prepossessions or any shirking of persistent 'whys'; for any notions we may have of a possible solution for a problem as yet unstudied should have at least the merit of being suggested by the inherent elements of the problem; and this being true, a statement of the possible solution and its reasons will certainly carry weight. Much more will an equally frank statement carry weight when the problem has been in all its bearings carefully considered and the best solution arrived at. In architecture, as in all other arts, it is granted that while reason may be pushed very far, it must finally stop short of full attainment, leaving this for the higher faculties of taste and imagination. Reason should lead the way, however, and imagination take wings from a height to which reason has already climbed. This reasonable plane for the contact of architect and client removes from between them much of that false view which assumes that art is an arcanum too profound for uninitiated minds, a Court of the Priests upon which unwashed feet may not tread. There is no danger that great things or even good things in art will ever be born to the sterile mind, or that the creative gift of a true artist will be profaned by a perfect comprehension of the unwashed.

"The art of architecture, moreover, is different from other arts in the largeness of this purely reasonable and (if the word be allowed) explainable side. Not to avail himself of this fact is for the architect a great mistake, for when the client has fully grasped the reasons for that part of a design which can be explained, he is inspired to completer trust for those parts which lie in the realm of the imagination and fancy. Often by such an interview floods of light will be shed upon questions otherwise vague and indeterminate, and methods of solving them will be indicated which will have a pertinence and beauty not otherwise attainable. It is not uncommon that an intelligent layman will have a breadth of view in architectural matters which will not be suspected if he be held rigidly to professional interviews. He lacks technical vocabulary; he fears perhaps to express an opinion which from a professional point of view will seem ridiculous; he hesitates to commit himself to what may be out of

Covered Court, Rookery Office Building

style. All this is wrong and should be discouraged. His opinions and tastes may be the result of careful study and close observation by a mind at once acute, discriminating and retentive; and, moreover, may have for the architect an especial value because they have been formed without professional prepossessions. The technical and professional point of view in art is not always the truest. Artists are often victims to artificially acquired judgment, when unaided vision in dry light should be the only communication with the mind. How great would be the value to an architect of being able at will to free himself from all the prejudices and theories which in his practice have grown about him, and for an occasional hour see as an intelligent layman may see! This is possible unfortunately only at second-hand, but at second-hand it is possible. If, however, it is to be done, care must be taken that for the time being the mind is not swayed by the very professional habit that prevents its own clear sight. Statements will be made, opinions expressed which will be shocking enough to archaeologists and art critics; questions will be asked impossible to answer; the profound student and brilliant designer of the moment before may find himself dangerously near a most unpleasant unmasking. This is as it should be and should not be shirked.

"The temptation is almost irresistible often to take refuge in the books, among the Greeks, among the French; to seek cover in the darkness of the middle ages, or concealment in the glitter of the seventeenth century; to quote precedents, and turn to buildings erected by great men. All this is nonsense. Be assured that no reason is good, no answer worth giving that does not spring from the present question and is not inherently connected with it. It is of course very easy to say what men of other times did, but it is not easy to tell whether our conceptions of those men and their surroundings are true to the life, or are pictures painted by ourselves and without models. No building nor architect of this or any other time can be a conclusive precedent until we get a stenographic report of the inter-

views which were held between the architect and his client, and even this is incomplete without a photograph of both.

"It will be seen that this tends directly against the literal use of historic styles. True. But so much the better for the styles as we understand them. A style has never been made by copying with the loving care of a dry-as-dust some preceding style. Styles grow by the careful study of all the conditions which lie about each architectural problem, and thus while each will have its distinct differentiation from all others, broad influences of climate, of national habits and institutions will in time create the type, and this is the only style worth considering. This position is reasonable and is susceptible of rational statement. It does not mean the monstrous method, sometimes advocated, which would gather fragments from all ages and build them into one hideous whole. It does not mean the reconciliation in one design of the 'chaste beauty of the Greek with the rugged strength of the Egyptian,' which is as if nature should essay a combination of the chaste beauty of the gazelle with the rugged strength of the rhinoceros. It means rather to use all that men have done, to use it all intelligently and consistently, with study and the nicest discrimination, and to make sure that the particular thing chosen for the given purpose shall be the best fitted for that purpose — shall in short grow out of it. This is as obvious as to say that a man's exterior form shall be the result of his interior structure, that his skin and hair shall be colored by the climate where he lives; and being thus obvious it becomes the true position to assume in relation to the client. Answers to his questions, corrections of his false, and approval of his right, tastes, estimating the value of his suggestions and the possibility of their realization — all these are possible upon this plane.

"Having thus mastered the outer conditions of the problem — its theorem — we pass to its solution. We sit down with the conditions before us. What next? The mind wanders; the question seems barren of interest. How shall we quicken and concentrate the mind — how give interest to the problem? First, saturate ourselves with it; fully realize all of its essential conditions. This may take time, which seems wasted, for meanwhile the design does not seem to grow. But wait: What sort of a town is the house to be in? How wide are the streets it faces? Where do the prevalent winds blow from? How much hot and cold weather has the town? How much rain? Which way is south? How far from the street is the house to stand? Has the town smoky or clear air? What are the native building materials? What is the character of the workmen likely to be employed? Is the occupant of the house a student? a family man? a public man with many friends? one who has many guests? who gives many entertainments? Is he a man fond of display, or one who shirks it and rather prefers the simplicity of 'solid comfort'? These and many other questions will suggest themselves, and being answered will, when added to suggestions obtained directly from the client, point out very plainly the general solution of the problem. This assumes that the architect will frankly accept the consequences involved in each answer, and also that he is not burdened by prepossessions so strong as to prevent his acting dispassionately.

"Before proceeding with our .design, one other point must be carefully weighed, as it will exercise upon the character of the building a very strong influence: —What sort of houses is the new house to have for its neighbors? Probably in no country in the world are architects so indifferent to this as in America. Here, if any attention is given to the matter, it is for the purpose of avoiding deference to the neighbors, of making the house as emphatic a contrast as possible. The existing houses are old and quiet? Then the new house must be as spick-and-span and as noisy and offensive as we can make it. The old houses are broad

Choir, St. Gabriel's Church [1]

and low? The new house must stand tip-toe to the clouds. The old houses are of stone? The new house must be of brick, and as red as possible. Thus we succeed in compelling every passer-by to stop and gaze upon our new house,

[1] Mr. Root's design for altar and altar rail has not yet (1896) been carried out.

but this gaze is too often that of baleful fascination, as one finds his eyes riveted by the antics of a drunken man. Any new design should be carefully adjusted to its neighbors. If out of key with them, it becomes invariably impertinent and offensive, be the design as clever as you please.

"Assuming now that the architect has been brought into entire sympathy with his client, that he has fully mastered the environments and conditions of his problem, he is prepared for its actual solution. The stage of mental preparation, based as it is upon the previous exchange of ideas between client and adviser, has undoubtedly brought about a tolerably trustworthy scheme of general procedure. We have now to determine more accurately what form our design shall take. It is not probable that any first study will be best, and for this reason it seems a waste of time even to consider the first study until several other sketches of plans and designs shall have been made, differing from each other as widely or as slightly as may be. Then an intelligent comparison becomes possible. To make this first comparison as little prejudiced as possible, it is wise to make each rough study independently, if possible with scarcely the memory of the others, and also (so far as the design is concerned) to make it as rapidly as possible. Thus the impression left upon the mind at the moment of production is less lasting, and the sketches come back to us from their temporary seclusion as if they were the work of another man. They can be criticised therefore without bias, and from among them can be determined more accurately the true path. From this test-sketching come new light and more accurate direction, and the design is ready to take on a growth more nearly like its full development.

"Further study will probably bring us to our libraries. Books are dangerous things and need most careful handling.

Reference to them will often tend to confuse ideas which before were well defined, and inject others totally irrelevant to the case in hand. In this hour with books, however freely they may have been used at other hours, reject as unworthy of consideration everything, however fascinating, which conflicts with the predetermined plan of procedure, and beware of a single detail which suggests itself as perfectly appropriate for our purpose. Nothing found in a book will add a feather's weight to a really good design if it be bodily transferred, or indeed transferred with anything of literal translation. For this reason the study of the hour should be close and sympathetic, continued until the mind is fully refreshed and inspired by a process precisely similar to that by which it became saturated with preliminary conditions. Then shut the book and do not go back to your design; do something else. After a day or two, find what impressions remain with you and work them out of yourself without reference to the originals. Any impression which remains so vague that reference must be made to the original source before it can be made to assume coherent and approximately satisfactory shape should be thrown aside as worthless. It is undigested food from which no muscle or vitality can be expected, and in the varied constitutions of men some mental foods as often disagree with individuals as physical foods. This fact is so palpable that it often becomes a question, not of accident but of constitution. Some architects can no more digest a bit of thirteenth-century detail than they can digest a nail. The only difference is that they readily learn whether the nail has been digested, while they may not know if the detail has been.

"During this time the critical study of the house plans will have been going on; each minutest point will have been discussed, and this not only in relation to the convenience and beauty of the interior, but also in its capabilities of artistic external treatment. The development of the design and of the plan should in all cases go on together; one should never get away from the other. No feature should ever be allowed to form into a plan, about the external treatment of which the architect has not a well defined idea.

"By study and sketching we are now prepared to make a somewhat carefully rendered design of the building as we intend it to be. At this stage of the design we are open to dangers which arise from several causes, different in architecture from other arts, but still dangerous. Several of these are loss of scale; over-application or wrong application of detail, and hence a loss of simplicity; loss of homogeneity. To avoid the loss of scale, it is of course necessary to realize through every means in our power the exact meaning of each part sketched in terms of the executed work; . . . and therefore not a single drawing should be made to a scale which has not been mastered.

"Over-application of detail will be avoided by similar means as loss of scale; but, beyond what may be taught by observation, is the simple law that beautiful detail is a precious commodity, not to be prodigally flung away, but to be used with wise discrimination. A broad wall surface should fairly cry out for an ornament before it gets one, and also a moulding or a column. In a drawing every plain surface or moulding seems of much less interest than when built or cut. Nature steps in here, and nature's decorations of sunshine and shadow, her warm glow of ever beautiful colors, varied and enriched by rain and wind, are always lovely, while our decorations often fall short of loveliness. . . . If, however, the mind is surcharged with brilliant inspirations, consistent, truthful, poetic, free rein may be given to it. But do not confuse the operation of the imagination with the operation of the pencil. Loss of simplicity does not necessarily follow when a design is enriched; it follows only when the design is falsely enriched, as when adventitious and impertinent products of ungoverned fancy interfere with the effect of some great and essential part. Adventitious features in a building should, like children, be seen and not heard.

"Homogeneity is in these days more difficult to maintain because the prevailing habits of the time have prevented architects from closely following traditions which would compel homogeneity, while no new habits dependent upon the nature of the case have taken their places. Every structure has some few conditions so far beyond all others in importance that in expression all others should be subordinated to them and influenced by them. These conditions may seem at first contradictory, but they can always be reconciled, and rightly considered will impress upon each detail of the design an effect distinct and unavoidable. The whole matter is summed up, as in painting, in the necessity of keeping a true perspective, giving prominence to objects in proportion to their importance. Yet nothing about a house is too small for close attention — for frequent revision and re-study."

Such points as the above were suggested by Root to the men of his profession as being "sometimes forgotten, not because they are unfamiliar, but because they are so well known." He concludes: "They are important, but beyond all questions of method in importance lies the inherent character of the architect. Architecture is so noble a profession that to allow its influence to be swayed by ephemeral fashions, to make its creations things lightly considered and cheaply wrought, is the basest of crimes."

In an essay on "Style," he attacks still more boldly, from

his standpoint of reason, some of the accepted conventions of modern practice. The essay reads as follows:[1]

"Is it not time that the familiar architectural word 'style' should be relegated to its proper meaning? As now used it has almost ceased to have significance even for architects themselves, while to the public at large the word has become a delusion. How often the architect of the day is compelled to strain his conscience in answering the familiar question as to the style of his designs, because he feels the necessity of calling by some traditional name designs often as unconventional as a chattering chimpanzee. For practical purposes, such phrases as 'Grecian Doric,' or 'Roman Ionic,' or any other names of the traditional styles have become impertinent, and are used only for lack of better terms.

"The word 'style,' as generally used by the public, has, on the contrary, with all its varied applications a very comprehensive significance, and is rarely misused or misunderstood; to say that a woman, a dress, or a yacht has 'style' is to convey an impression which is understood with moderate accuracy. Thus used the word carries a deeper meaning than mere adherence to given fashions, even if the latest; as in the case of many women who devote an energetic existence to the latest styles, yet are never accused by anyone of having 'style.' This quality has a wider sweep; it lies far beyond the creative power of a Worth or a L'Archevèque. It is inherent — a thing of the head and heart, not of the epidermis. It shines out from beneath a beggar's rags; it reveals itself in the touch of an inexperienced pianist, in the 'handling' of an untrained artist, in the lines of a thatched cottage. We find that among the work of architects it is present in one building and absent

[1] Paper read before the Chicago Architectural Sketch Club, January 3, 1887, and published in *The Inland Architect*.

in another. Often it characterizes an architect's smaller buildings and is absent in those more important, or vice-versa. In the progress of a design it frequently happens that a preliminary study will be full of 'style' and the final design have not a bit of it.

"Now, this common word 'style' is manifestly not of the same signification as that used in architecture — as when we say that buildings are in the 'Grecian Corinthian style,' 'the style of François Premier,' or 'the French Gothic style of the thirteenth century.' With this special use of the word each one of us is presumably familiar, and I wish for a moment to call attention to 'style' in its larger, fuller and more widely understood use.

"And first let us note that so far as art is concerned, few created things have ever lived beyond the age of their creator that lacked this precise quality. Occasionally some titanic and monstrous mind will throw upon the world intellectual spawn which will live for ages because of the tremendous power and vitality which have been injected into it. But these phenomena are too infrequent to be worth discussing, and constitute only rare exceptions to a universal law.

"Of all great works of art which have come down to us, spared by the tooth of time, we confess now what was confessed in each age before us — they have 'style.' This, in spite of the fact that the architectural style may be one we despise. Pierre de la Vallé probably had no warm admiration for that Gothic style which is built in the apse of Notre Dame de Paris; Christopher Wren certainly cared little for the similar style of old St. Paul's or Westminster Abbey, or the later Gothic designs of Oxford which he so mutilated. But I do not doubt that both architects would have admitted that the buildings which they did not admire had the kind of 'style' we are discussing. Why was this? For a reason precisely similar to that which saves a gentleman of the old school from the ridicule of a gentleman of the new. You may feel that the manners of the *grande ècole* are out of key with our jaunty flippancy; but there can be no doubt that they fitted a different, and perhaps better mode than ours, and in all essential things, all things of the heart, the two gentlemen are at one.

"Thus, although Notre Dame de Paris and the Hotel de Ville are two buildings of different ages, as widely apart in manner as St. Louis and Henry IV., you will note how alike they are in certain respects. See the noble gravity with which in them large matters are treated; the sweet repose of manner in every-day affairs, the airily graceful and fantastic touch which enlivens lighter subjects. From the noble sweep of the centre door arch to the great griffins that from its tower-tops grin out over Paris, Notre Dame has this fine, gentlemanlike style. There are no solecisms. Everything is fitting; temperate when most exuberant, contained when most severe.

"What is this fine style? How did these architects get it? How is it that all over the world — where the gleaming domes of Taj-Mahal sleep in the white sunshine; where gray pylons of Egypt enclose their depths of luminous shadow; where the pink pentalic columns of the Parthenon lie scattered on the Acropolis, bleaching like the bones of a dead demigod; where the dim, echoing aisles of Chartres filter from the sky its most heavenly rapture to pour it on the humbled worshiper — how is it that everywhere men have fixed in stone and wood and glass this quality, so subtle that to us it often seems the most refined essence of art?

"Any competent answer to this question will necessarily

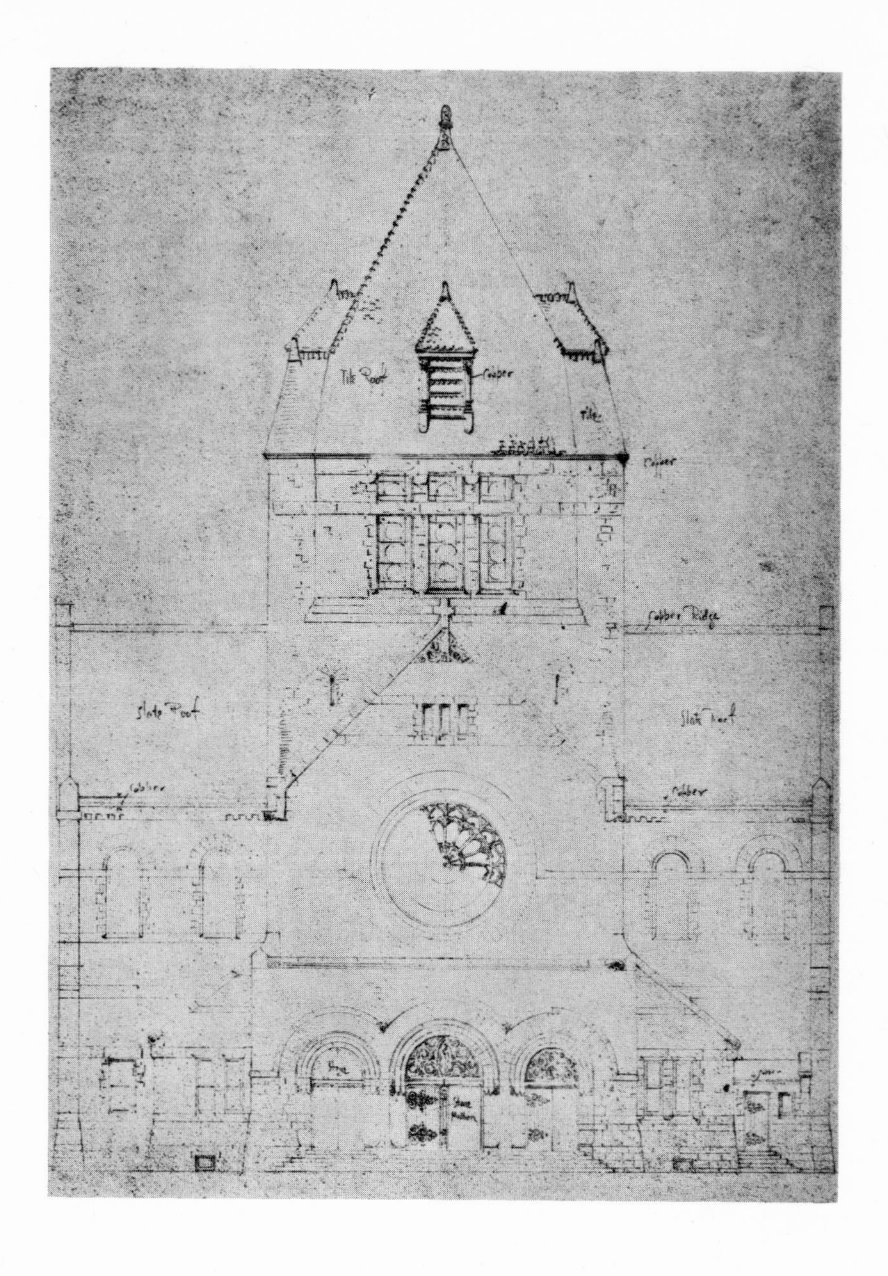

ST. GABRIEL'S CHURCH, STUDY FOR FRONT ELEVATION

Facsimile Reduction of Mr. Root's Sketch

touch upon a field of ethics not confined to architecture alone, nor even to the arts alone, but pertaining to humanity itself. The arts, architecture among them, have been called polite. Perhaps in the earlier stages of this politeness architecture takes precedence of all others. Painting and sculpture began their career with no distinct debt to humanity; but architecture was, at its birth, shouldered with a large obligation, which it was in decency compelled to pay. Every house built to shelter man from the elements was a thing not to be avoided by its neighbors. It not only partially shut out from them grass and trees and sun and sky, but, by virtue of its very bigness and fixity, it became, whether a thing of beauty or not, a thing of prominence. This fact has made Mr. Garbett call architecture 'the politeness of building.'

"Accepting this definition as sound, let us note some of the qualities which we find in a gentleman, as we understand the term, and see if they are not equally applicable to good buildings. These are: Repose, Refinement, Self-containment, Sympathy, Discretion, Knowledge, Urbanity, Modesty.

"Repose. Quietness of body and mind; not phlegmatism, but enforced quietness, as in the poise of a gladiator. The mind becomes finely receptive when held in this calmness of attitude.

"Refinement. In which all things tend toward the loss of asperity, not loss of power nor of value; gaining in that smoothness of surface, that crystallineness of composition which give added currency and beauty to the thing refined.

"Self-containment. Which avoids a too ready utterance of the momentary thought; which spares other people a swift infliction of all of our knowledge; which inwardly debates before answering grave questions.

"Sympathy. Which 'puts yourself in his place;' which readily accepts a point of view; which quickly adjusts itself to its environment; which gives gravity for gravity, lightness for lightness, tears for tears, laughter for laughter.

"Discretion. Which seeks always the fitting thing to do, thus supplementing sympathy; which holds its tongue when speech is unnecessary; which knows nothing when forgetfulness is a virtue.

"Knowledge. The care of speech; the loving selection of words; the scrupulous nicety of grammar, the fullness of idea and illustration that decorates each subject touched.

"Urbanity. As the name suggests, a quality begotten in cities; suavity; the faculty of avoiding friction; the knack of easily getting about in crowds of men; the attitude of deference to their weaknesses; the power, without creating offense, to ward off their aggression.

"Modesty. Without which all other qualities may become offensive. Not affected modesty; not Uriah-Heepness; but the genuine self-esteem which, in justly valuing self, puts as well a just value on others, and thus confesses that self is small in many comparisons.

"Now, what are these qualities in men that they are not in buildings? Their sum total makes a perfect gentleman. The sum total of their analogues makes a perfect building. As a man may lack some of them and still be a very good fellow, so from a building a number of these elements may be omitted and still the design not be utterly damned.

"Let us now proceed to apply these gentlemanlike qualities to a test of buildings.

"As to repose. It seems at present heretic to say that it is the most essential of all qualities, but the fact remains that it is. The instinct of the world has decreed that all large things should be quiet or slow-moving, and that only little things like bees and butterflies may flutter. The world has also noted that all large things are soberly, even if richly, colored, and that in form all of their lines tend to the expression of the quality of repose.

"Since, therefore, buildings are the largest things made by man, a deviation in them from this universal law is the most elemental of mistakes, increasing in enormity as the building considered increases in size. Both in this and other respects many things may be pardoned to a little house, or one without public significance, which become unpardonable in a larger or more important building.

"I am aware that you may summon as apparent witnesses against me many of the notable buildings of the world, but even in these I think a close study will show that the principle is sound, and is carried out. As a matter of fact, so general a law as this always has within it a lesser principle which determines the exact application of the law, and in this case the inner principle is simply this: What sentiment is the building designed to convey? Is it the restless aspiration of the soul after God, as embodied in the mediæval cathedral? Is it the expression of the power and stability of a great corporation, as expressed in its office building? Evidently there must be very different treatment of the two classes of design, but it seems equally evident that both designs must consider the outer and elemental law to as great extent as is consistent with the expression of purpose.

"Practical applications of this law a little reflection will show us, and it is worth while, therefore, to mention but a few. Probably nothing about a design is more expressive in this respect than the management of roof or cornice lines. In a small house, or one that is greatly varied in plan so that each of its parts is small, a very broken and even restless outline may be good. But even in this case, there should be sufficient allowance of quiet and unrelieved background to offset fully its whimsical features. In large and important buildings, however, especially those built for commercial purposes, I believe that experience will show simple sky-lines to be best, as best conducive to the quality of repose; and more than this, because a very broken sky-line is apt to suggest multiplicity of subdivision or function, and should, therefore, be coincident with these subdivisions or functions. This in commercial buildings can rarely be the case.

"The value of plain surfaces in every building is not to be overestimated. Strive for them, and when the fates place at your disposal a good, generous sweep of masonry, accept it frankly and thank God. If this goodly surface come at the corners of your building, so much the better; for there can be no better guaranty that the house will 'stay where it was put' than the presence in it of masses of simple masonry at its angles.

"As to repose in color, you will know at once all that can be said by me, and will sympathize with the utter condemnation of the use of sharply conflicting colors in any structure of considerable size.

"In general, our whims of all sorts, our fanciful vagaries, whether in color or form, may be put, perhaps safely, into small buildings, but if they go into large structures, they should be kept well subordinated to the general mass, whose largeness and dignity should be expressive of not only sober thought, but of the gravity becoming all great things.

"Refinement is a quality whose importance will be at once apparent. Of late it has at times seemed obsolescent, but always in work which can never have permanent value. Refinement in architecture means not only the careful consideration of each detail in itself, but also the relation of each to its neighbors and to the whole. For what may be well enough in itself may be utterly vulgar in juxtaposition with other things.

"The laws by which refinement in a building is reached, would be most difficult to state; but apart from that close study which is necessary for each good element in a design, the mysterious thing called taste is of vast importance here; and the acquisition and cultivation of this is a matter to be constantly followed. In this pursuit not only is it wise to familiarize one's self with confessedly great architectural examples, but with all great art work. As much may be learned of color from one great canvas of Paul Veronese as from all the books on the subject ever written, and the study of the contours of Greek vases will do more to cultivate a niceness of taste in outline than many profiles purely architectural.

"More than all others, however, the human form must remain the supreme school for the study of form and proportion in its most refined and significant expression. Here, as all artists have insisted, the methods of nature have their fullest revelation. This is the divinest design for any structure; this is the most pregnant essay on the much vexed questions of Proportion and Scale; here is a perfect solution of the relation of exterior expression to interior arrangement, and here is a demonstration of the fact that the utmost refinement may be combined with herculean strength. When fully expressed in architectural design, this refinement means all that it suggests in the human form itself. There is the same careful avoidance of useless features, the same perfect adjustment of each part to the function performed by it. Elephantine columns are not used to do the work of mice; necessary structural features are not emasculated by ornament too delicately wrought; purely decorative features are not so formed as to give a false suggestion of vital necessity.

"Like the refinement of a man of the world, the refinement of a design will suggest itself through a thousand channels, sometimes through a direct appeal, sometimes through an indirect insinuation, sometimes through an effort to conceal some necessary weakness or misfortune, so as to spare needless pain to the observer. In all cases the quality has the true ring when it springs from soundness of purpose — from the heartfelt desire to please; and it becomes false and hollow in men and in buildings whenever it is an affectation.

"Let us glance at the next attribute of a man or building of 'style,' Self-Containment.

"Whenever we meet a man who impresses us as burning with the wish to tell all he knows, let him be as graceful in speech, as wide in knowledge, as polite in manner as may be, we feel that he lacks a most essential element of 'style.' So with a building. Nothing is more offensive than those verbose and overdone designs which are not only mere *tours de force*, but which suggest the anxiety of the architect to tell all that he knows in one design. Very successful buildings have the quality of temperance, of self-containment. Even in the most exuberant French or Flemish Gothic, the exuberance is a part of its age, and comes as a natural outgrowth from it. In good examples of these types there is no straining for effect, nor anything theatrical or merely declamatory. There is always the feeling that, however much the architect may have chosen to say, he has exhausted neither himself nor his subject, but kept in reserve a thousand strong images or quaint conceits for some future use.

"In these days, when what we call 'originality' is so much desired, self-containment is perhaps more difficult to attain than ever before. But we must learn it, distrusting the merit of any of our designs which seem labored to us, in which effort is made to express more than we really know, being assured that all over the building executed from such a design will be the painful traces of labor and sweat. In the varied solutions possible to a problem, the true labor to be expended is in first determining which one is best, then evolving it when it is found. The best solution will always be the simplest, and its full growth will follow with a directness and ease which suggest the budding of a flower rather than the forging of a columbiad.

"Self-containment in the expression of a subject always means its thorough digestion. In conversation we may be pardoned if we occasionally think aloud, thus uttering many irrelevant or tentative remarks. Our buildings are much more serious things, for however much they may deserve oblivion, the fact that most of them remain standing after we are through with them prevents people from forgetting them. Every intemperate and hastily uttered thing about them remains to our discredit. We may not all succeed in doing original work, but each of us can do well considered work, expressive of that self-containment which thinks first and speaks afterwards.

"Sympathy, another quality necessary in the gentleman, is also necessary in a building, and this means, of course, in an architect as well.

"In each community there are certain tendencies of the people, certain peculiarities, full sympathy with which is essential to the successful designer. This is a point we are apt to neglect. Our work has too much of the transplanted look which comes from the absence of this active sentiment.

Touched by the warmth and sunshine of an outgoing and vital sympathy, all styles of architecture become quickly acclimatized and characteristic. Yet it seems sometimes that one of our greatest efforts is to prevent this acclimatization by rigorous insistance upon mere traditions, too tenaciously holding to the dry canons of mere architectural style. This is altogether a mistake. A great type in architecture, like that of the Parthenon, becomes great not only because of its perfection as a solution of a given problem, but because in a hundred small respects it expresses the immediate influence of essentially local conditions.

"This variation because of environment always comes about of itself in time, and this may be in spite of architects. No importation of Greek architects could save Roman work from swift differentiation from Greek work. Our attitude should therefore be one of readiness to accept and help forward the inevitable. By doing this we can insure that it will be the finer national characteristics, rather than the grosser, whose influence will be manifested.

"Passing from this wider view, we must also note that sympathy is equally essential in considering the purpose of each building, and the idiosyncrasies of each owner. Many a most brilliant feature has been the outgrowth of what at first seemed in a client an idiotic whim; and many most successful buildings are so because they reveal on the part of the designer a point of view in warm sympathy with their intention. If the building is a warehouse, a dry-goods store, an office-building, or a hotel, the true points of view in designing them will be largely determined by these various commercial considerations.

"The architect occupies a position in this respect different from all other artists. He can never afford, even when the artistic expression of his design alone is considered, to neglect a single condition not only in the larger matters of climate, national characteristics, general purpose, etc., but also in matters apparently very trifling. I am confident that an architect designs a better grocery-store, if into his own professional view of the problem he will admit in all possible fullness the grocer's view. More than for all other artists does success for the architect depend on the activity and warmth of these sympathies.

"But sympathy is a very dangerous thing without discretion. Sympathy leads us onward; discretion pulls us back. Without discretion architecture is like a machine without a governor.

"Many houses suggest a clock in the act of striking twenty-four, or a locomotive driving-wheel whirling around on a slippery track. How many buildings do you know of in Chicago, against whose discretion no charge could be sustained? Of course, I do not mean the large class of tramp and bummer houses which, if justice had her way, would always be in the lock-up, on charges of 'drunk and disorderly:' I refer rather to houses of avowed morals, who profess not to stay out nights, and in whose daily and nightly life the latch-key has no place. In even these professedly good houses, how many skeletons dangle from the cornice, perch on the roof, hover about the doorways or crouch at the basement. What we need now more than anything else is 'proper' houses, whose real discretion is what it professes to be. What would you think of a man who should wear his religion in the band of his hat, and yet get drunk, and not care enough about it to go home in a cab? This is exactly like the indiscretion of our houses. They are always doing indiscreet things. Columns, roofs, gables, balconies, are all over them, each loudly swearing it is what it pretends to be; and yet a blind man could see there is not a word of truth in it. In their anxiety to induce belief by volubility of protest, many of them look as if the source of their design had been a firework pin-wheel, while some assert by their cumbrous features, by their heavy brows and wrinkled skins that they are great giants of houses, when it is evident that they are only wretched little pigmies.

"Seriously, discretion is our crying need — the doing of the right thing in the right place and time. What discretion have we, when we assume in the prevalent craze that because a type of design is good for a house 100 feet wide and high, it is equally good for a dwelling 25 feet wide and 30 feet high? in other words, that the limbs of an elephant are good enough for a greyhound; or that nothing is so beautiful as the torso of the Medici Venus on the legs of the Farnese Hercules. This sort of thing is no more true in architecture than in any other art or in nature itself. As the fond mother said of her hopeful son's 'swear word' — 'It 's worse than immoral — it 's ungentlemanly.'

"Nor is it true discretion to assume that the same kind or scale of detail is equally good for all buildings. We don't sing Schubert's 'Lorelei' on the floor of the board of trade, nor shout the price of grain in our music-rooms. And yet we spend a wealth of delicate ornament on our down-town edifices, and build our dwellings like Stonehenge. It would seem that ordinary discretion should teach us that the relation between dwellings and trade-palaces is the relation between an orchestra and a brass band. Whatever is to be spoken in a commercial building must be strongly and directly said. The very style of the ornament should be simple enough, and the scale large enough, to be easily comprehended. If not, if the unseeing eyes of busy men are daily saluted by delicate details, not only are the details wasted, but they are so far vulgarized as to become impotent to produce pleasure even when men have leisure to contemplate them. In the exercise of this discretion, let us consider each quality our building will express, making sure that its expression be appropriate, and that it be well adjusted to the mood of the spectator; not lowered down to his plane, but, although above the sordidness of his daily thought, sufficiently in recognition of it to escape total neglect. Our architecture will never live beyond our own lives until it loses much of its hap-hazard, hit-or-miss indiscretion.

"Knowledge, if essential, is also obtainable. Genius is beyond most of us, knowledge is accessible to all of us; so that in this age of light, ignorance has become a crime. Occasionally we hear a certain kind of man deliver himself something after this fashion: 'Knowledge is all very well if a man does not know too much.' Then he will cite instances of college men who are starving on ten dollars a week, and of men like himself without education, who are 'climbing to the top of the ladder.' This sort of talk means nothing. Granting, for the moment, the point that starvation of the body is worse than starvation of the mind — that not to know mental hunger is to be well fed — it remains true that the college man is not necessarily better educated than his more successful critic. There are many men to whom ideas come freely and graphically through things, and with slowness and dimness through books. Viewed from what point you will, every man is distinctly the gainer by acquiring knowledge, and no man more than the architect. Every building bears the impress of the knowledge or ignorance of its designer, not of necessity in any one of its details, or even in the composition and adjustment of them all, but certainly in the subtle essence which we call 'style.' The profounder the knowledge, the fuller and richer the result.

"It is valuable to know that architects of a certain age designed buildings after a certain fashion, and adapted to this fashion the various details of these buildings, but it is much more valuable to know the causes which lay back of these results. The mere facts, though significant, are bald and unproductive without their antecedent causes. To have mastered fully these causes is to be able to produce results analogous to those first produced — not in the dry and formal manner of the mere copyist, but with the fire and force of the original. No period of college or school training can do more for the architect than beget in him the sacred thirst of knowledge, which it should be his life work to gratify. Apart from the pleasure to be derived from consciousness of this knowledge, is the certainty that every design he makes will bear the impress of it. It may be in the selection of means to ends, it may be indicated only in certain turns of profiles, in certain delicate adjustments of parts, where a different treatment would have been only less good; it may be in still remoter ways; but everywhere will be shown the grasp, the copiousness of thought, the richness of apt illustration, born only of full knowledge. Just as in a critical essay by Matthew Arnold or James Russell Lowell, every sentence reveals the wealth of learning that lies back of it, so plainly does the architect reveal his knowledge in his work.

"In the absorbing cares of an active life, those forms of knowledge whose bearing seems immediate, or as we say, 'practical,' will be most naturally acquired, but it is a misfortune to any architect, and an appreciable loss to his work, when he ceases to acquire that form of professional knowledge which is entirely literary, and which may be related to his profession only by some side-light shed from another art, which architecture may borrow. The so-called 'practical'

THE ART INSTITUTE, NOW THE CHICAGO CLUB

architect, who knows nothing of his art beyond what has been grafted into him by the surgery of dry practice, is passing away. Large and acute minds there are, in whose work you see the result of ripe wisdom and nice taste acquired by long experience and observation alone. These are not the men, however, who will deride that wideness of knowledge which is here commended. They are rather men who will point us to their earlier work as monuments, not to their glory, but perhaps to their shame or misfortune, and warn us to push with all vehemence our acquisition of the knowledge thus early denied to them. Our profession is rich enough to range and feed in during all our probable lives, without ever getting into our stomachs the indigestible food of 'mere theory.'

"Urbanity is the next phase of politeness to which your attention is called.

"If sympathy is fellow feeling, urbanity is the expression of readiness to extend sympathy even before it be asked. Time was when urbanity in a house was as unsuitable as a silk cap in a jousting tournament. The house was a castle, its owner its warrior defendant, and everybody outside it possible besiegers. But with the dawn of day after the long dark feudal night, the dwelling opened outward like a rose in the sun. Men like Jacques Cœur of Bruges built houses in which they delighted to express to all who passed the new-found peace and friendliness. In such houses was the frankest avowal of good fortune, the most charming confession of a desire to please. So that these newly blossomed dwellings had the native charm of a lovely *débutante* who delights that others shall admire her beauty.

"Is not this the typical attitude of the nineteenth-century dwelling? Certainly no menace threatens our houses which stone walls can ward off. The brigand of to-day gains access wherever he can enter. We do not generally build our houses among people we don't speak to. Whence, therefore, the sudden growth among us of mediæval castles, whose only lacking detail is a shriveled head thrust over the cornice on the end of a pike? Are we so badly put to it for ideas that we must not only borrow from the eleventh century, but add to the mediævalism of it? Surely if this sort of thing was good when men went about in steel, sword in hand, it is not good when men wear silk hats and smoke cigarettes. We may be aristocrats by instinct, but need we write over our doors, '*Odi profanum vulgus et arceo*'? In other words, should not our houses follow our personal example, if we be gentlemen, and doff their hats to their neighbors?

"In my business hours I may perhaps be pardoned if I am sometimes brusque, and hence my business house may follow me in the expression of this. But am I equally pardonable if my churlishness is not only carried into my house, but is thrust upon the street offending my neighbors? Not so; the courtesy I expect I should extend, and the house in which I live should say plainly to those who can less escape the daily sight of it than of me, 'Here lives a gentleman.' This does not mean extravagance of ornament nor lavish outlay of money nor vulgar solicitation of notice. It is beyond and above these, and rather scorns than courts them. It is simple urbanity. It is the natural grace of a graceful society, to which every man in it owes allegiance.

"And this allegiance suggests the last quality which we may consider — Modesty.

"What man so great as to escape its obligation? what building? To-day we expend our labor upon some carefully considered design. It is carried out, and becomes what we and perhaps the world call our masterpiece. This last creation, emanating from our highest powers, furnishes to some stronger contemporary just the suggestion he may have lacked, and forthwith our masterpiece is eclipsed, and no one is the wiser as to how it came about. Our work once done becomes the world's property, and is judged not by the impression of the moment but by criticism matured through long time — criticism in which often we become witnesses against ourselves.

"The self-assertion of a man or of a design has in this calmly pronounced criticism no chance for favor nor for fame. All its cheapness and all its arrogance are revealed, and at last it stands forth a bragging humbug. Look at the splendid architecture of the second empire in France. Men of great talent created it. Millions were spent upon it. Why did it fall short of enduring fame? It is not modest, it protests too much; it claims too much. It has the cheap bluster of a hired bravo, and the false beauty of the street cocotte. We must learn to suspect in our designs all that directly demands admiration as its right. Ours should be rather the ambition to erect buildings which are said to 'grow upon one.' Not all of the buildings which have carried the world instantly by storm have held their place in its esteem. Most of them, in spite of pride and self-assertion, have fallen to their proper level. Fustian is always ephemeral, and brag is no more permanently effective in stone than in words.

"All that has been said, all that might be said, only brings us back to well-known principles, and we find at last that the summits of a great profession are achieved only by a persistent course and hard climbing; by self-denial and steady self-analysis; by wide and catholic views and finely tempered taste. But we may be sure that our work will never rise higher than its source; that no great creation comes from a small man. Such qualities as we have considered do not get into the building except through its architect; so we see that a gentleman among buildings means a gentleman among architects. Remember it was not Michael Angelo who did the talebearing or indulged in the loud recrimination when St. Peter's was building."

In another paper, read before the architectural class at the Art Institute, and printed in the "Inland Architect" for June, 1890, he discusses, more specifically, "a great architectural problem"—that of the design and construction of a large modern office-building. Its minute description of the system of "Chicago construction" cannot be omitted, because this system was partly his invention and his firm was among the first to use and develop it. The paper begins by pointing out the growing complexity of human habitations. "In the great monuments of early Egypt, of Greece and even of mediæval Europe, as well as in such smaller buildings as have survived to this day, very few and very simple ideas dominated the whole structure as well as its art expression. . . . It was the Renaissance, with its wonderfully vital and complex thought, which first began to impress upon architecture the stamp of individual whim or desire. . . . And with the enormous growth in wealth and civilization since the Renaissance, especially since the beginning of this century, the change has been beyond the wildest flight of the imagination. The luxuries of kings are now necessities of life to the day-laborer; and following every modern necessity is a vast nebulous train of luxuries, all in their turn to become fixed and solid as necessities. These all demand accommodation and expression in modern architecture, and architecture must meet the demand."

He points out that "sufficient time has not yet passed for this expression to be fully wrought out," and continues:—

"Architecture is, like every other art, born of its age and environment. So the new type will be found by us, if we do find it, through the frankest possible acceptance of every requirement of modern life in all of its conditions, without regret for the past or idle longing for a future and more fortunate day; this acceptance being accompanied by the intelligent and sympathetic study of the past in the spirit of aspiring emulation, not servile imitation. If the new art is to come, I believe it will be a rational and steady growth from practical conditions outward and upward toward a more or less spiritual expression, and that no man has the

Ornament of Capital, Rookery

right to borrow from another age an architectural idea evolved from the life of that age, unless it fits our life as normally and fully as it fitted the other. I say practical conditions, and this is fully meant — practical conditions without qualification or abridgment. Whenever in the past such a full acceptance occurred, and a building was erected in the effort frankly to express the conditions thus accepted, art has been willing and ready to consecrate the effort. But, on the contrary, whenever art has been evoked to abridge in architecture one of those normal conditions, she has been distant and cold. . . .

"We live in an age beyond all others reasonable. The ethical and art status apparently reached by the Greeks and

Venetians through processes almost intuitive, must be reached by us, if at all, through processes entirely rational. If the problem before us were the design of a temple to Jupiter, with its simple portico and cella, the whole attitude of the mind would be different from that which is demanded in the effort to design in homogeneous and expressive form a great and complex office-building of twelve stories, constructed of steel and terra-cotta. Here the pure art expression can never be so high, perhaps, as in the simpler problem for reasons inherent in the problem; but if it is to be truly an art expression worth considering, it will be reached at the point where intellectual action, intensely concentrated upon vital conditions about and within us, passes into an unconscious spiritual clairvoyance. Here is the path which will lead us in the right direction, though we may not reach the end of it. . . .

"The subject, then, of this paper is some of the processes by which a large office-building in Chicago is evolved, from the time when the site is determined to the time of its occupancy. The subject is chosen because no class of buildings is more expressive of modern life in its complexity, its luxury, its intense vitality. The purely artistic side of the question will not be enlarged upon, because, as I have said, it is the practical and even commercial sides which at this moment need special attention, not so much for themselves, but as factors, and most important factors, in every aspect of a great problem; occupying a much greater and more significant relation to the ultimate art expression than has generally been conceded to them.

"How much 'per cent.' has always been considered foreign to art, and generally it is. Yet, curiously enough, it may sometimes guide art, if not positively foster it. Art has never grown vitally without some sort of check, whether in the limitation of the age, the narrow yet intense idea which was the inspiration of the epoch, the specialized occupations of the moment, or some other equally valid cause. And in this age the question, purely commercial, of 'per cent.' often intrudes itself at a time when thoughtfulness is about to give way to mere lavishness, and asks of the mind the pertinent question 'why?' At the moment when an architect is intrusted with work to be executed by him 'regardless of expense,' let him beware that he lose not the thoughtful temperateness which should underlie even the most splendid effort. But when a certain income must be derived by revenue from the building designed, every question must be carefully weighed, investigated in every possible light, and the result is apt to be interesting, at least as expressive of thought; and if solved with truth and imagination, it will be interesting also from an art standpoint, as art in architecture is merely the expression in solid material that some one has thought for our comfort and delight.

"Let us begin, then, at the moment when the questions involved in such a building arise and are propounded to the architect for solution.

"Let us suppose that in the business centre of this city a piece of ground has been purchased, lying upon the corner of two prominent streets, the dimensions of the ground being 150 feet north and south, 100 feet east and west, with a 16-foot alley on the south. It is surrounded by buildings averaging in height nine stories, and the average width of the streets on which it fronts is 70 feet, being in one case 66 and in the other 80. Of course, the first radical question to suggest itself is that of light, and this will at once dictate certain general and preliminary conditions of the plan upon the ground. Experience has demonstrated that all spaces within the enclosure of four walls which are not well lighted by sunshine, or at least direct daylight, are in office-buildings non-productive. The elementary question, therefore, is how to arrange the building upon its lot so that every foot within it shall be perfectly lighted, and all spaces which would be dark thrown out.

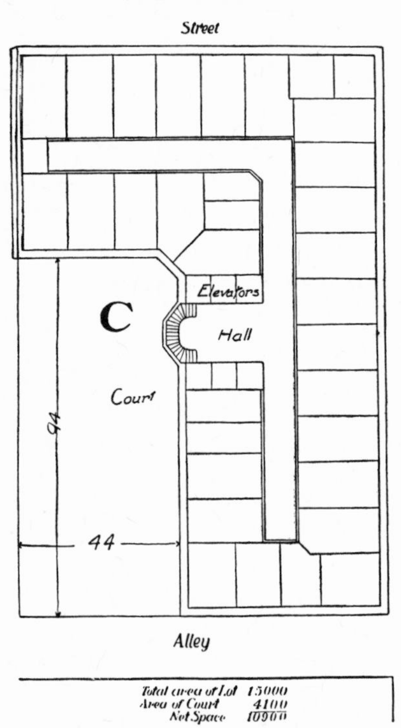

Plan for Office Building

Three floor-plans are then presented and minutely discussed with reference to this problem of light, the decision resting upon the plan shown. The writer continues: —

"The next general question is the number of stories, and in Chicago, at present, the difficulty is not to determine how few, but how many. Nothing to a stranger seems more irrational than the present rage in Chicago for high buildings; but the reasons for it are obvious and the fact apparently fairly well established, so that we must accept it. Let us assume that twelve stories are determined upon.

"The next step is to approximate the cost of the building; a question of keen interest, and one in which it would not be conceded generally that the architect puts his best foot forward. Here experience has shown that the cost may be obtained within a very small fraction by ascertaining the gross cubic contents of the building from the bottom of the foundations to the top of the roof, and inclusive, also, of all the space enclosed within walls in the shape of areas, etc. Dependent upon the elaborateness of finish, the cost per cubic foot of such a building will vary from 25 to 40 cents, although in Eastern cities the latter figure is often greatly exceeded. Thus, a building of this sort, containing 2,500,000 cubic feet, will cost, according to its elaboration, from $625,000 to $1,000,000, the average being about $750,000.

"The general plan being now determined, and the question of cost discussed, we proceed to other points relating more in detail to the arrangement of the building, and which still have especially to do with the question of revenue."

The writer then discusses nine such points, embracing height of stories, character of the main entrance, number and size of elevators, position of pipes and shafts, toilet-room and barber-shops, burglar-proof vaults, space in basement, plumbing and steam fixtures, and spacing of windows. He continues: —

"Think of the feelings of an Athenian architect of the time of Pericles, to whom the problem should have been presented to design a building of fourteen stories, imposing the following conditions: All of the stories except two to be ten feet six inches high, all window-sills to be exactly two feet from the floor, all lintels to be six inches from ceilings, and all windows to be in width not less than four and not more than six feet, and to be situated at distances apart of not more than six feet. If these conditions did not paralyze the architect, give him a few more: That all windows should have flat lintels, and that he must avoid as much as possible all projecting members on the façade, since these catch dirt and soot; and give him instructions to put on a few ten-story bay windows.

"The next group of questions of vital importance relates to structure. The building must be fireproof. . . . The present fireproof structure is provided with metal columns and beams, all of which are enclosed in an envelope of hollow terra-cotta, which is fastened securely to the supporting metal. By this device heat is kept away from all metal work, and absolute safety is secured. (Fig. 1.) Steel columns are coming rapidly into use instead of cast iron, for the reason that iron presents many unreliable features in the difficulty of obtaining perfect castings, and of ascertaining certainly whether the casting is perfect or not. The steel columns are made of rolled plates of steel which are bent into proper form and riveted together. Thus they may be inspected thoroughly, and they are absolutely trustworthy.

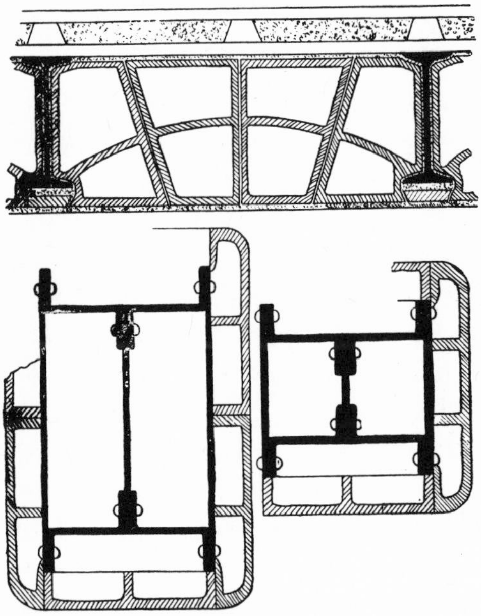

Fig. 1. Construction of Fireproof Column

"In the enormously tall buildings now erecting, scarcely any form of masonry is strong enough to use alone in the construction of the fronts; when, as noted above, windows must be placed at distances not much more than twelve feet apart, and should be at least four feet wide. This leaves a pile of not more than eight feet at best, and this is often not strong enough to carry its load unless one makes it very thick, or strengthens it with metal. The first is costly, both in itself and because of the renting space it consumes. The second is entirely practicable and satisfactory. An iron or steel column is placed within the masonry pier, attached to it by anchors which do not interfere with any difference of expansion of the metal and masonry, and this column carries the loads of the various floors, the masonry being a mere protection against fire and weather. Another and still simpler method is to enclose the metal column in an envelope of hollow terra-cotta supported at each story on the column itself by brackets. In this case the column does all of the work, and any portion of the terra-cotta covering may be removed without injuring the structure.

"Beneath all of these various supporting members foundations lie, which present some of the most interesting features of Chicago architecture or engineering. The greater portion of the centre of the city is built upon a bed of clay, more or less soft, the firmest part of which lies at an average depth of 12½ feet from the grades of streets. . . . By tests made by the government, and also by individuals, this clay is found to be capable of carrying loads of not more than three and a half tons to each square foot. Practically this is greater than is safe, and the load generally assumed as conservative varies from one and a half to two tons, as greater loads per square foot create settlements so large as to be embarrassing. Into this clay, every building built upon it settles to a greater or less degree. In several cases this settlement is considerably over a foot.

"The general theory of the foundation plan is to exactly proportion the area of each foundation pier to the amount resting upon it, keeping it free from every other foundation pier, so that the whole settlement will be equal, each pier being entirely independent. Thus a pier weighing, with the floors supported by it, 150 tons, should have footings of 100 square feet, and one of 75 tons, footings of 50 square feet. Several very nice variations must be made from this general law, but this is the rule.

"How best to construct this floating raft is the vital question. Formerly it was made in the shape of a pyramid of stone laid in cement, but this is costly, filling up the basement with its bulk and adding often twenty per cent. to the gross weight of the whole pier. The present method is to lay down upon the level clay a thin bed of cement upon which are placed steel rails or beams, spaced at closer or wider intervals, according to the weights to be carried and the length of the beams. The rails are then filled between and covered by cement, thus excluding air and water; another set of beams are laid upon them, somewhat less in area, and so on, the whole forming a solid mass of cement webbed with a mesh or grill of steel, giving it very great transverse as well as crushing strength. (Figs. 2 and 4.) Such a foundation is made, covering areas of 20 feet square or more, the total height of which is not over three feet six inches, thus leaving the basement unobstructed.

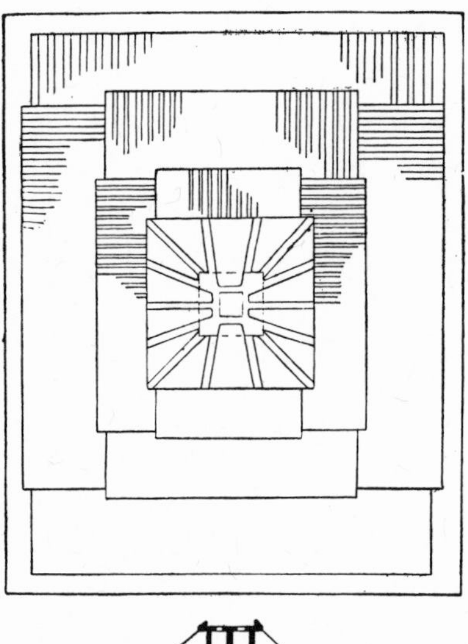

Fig. 2. Steel and Cement Foundation

Under the old system of construction a stone pyramid 12 or 14 feet high would have been necessary to do properly the same work, and this would have filled up not only the entire basement, but some of the first story also.

"I have said that whatever construction of foundations be employed, some settlement of the building takes place. This creates several very delicate and interesting problems. It frequently happens that a very heavy building is to be erected by the side of another already completed. The new building will, of course, settle, and in doing so will work injury to the old one, cracking its walls, destroying the level of its floors, etc. Besides this, the old foundations are not large enough for the new and larger weights. To overcome this difficulty arrangements are made to underpin the old wall, and support it temporarily with heavy timbers extending far enough east and west to span the width of the proposed new foundations. While the wall is thus supported the new foundations are put in place, and that portion of the new wall begun which is needed to make, with the old, a composite wall strong enough for all of the work. The old wall, up to this time carried on timbers, is not reconstructed for some time, but instead of the timbers originally used jack-screws are substituted. (Fig. 3; see following page.)

"As the new construction proceeds, the new wall, with its foundations, slowly settles, and to hold the old wall and the building to which it belongs in place, the jack-screws supporting it are turned from time to time, becoming slightly lengthened, and thus keeping the former levels undisturbed. This it will probably be necessary to continue for a year or more, as the new building will continue to settle for that time. When all settlement has ceased the jack-screws are removed one by one, and the space occupied by them filled with brick.

"This is simple enough; but sometimes it happens that the old building adjacent to us is so occupied in the basement that we may not go into it without underpinning, and are thus prevented from using the above device. We cannot rebuild the foundations, yet we must not add to the load they carry. Here comes in one of the architect's best friends, the 'cantilever.'

"Some distance from the old wall, columns are placed which are used as fulcrums of a lever. Farther away, on the long arm of the lever, another line of columns is placed, and against the old wall still another. Beneath these a foundation has been built, widest under the columns next the wall, and narrowest beneath the columns farthest from it. The columns next the old wall will carry, on beams connecting them, whatever height of new wall we may require to be added to the old for the completion of our building. A very heavy girder runs beneath these three columns, and you will see by this diagram that if our calculations be correct, the column A will tend to settle most, the column C least, and the intermediate column B should settle exactly like all columns carrying simple and direct weights. Thus we carry our own new wall from within, and in no way disturb the neighboring building. (Fig. 4.)

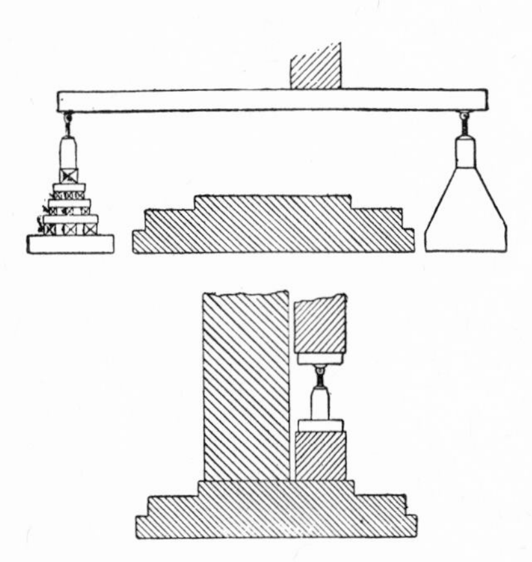

Fig. 3. Temporary Support of Old Wall

"When the foundations are completely built, as I have indicated, large cast-iron shoes are put upon them to receive the base of the steel columns and distribute the loads carried by them over a larger area upon the footings. (Fig. 2.) When the steel columns have been placed upon these shoes, and the structure has reached the first floor, the steel or iron beams are all bolted to the columns through wrought-iron brackets, and each beam is bolted to the next, forming a perfectly rigid skeleton of metal. To guard against all lateral movement from wind pressure or other causes, diagonal braces are carried along the tops of the beams between

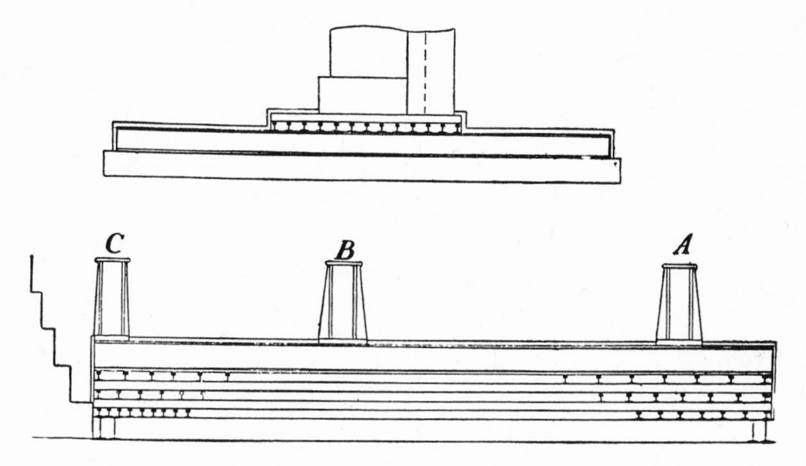

Fig. 4. Cantilever Support of Old Wall

extreme points of the building, so as to tie the whole structure together like a truss. So strongly may this be done that a section of floor framing might almost be turned on edge and hold itself intact like a bridge truss. Thus, this great iron skeleton is slowly articulated from story to story, and during this process the flesh and skin begin to grow upon it.

"It will not do to wait till the roof framing is done before covering the anatomy of the building with its fire-clay, for here a nice point peculiar to our soil comes in. The plans of our foundations have been made necessarily for the completed building, and at each stage of the construction the same relationship, as nearly as possible, between the weights of each pier must be maintained as will ultimately exist in the completed building; otherwise one part will settle lower than another, and needless strain be imposed upon the building. If the soft clay kept its original condition after the completion of the building, the whole structure might resume its levels with completion, though, as just remarked, with considerable strain; but the clay is compressed by the loads placed upon it, and is drained of its water to some extent, thus becoming harder and capable of resisting greater pressure. Those weights which are placed upon it last do not settle so much as those placed upon it in the beginning. The whole construction of the building should, therefore, develop at the same time.

"All that has been written relates to those portions of the building with which the public at large can have but little interest, but which are the inner and significant principle about which every external aspect must arrange itself. The truest and best forms which this external aspect is to present will be found by a reasonable appreciation of conditions of our civilization, of our social and business life and of our climatic conditions. Even a slight appreciation of these would seem to make it evident to every thoughtful man in Chicago that all conditions, climatic, atmospheric, commercial and social, demand for this external aspect the simplest and most straightforward expression. Bearing in mind that our building is a business building, we must fully realize what this means. Bearing also in mind — though this, like the other conditions, is not likely to escape us — that dust and soot are the main ingredients of our native air, we must realize what this means. Both point the same way. Every material used to enclose the

MILLS BUILDING, SAN FRANCISCO

structure we have seen raised must be, first, of the most enduring kind, and, second, it must be wrought into the simplest forms.

"These buildings, standing in the midst of hurrying, busy thousands of men, may not appeal to them through the more subtle means of architectural expression, for such an appeal would be unheeded; and the appeal which is constantly made to unheeding eyes loses in time its power to attract. In them should be carried out the ideas of modern business life — simplicity, stability, breadth, dignity. To lavish upon them profusion of delicate ornament is worse than useless, for this would better be preserved for the place and hour of contemplation and repose. Rather should they by their mass and proportion convey in some large elemental sense an idea of the great, stable, conserving forces of modern civilization.

"Enough has been said to suggest how radically new in type such edifices are, how essential is the difference between the modern and any of the preceding recognized architectural types.

"One result of methods such as I have indicated will be the resolution of our architectural designs into their essential elements. So vital has the underlying structure of these buildings become, that it must dictate absolutely the general departure of external forms; and so imperative are all the commercial and constructive demands, that all architectural detail employed in expressing them must become modified by them. Under these conditions we are compelled to work definitely with definite aims, permeating ourselves with the full spirit of the age, that we may give its architecture true art forms.

"To other and older types of architecture these new problems are related as the poetry of Darwin's evolution is to other poetry. They destroy, indeed, many of the most admirable and inspiring of architectural forms, but they create forms adapted to the expression of new ideas and new aspects of life. Here, vagaries of fashion and temporary fancies should have no influence; here the arbitrary dicta of self-constituted architectural prophets should have no voice. Every one of these problems should be rationally worked out alone, and each should express the character and aims of the people related to it. I do not believe it is possible to exaggerate the importance of the influence which may be exerted for good or evil by these distinctively modern buildings. Hedged about by many unavoidable conditions, they are either gross and self-asserting shams, untrue both in the material realization of their aims, and in their art function as expressions of the deeper spirit of the age; or they are sincere, noble and enduring monuments to the broad and beneficent commerce of the age."

Railway Station, Buena Park

I am conscious of having preferred to quote from Root's essays passages which show his rebellion against the dry conventions of his art, and of having suppressed those which insist with equal emphasis upon a complete and thorough scholarship in its history and traditions. Such arguments as those I have omitted are more familiar, and may, perhaps, be left safely to the reader's intelligence. What I have wished chiefly to show here is the alert modernness of this man's sympathies, the broad foundation of humane reason from which his imagination took its flight.

V

HIS WORK AND ITS RESULTS

I HAVE permitted my hero to give unawares an analysis of his artistic conscience, of the motives of his work and its aims. It remains now to consider what he accomplished. Here I get no help from him; and indeed I can almost hear his voice in protest. "All that I did," he would say, "was hastily done; tentative, immature, imperfect; give it the charity of silence." When the projectors of the First Regiment Armory suggested that the signature of the firm be carved into its corner-stone, Root refused; adding with one of his swift smiles, "We may do better ten years from now." None thought so lightly as he of his achievements. Two months before his death, in an anonymous review of Chicago architecture, he described John Root as "the victim of his own moods — too facile always carefully to reconsider his designs." "Much work by Burnham and Root," he said, "is suggestive and has borne its part in the architectural movement of the day, while much of it reveals crudities begotten of the haste or indifference of the hour." It happened sometimes that a building was put through so rapidly, or under such severe limitations, that the result did not fairly represent the designer. Looking from the windows of his office one morning toward one of his tall structures, he said, "What blamed architect is responsible for that? I don't know him." And others of his buildings palled upon him so cruelly that he would go around the block to avoid passing them. In the rapid growth of his mind, its expansion in creative power, his past work soon ceased to satisfy him. He would turn aside compliments of his most successful designs by saying that no one could tell whether they were good for anything until they had been tried by time. He longed to revise the building of last year by the knowledge of this, and his mistakes became demons which mocked and tormented him from many an edifice, rebuking all temptation of pride. And besides, his modesty went deeper. To his instinct, self was not the fixed centre of the universe, but merely a clear medium through which strange forces flowed and ebbed. Any impression which his individual mind might make upon these forces seemed too slight a thing in comparison with infinite possibilities to be worth talking about.

But "the man who does not make mistakes very seldom makes anything." Root's work had the spirit of youth in it, and its faults were errors of strength rather than weakness; cast off as impedimenta, leaving the runner ever more free for the race, and suggesting the hope of athletic completeness in that great future which death robbed us of. Although time often failed to ratify his work in his own mind, the cases were few, in spite of the enormous pressure upon him, in which a building went out of the office without representing his best thought at the time. "He had a kind of pride," say his brother and others, "in being personally responsible for nearly if not quite all designs executed in the office. His genius was so impressed upon his employees that the individuality of nobody else was expressed in the designs." This was regarded by many as a mistake; "with his extraordinary fertility and versatility, he attempted to do too much." One of his friends writes that he "tried to induce him to interpret his studies in free hand and not make such careful drawings; to spend his time more on the mass than on the detail. But he replied, 'Who will dot the i's and cross the t's of my buildings when they get my drawings in the draughting-room?— they rub off enough as it is.'"

An architect who was four years in Burnham and Root's office, part of the time at the head of the draughting-room, says: "Mr. Root was the swiftest and most accurate draughtsman I ever saw; he could make, did make constantly, quarter-inch-to-the-foot scale drawings off-hand." Another, who has had much experience in making perspectives for various architects, dwells upon the accuracy of Root's drawings. "Most architects make little sketches," he says, "and the draughtsmen fill them out. But I tell you, when I got a drawing from John Root to make a perspective of, I had to knuckle down and do as I was told. When he had a new job in his mind he would sit and think it over quietly; and then perhaps he would pull down a book of photographs in the style he wanted; and he would give just a glance to each picture — never stopping — go through the whole book in five minutes, turning the leaves just as fast as he could with his funny chubby fingers. And then he would shut it up and say, 'demmit!' under his breath — (he used to say 'demmit' like Mr. Mantalini; it was his only profanity) — still turning the thing over and over in his mind. And in a day or two he would see that building in front of him, and throw it on paper like lightning. He used to hate to do perspectives — said he was too stupid. But just look at that one — he could do them better than any of us when he cared to try." Thus

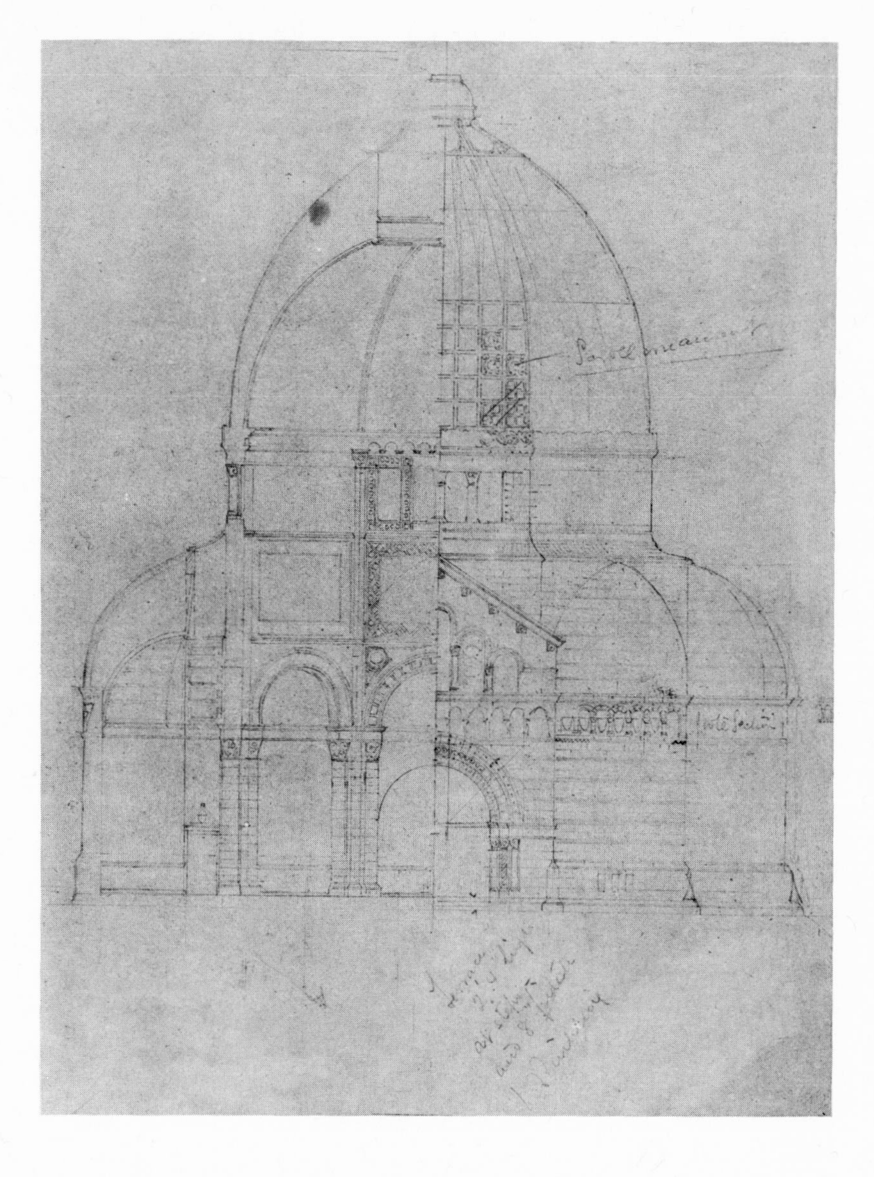

CROSS-SECTION, INDIANA SOLDIERS' AND SAILORS' MONUMENT

Facsimile Reduction of Mr. Root's Sketch

we are assured that the essay, "Hints on Design," fairly describes his own method of work.

He drew usually on large sheets of heavy light-brown paper spread out on a wide table. When his drawings had served their purpose, he did not care what became of them, and, as a rule, they were destroyed. Many of the earlier ones were burned in 1885 with the firm's offices in the Grannis Block; and the later drawings were left to the mercy of chance, for only during the last months of Root's life did the firm begin to awake to the advisibility of filing them. The greater portion of those which still exist are studies for buildings which were never erected — studies which, never having been used, were preserved for future reference.

He drew with incredible rapidity; never in a tentative, fumbling way, as though searching for an idea, but boldly, as though he were sketching a completed edifice. He had the rare power of seeing the finished building with his mind's eye before he put pencil to paper — a complete architectural prevision. A word, a hint, a sudden thought, would send a great structure shooting upward in his imagination, and a rush of swift exact strokes on brown paper would make it a reality. "He could really see it," says Mr. Burnham; "I have never seen any one like him in this respect. He would grow abstracted and silent, and a far-away look would come into his eyes, and the building was there before him — every stone of it." Doubtless this vigor of imagination accounts for the feeling of spontaneity and enthusiasm which all observers find in his best designs. "His works are full of life; they seem to breathe," said Mr. Frederick Baumann at the Columbian Congress of Architects. A vivid joy went into them — the ardor of a mind too full for utterance, the thrill of a keen and vital inspiration.

It was as much in construction as in design that Root proved his inventive genius. The mathematics of his profession interested him as deeply as its art. As an engineer, he was always venturesome: because a thing had never been done before was no reason, in his mind, why it could not be done safely, provided the figures authorized the experiment. Early in his practice, when the South Park stables were built, Root carried the large roof on a kind of truss new in Chicago, which the contractors were afraid of. When the time came for removing the scaffolding, the men predicted that the roof would collapse; so the young designer himself took out the last screws and gaily waited for the catastrophe.

"For the Montauk Block, as well as others of his earlier tall buildings," writes Mr. Walter C. Root, who, from 1879 to 1886 was in his brother's office, "John personally calculated the footings and laid out the constructional drawings." This seven-story block, built in 1882, the first high office-building erected by the firm and the lowly leader of the sky-scrapers, embodied an experiment destined to revolutionize the entire system of foundations for heavy buildings. In the planning it was found that stone piers, of the size necessary for supporting a heavy column of fire-proof vaults, would seriously obstruct, not only the basement, but also the first story. Mr. Owen F. Aldis, one of the owners, mentioned this objection to Root, and told him that he must make room somehow for the dynamos. "A day or two later," Mr. Aldis reports, "he said to me: 'I believe we could make the piers smaller without loss of strength by buying old steel rails, which would be cheap, and laying them row on row, with concrete around them to prevent rust.' He made preliminary calculations then and there, and decided that it would be feasible. With his concurrence I called in an expert engineer to go over the foundations, because of the unusual height of the building. The expert approved all the figures except for one pier, but on review he found that Root was right and the error was his own. In carrying out the plan, we were surprised to find that the new kind of foundations was cheaper than the old." The experiment aroused great interest and grave criticism at the time. I myself remember Root's certainty the steel-rail-and-concrete system would prove a success, and his laughter over the croaking of doubters.

Façade, House of Reginald de Koven

It was not the first time that iron had been used to strengthen foundations. One such instance occurred in the '70's, when Mr. Frederick Baumann, one of the veterans of the profession in Chicago and a man of great ingenuity and skill, being summoned to bolster up a settling building, constructed new piers beside the old ones, strengthening their foundations with iron beams. But Mr. Baumann states that no concrete was used by him, that his parallel beams bore little relation to Root's mesh of embedded steel, and that Root never knew of his experiment with metal until he told him about it years after.

In the Montauk Block the new foundation was used merely as a temporary expedient, with no thought of extending the system to other buildings. But after the Insurance Exchange had been built in the old way, the firm found that there was scarcely room enough in its stone-obstructed basement for necessary machinery. Resolving not to be caught in that way again, they studied various expedients for gaining space without digging deep into the earth, which the conditions of our soil make inexpedient. The old Montauk experiment recurred to their minds as the most available plan, and accordingly they determined to use steel-rail-and-concrete experiments throughout under the tall buildings then in the office — the Rialto, the Phœnix and the Rookery. This system enabled them to save much time by doing the work in winter. Thus, instead of great derricks handling immense stones, the astonished people of Chicago saw on these lots low wooden roofs pierced by numerous chimneys, under which were being laid quietly and comfortably the foundations for eleven-story buildings.

The success of this system has been proved by time: to-day the Rookery shows a variation of less than an inch in settlement. It opens large spaces for rental in the basements of heavy buildings, which, under the old system, would have been filled up by piers, even to the exclusion, often, of the necessary room for boilers and dynamos. But I need not dwell on its economies of space, time and money, upon its stability and fire-proof quality. Mr. Dankmar Adler, of the firm of Adler and Sullivan, took occasion, soon after the completion of the Rookery, to express most felicitously to Root the thanks of the profession, telling him that he was "entitled to the same praise which is accorded the man who makes two blades of grass grow where one grew before."

Other problems arose in regard to foundations, especially in planning high buildings adjacent to lower ones already built. The firm was the first to use the cantilever arrangement of steel footings, by which a heavy party wall could be supported back of the ground directly under it. Mr. Walter C. Root writes: "Some very difficult cases arose: old party walls had to have footings removed, and had to be reënforced or added to in thickness. Into this field of comparatively untried engineering John pushed easily and with invariable success. To one who has 'grown up,' so to speak, familiar with these problems of calculating footings, reënforcing party walls, planning steel foundations and steel buildings, they seem not especially complicated or difficult feats of engineering. But to start into this field, hitherto unexplored, develop these new schemes, push to logical conclusions old principles, and accomplish so easily and successfully these large results, certainly showed a constructive mind of great imagination and grasp.

"In a technical and narrow sense, John's mathematical and engineering abilities were deficient. He had not time to learn and keep up the many branches of constructional detail. He was rusty in his calculus and trigonometry, ditto much of his applied mathematics. I do not believe he would have cared to trust himself to calculate an important truss; it was not necessary nor desirable that he should. With the increasing press of work in the office, the custom developed rapidly of having specialists work out the various problems; for example, after an idea like the steel-rail footing had been developed, engineers were consulted as to the best methods of execution. But John had such a quick perception that he could suggest to a specialist an idea which would illuminate him, and enable him to work out a solution of a hard problem in a new and brilliant manner.

"Captain Eads, I think, was not technically informed in the details of his own work, yet he is considered by engineers one of the greatest lights in the profession in his day and generation. He could not calculate a complex truss, but he could develop the general scheme of an enormous and difficult bridge and see its practicability when others felt discouraged. So with the Mississippi jetties. He had the ideas and he could find the mathematicians. This illustrates what I mean when I say John was not an engineer or mathematician in a technical sense. Emergencies such as those in Chicago required a great deal of judgment in addition to figures. His judgment of these constructional problems in general was the quickest and best I ever saw. That is imagination — imagination as shown in the conquest of a practical and unpoetical problem."

After being used successfully in foundations, metal beams climbed rapidly up the walls. Mr. Walter C. Root continues: "Mr. Jenney, in the Home Insurance Building, was the first architect to build any extended piece of wall with iron columns encased in brick, although such columns had been used before in special single piers. The diminished price of steel, certain object-lessons in the unreliability of cast-iron, and criticisms of engineers, determined the use of rolled steel exclusively in later buildings than those of the Rookery period." Messrs. W. A. Drake and P. B. Wight contributed the invention of steel columns having air-chambers and fire-clay around them, and as the buildings climbed higher and higher, the system of steel construction developed rapidly towards its present completeness. The devices by which his sky-scrapers were tied together vertically, horizontally and diagonally, against all possible resistance of weight and fire and cyclones, were always an engrossing study with Root. When I resented one day his preoccupation with these commercial buildings, he replied, "But I rather like to make them stand up." He felt that in the art, or, rather, the science of building, invention has not kept pace with its nineteenth-century progress in other sciences, and he was always trying to think of new devices, and to lengthen the list of available materials. He valued brick, and used it with straightforward directness, and in various buildings he proved the effectiveness of carved and molded brick for ornament. He appreciated the lightness and adaptability of terra-cotta, and was the first to erect an entire facade of this material. "We are now closing up the Rand-McNally Building," he wrote to his wife in August, 1889, "and I am glad to say that we have succeeded in keeping both fronts entirely of brown terra-cotta."

These various innovations were not accomplished without much criticism. Rival industries were antagonized even to the point of accusation. But, strong in honor and reputation, the partners cared little if their motives were impugned. "No man, who for the moment seems to be successful," Root wrote to his wife in the summer of 1890, "can hope to escape abuse of some sort."

He used to talk almost as much about the engineering problems as the artistic ones, and his office letter-book proves his close attention to them. The subject interested me, and several times he gave me a minute description of some new device. When the late H. H. Richardson, who left this branch of the profession to his engineers, was designing his massive granite building for Marshall Field & Co., he entered Root's private office one day and questioned him about soil, foundations, etc., in Chicago. Root thereupon accommodated him with an hour or more of his lucid talk upon technical details. He once detailed to me, as he did, presumably, to the great designer, the elaborate series of fine balances by which a heavy building is adjusted to our uncertain soil. A letter in his handwriting, written in June, 1889, in answer to certain criticisms of the owner of the newly planned Monadnock building, is in point. He says—(I quote only the essential paragraphs):—

"The system employed for these foundations is exactly that used here (Rookery) in all respects except where beams are used in the lower course of concrete. This latter detail was employed after a conference with Gen. Sooy Smith, who endorsed it as superior to the use of concrete alone.

"As to the variation of loads between large and small piers (foundations) the same variation is employed here and in the Phœnix with success, and originated in a discussion between George Tapper and me several years ago. The theory of it is that by increasing the weight per foot on small piers and diminishing it on large piers, the tendency to 'punch up,' or be lifted by the downward movement of large piers, is lessened. Experience in this building (Rookery) having demonstrated that the theory here employed was sound, we do not like to make any arbitrary variation from it; especially as the system is the result of experience beginning at the old Grannis Block and carefully tested by actual practice through many other buildings."

The combination in one mind of ability as a designer with ability as a constructive engineer has always been rare among architects. The essay on office-buildings, quoted in the previous chapter, sufficiently proves Root's scope and exactness in the mathematical part of his profession.

It is characteristic of him that, in describing the various devices, many of which he had invented or developed, he should make no personal claim to them.

Root's freedom and fecundity in his specialty were made possible by his partnership with a man of strong executive capacity. Alone, he would have been embarrassed by

Hall, House of Reginald de Koven

many details wholly obnoxious to an artist of his temperament. It was Mr. Burnham, as a rule, who created opportunities for the designer, especially before the reputation of the firm was fairly established. It was his important function — the most important of all in the opinion of many an architect, certainly the fundamental one — to "get the jobs." In a letter to his brother written in November, 1887, Root says: "We have just had very good luck in saving the Cleveland Building, which I feared had gone up the flume. Burnham took a lot of studies I made, and with them and his own nerve carried the committee gaily into camp." In many of the stock-companies which erected the largest buildings, Mr. Burnham was a director and the principal organizer. Though the partners conferred continually in regard to the conduct of the office — its relations with clients, contractors and draughtsmen, and other matters of general policy or of detail, it was Mr. Burnham who carried out their conclusions, took the brunt of the negotiations with contractors, and, except in the department of design, managed the large force of employees. He relieved Root also of much conference with clients, although, toward the end, these gentlemen were invading the latter's private office more and more. In a letter of July 12th, 1890, we find Root lamenting: — "D. H. B. has been away — first in New York and now in San Francisco, and this compels me to do much more of the 'jaw' work than I enjoy, and tends also to keep down something of the efficiency of my proper work."

Mr. Burnham had unflinching courage and an abiding faith in men and in large projects which inspired all who were associated with him, compelling them to live up to his expectations. His judgment and taste were good, and as a critic he was very suggestive. "He would lean over John's drawing-board," says a gentleman long in their employ, "and say, 'John, I don't like that very well.' 'Well, what's the matter with it?' John would say. And then Dan would point out something: tell him to fix up that corner, or change the grouping of those windows, or strengthen the sky-line, or do something else with the drawing. And John would reply that he thought it was pretty good as it was. But invariably after Dan had left he would fall to studying over the drawing, and would end by strengthening the weak places as Dan had suggested."

Mr. Burnham was skillful in laying out a building. Root did not enjoy this part of the work, and rarely assumed it, except in the case of buildings which presented novel problems, or in which he felt a special loving interest, such as the Art Institute, the Woman's Temple and many residences. When a building came to the office, Mr. Burnham, as a rule, laid out more or less roughly ground and floor plans. Frequently he made many such studies, the partners deciding together upon the best one, which Root would use as the first element of his problem in designing the exterior. The senior partner influenced strongly Root's exuberant imagination both as a stimulus and a check. Root often felt a certain reluctance in initiative. His mind was of the Shakespearean type: it could build temples, towers and palaces upon a hint; but it craved the hint, as Shakespeare craved his plot, for the starting-point of his dream. Usually this hint came from one or more conditions inherent in the problem: such as shape of ground, proportions of building, kind of material to be used, amount to be expended or some other element of the equation. Sometimes the suggestive word came from a client, oftener from his partner, or perhaps the latter would embody it in a sketch drawn in a few rough lines. And from such a seed the plant would grow and flower in Root's brain as swiftly as a magical mango-tree. Out of the long list of the firm's work, the buildings in the exteriors of which Mr. Burnham claims a share, by virtue of rough sketches embodying the starting-point of an idea, are the Monadnock, the

Insurance Exchange and the Woman's Temple, a water-tower and office-building at the Stock-yards, the Montezuma Hotel in Las Vegas, the First Regiment Armory, St. Gabriel's Church on Forty-fifth and Wallace Streets, the design (never executed) for the San Francisco "Examiner," and five residences, two of them — Mr. Hale's and Mr. Kent's — being of considerable importance. In the cases of the Insurance Exchange and the Montezuma Hotel, Mr. Burnham finds that the relationship between his suggestion and the final design was slight, while in those of the Monadnock and the First Regiment Armory it was closest.

The evolution of the beautiful design for the Woman's Temple illustrates the hospitality of Root's mind to criticism and suggestion. The first sketches seemed perfunctory, lacked inspiration — a square tall office-building, nothing more. Mr. Burnham was the first to view and object. "If that is honestly your idea of what this building should be, go ahead with it," he advised in his large serious way; "but if you are not yet interested, if you have not put your soul into it, try again." And he urged a change of form, made a rude sketch showing an exterior court, a change which Root embodied in the second drawing. Root was always ready to show his studies and eager for criticism; so one evening about this time, when the partners had invited a few friends to their office for a bit of hilarity, he brought out this large drawing and asked two or three of us what we thought of it. At that time it was roofless, and we complained that it expressed no idea except that of a commercial building. "That's what it is," said Root. One of us retorted, "But it is something more as well; these women have higher hopes for their temple — it should express their aspiration." "Why don't you give it a roof?" said another; and so the talk went on. In a few days he remodeled the upper stories, and added the beautiful roof and a slender upward-pointing flèche as well. The design was complete in the form it will assume when the money for the flèche and for the sculpture over the gateway shall have been appropriated. For this building Root made ten or twelve different studies for ground and floor plans, and Mr. Jules Wegman, then a draughtsman in the office, made tracings from them which are still in his possession.

Mr. P. B. Wight, from whose office Burnham and Root passed to their own, wrote after Root's death that "the key-note of his great versatility in design" lay in the fact "that he was quick in seizing on the capacity of all building-materials for architectural expression, that he designed for the materials, and did not have to find materials for carrying out his designs." He continues: "Root was consistent in his ideas from the time that he first put pencil to paper, and continued to develop them to the end." In other words, he was constructively, as well as artistically, an architect. His feeling for design was always based upon a profound sense of structure. He built up a design from its bones, felt the anatomy of his buildings in every stroke of his pencil. To a man so constituted, architecture could never be defined as a decorative envelope applied irrelevantly to the structure of a building; on the contrary, every lightest ornament must grow out of structural conditions as naturally and inevitably as a flower from a plant.

Thus the secret of both his versatility and his consistency—I cannot emphasize this trait too strongly—was his love of truth, his feeling that beauty can be attained only through truth. A building, he thought, should frankly express not only its structure, but its purpose; it should choose the materials most expressive of its purpose. A purely commercial building in a smoky city should not be carved out of monumental stone and loaded with mouldings and meaningless ornament. Dwellings might flower in delicacy, temples of art and religion might draw upon the most precious treasures of beauty; but commerce should be content with simpler forms. His desire for truth, however, was wholly free from that conscious striving for originality which comes from the egotistical thrust of self into the equation. He felt the necessity for thorough scholarship. "No lasting success," he said, "comes to an artist who is not grounded in classics. Life is not long enough for one to discover for himself those laws of beauty which thousands of years have evolved for architecture."

It may be said, in general, that his quest of truth in an architectural expression of our modern civilization took, as its point of departure, the Romanesque churches and castles of southern France. Like Richardson, Root recognized in these a style arrested before completion, while still in the process of healthy development, and he found the spirit of it singularly suitable to the conditions before him. Though never limited to it, he based much of his work upon this early mediæval system of design, adapting and moulding it to his complex purposes with a fertility and energy of creative imagination which amazes those who try to follow the double-quick pace of his last ten years. Can this be the idle dreamer whom his father despaired of, this the lazy student who divined knowledge without digging for it? — this, one of the most prolific workers of his time!

Thus his more important work is based on romantic, rather than classic motives. "Richardson introduced the Romanesque revival," wrote Mr. Henry Van Brunt in his able review of Root's work, "and through the unexampled vigor of his personality, had already led it on to an interest-

THE WOMAN'S TEMPLE, CHICAGO

ing point of development when his career was interrupted by death; Root carried it still further toward the point of its establishment as the characteristic architectural expression of American civilization. The former conferred upon it power, the latter variety, and both, with their trained coadjutors in the profession, have already proved that the experiment is not merely a revival, barren of results, . . . but the introduction and probable acclimatization of a basis of design. . . . It seems to have been nearly proved that,

Fireplace, House of Reginald de Koven

in the hands of such a man as Root, upon this basis can be built an elastic system, capable of expressing any degree of strength or lightness, simplicity or complexity, force or refinement. It has also been proved, largely by his efforts, that the maintenance of the essential principles of the style does not depend upon the preservation of its peculiar original archaic character in structure or ornament, but that it can amalgamate elements from classic, Gothic, Saracenic, or even Indian sources without being diverted from its strong natural growth."

Root's allegiance to the style which he used with such freedom and boldness was by no means exclusive. Unlike Richardson, he did not confine himself to it, and he would have been the last to assert its superiority for all purposes. His work shows essays in many directions — in the style of Queen Anne, of mediæval Holland, of the royal châteaux of France, of (freely adapted) colonial America, of Byzantine and Indian motives — some of these being among his admitted successes. The Flemish Gothic especially he delighted in; I think he would have confessed that he welcomed more than any other opportunity a subject which admitted of this motive. Its range was narrower than certain other styles, but he loved it. "We must beware," he wrote once, "of the servile imitation of those greatest and completest styles which mark the end of long periods of architectural development. To the use of these we have no right unless we shall have realized in our own mind the series of transitions by which the style was evolved, and for this reason it will be found often that a study of a transitional period is much more suggestive than a study of a complete style. Unity of design we must have, but unity must spring from within the structure, not without it. The great styles of architecture are of infinite value, but they are to be vitally imitated, not servilely copied. We must return continually to nature and nature's methods."

Up to the time of his death he had experimented little with the classic and its Renaissance outgrowths. Appreciating fully the beauty of Greek architecture, he felt, with Mr. Montgomery Schuyler, that "this very perfection, which was only attainable when life was simple and the world was young, this necessary relation between the construction and the detail of Greek Doric, makes it forever impossible that Greek detail should be successfully 'adapted' to modern buildings." Yet perhaps "forever impossible" is too strong a phrase to express a mind so unprejudiced, so open to impression and conviction, as his. One cannot lay down limitations for the course his mind would have taken through the coming years. Many persons close in sympathy with him believe that he would not have continued to exclude the classic from his architectural repertory. One of these, a gentleman long in his office, says: "He didn't use the classic much, thought there wasn't much in it — for us. But how prettily he was playing with it before he died! — it was just beginning to tempt him a little. If he had lived, and people had begun to demand the classic from him, he would have given them better and fresher classic than they have had for centuries." I have heard him speak appreciatively of colonial architecture, of the skill of these isolated designers, who, in translating into wood a style created for marble, introduced modifications suitable to the expression of the lighter material.

But I am lingering too long with generalities. In reviewing Root's work, swiftly and most untechnically, I shall make little attempt to decide upon the merits of the respective buildings, or to fix their place in the development of American architecture. All that must be left to time and the critics. I shall trace merely the course of his work through the designs which have been generally accepted as representing his best thought.

From the first he led his profession in Chicago. One of his first dwelling-houses — a little red-brick residence on Michigan Avenue, near Van Buren Street, which has since given way to commerce, had the best façade in town at that time. A larger house at 2100 Prairie Avenue — the firm's first important commission — was much discussed at the time of its erection in 1874 for its departure from prevailing types. It was revolutionary, epoch-making, though now it seems simple enough by comparison with the later essays of various architects which surround it. Some of the houses of that period still hold their own as good pieces of design, and already they showed great diversity of motive and treatment. No details of situation, material, or character of owner were neglected by Root as hints for an architectural motive, and there was little in the architecture of the time or place to make him respect precedent. In those days he was, perhaps, the only man in Chicago who stood for his new art — the modern progressive art, realistic in its truth to the life and the needs of its own time, idealistic in its revelation of the beauty of this common life, the spiritual poetry inspiring it. Other men came afterwards who felt the new influences, but to the day of his death none ever disputed his lead.

The first office-building in the firm's long series was the Grannis Block, erected in 1880, at 115 Dearborn Street. This was burned a few years later, but restored according to the original design, with the addition of two stories, and re-named the Illinois Bank Building. The use of brick for a down-town office-building was an innovation at the time among the conventional façades of cut-stone. In design the building showed many points of innovation; in small matters as well as great, Root was always striking out from the old ruts into new paths soon to be widely followed.

During the winter of 1881 occurred the long and disappointing competition for the Chicago Board of Trade.

The members of this great corporation, resolving to seek larger quarters, bought the lot at the foot of La Salle Street, commanding its long straight vista, and selected a building committee of five gentlemen, who should secure plans and carry on the work. The majority of the members of this important committee seem to have been chosen because they had time to give to the delicate task, fitter and abler men being completely engrossed in business and unwilling to serve their society and the public. Thus the committee did not fairly represent the corporation it served in either knowledge or taste. The committee ordered a general competition, and paid five of the leading firms of Chicago a thousand dollars each to compete. At this invitation, Root set spurs to his quick imagination, and in an incredibly short time three designs, each with its complete set of drawings, water-color perspectives, etc., were prepared and submitted from the office of Burnham & Root, in competition with many others. Two of these plans followed the usual conventions in combining under one roof the great hall and the offices which were to be used for rental. The third, which was presented as the firm's idea of the building, differed from all others in making separate architectural features of the two, uniting them by a corridor. This design was much admired during the public exhibition and the new idea of the building was endorsed by the committee, several members of which heartily congratulated Burnham & Root upon the unchallenged superiority of their plans. After a time, however, these committeemen rehearsed to the firm the complaints of the other architects, who objected to the acceptance of a design which was based on an idea so little in accord with precedent in such buildings — so original a departure. The committeemen begged the young men, "merely as a matter of form" and in order to satisfy the objectors, to go into a new competition on the basis of their own idea. This was disappointing, but the committee's reasoning was so plausible that Burnham & Root made the mistake of consenting to a new competition based avowedly upon their plan. The new design which Root evolved was a more careful study than the other, developing out of it. Though accepting the round-arched Romanesque for its motive, it treated the style with great freedom and boldness, enriching the façade, for example, with a flowery exuberance of decorative sculpture, for which Mr. John Donaghue made sketches with all the enthusiasm of his brilliant youth. It was sculpture loyal to its modern subject, showing Chicago, crowned with elevators, whose form became as decorative as battlements, receiving the products of the world.

A long wrangle, growing ever more bitter, now commenced in the committee. Two plans were finally preferred — Burnham & Root's, for which Mr. Charles Counselman held out valiantly to the end, and a hocus-pocus sort of whispering-gallery affair, suggestive of the Mormon Temple at Salt Lake City, which was designed by a local creator of abominations. Experts, who were summoned to estimate upon cost, found that either building, if erected, would not exceed in cost the million dollars appropriated.

Burnham & Root at first took this rivalry as a huge joke, but when their opponent secured four votes in a committee of five, it became apparent to the members of the Board of Trade, who from the first had strongly favored the firm's plan, that the danger was serious, and a petition was circulated and generally signed on the floor against the acceptance of the absurd design. The committee, not daring to disobey this mandate, compromised upon a commonplace design upon which no estimates had been made, and whose cost afterwards outran the original appropriation by about seventy-five per cent. By this questionable proceeding the city was again saddled with "several million dollars' worth of hideousness," and the long vista down La Salle Street, which might have been an inspiration of beauty forever, has become an eye-sore and a disgrace. The building soon began to settle unequally and show great gaps and slants;

Project for Boatmen's Savings Bank, St. Louis

and when, about twelve years after its erection, the stones began to fall out and threaten the lives of occupants and passers-by, it was found necessary to remove the tower. Its great clock now looms from the top of the low central window, like the single eye in the forehead of a Cyclopean monster. Unfortunately the beauty of Root's design for this building cannot be put in evidence, as the drawings were all burned in the destruction of the firm's offices in the Grannis Block. Mr. Burnham says that it was one of his partner's most brilliant works. His memory prefers the first design for the wonderful spontaneity, the swiftness of inspiration it showed. The second, which grew out of it, though more carefully studied, more complete, lost, to his mind, something of this intensity of feeling. In the second, Root placed a great tower over his connecting corridor. Neither the first nor the second design could be classified with exactness under any historic style. Both contained crudities, as most work does which springs from a direct and vital inspiration, but the completed building would have carried boldly any defects of detail, and, in the opinion of those who remember it, would have won the admiration of all critics as one of the best works of modern architecture.

But if the firm lost the Board of Trade, they received commissions for many of the large office-buildings which were needed around it, in a district of the city which, at that time, was little improved. Their first high building had been the Montauk Block, but this was designed under limitations so severe as to make Root rage at the time; various designs being rejected as too ornate, he made one in sheer desperation at last which he called a "sugar-factory," and this was approved. When completed, the building seemed to beetle over the street at the top; and thereafter he made the walls of tall buildings recede an inch or two as they grow thinner at each architectural story — a device which conquers the defect without being apparent to the eye. In the office-buildings which now followed in rapid succession — the Insurance Exchange, the Rialto, the Rookery, the Phœnix, the Rand-McNally, the northern half of the Monadnock, the Woman's Temple and the Masonic Temple, in Chicago; the Society for Savings and the Cuyahoga, in Cleveland; the American Bank Building in Kansas City; the Chronicle and the Mills Buildings in San Francisco, the Equitable Building in Atlanta, and many others — he proved his power of luring beauty to the service of commerce. The charm of these is in their fitness, their business-like simplicity, the frankness with which they accept limitations and use them as inspirations. The strong proportions and mighty lines of some of them express the relentless power of the spirit of modern commerce; of others the greater delicacy and grace set forth its broader human sympathies, its close alliance with all phases of human life. They were always planned rigorously for light, convenience, and economy of space, having courts either interior or exterior, and elevators carefully located and grouped. In them the stairway loses the commanding position which it has held in architecture since the dawn of the Renaissance, its place of honor being assumed by groups of elevators, its windings by the lofty vista of many-storied courts. That able and scholarly architect and critic, Mr. Henry Van Brunt, wrote thus in 1889 of the strenuous conditions out of which these works of art have sprung:[1] —

"A ten-story office and bank building, fire-proof throughout; with swift elevators for passengers and freight, a battery of boilers in the deep sub-basement giving summer heat throughout, and supplying energy for pumps, ventilating fans, and electric dynamos; equipped like a palace with marbles, bronze and glass; flooded with light in every part; with no superfluous weight of steel beam, fire-clay arch, or terra-cotta partition; no unnecessary mass of masonry or column; the whole structure nicely adjusted to sustain the calculated strains and to bear with equal

[1] "Architecture in the West," *Atlantic Monthly*, vol. lxiv, p. 772.

stress upon every pier of the deep foundation, so that no one shall yield more than another as it transfers its accumulated burden to the unstable soil beneath — such a problem does not call for the same sort of architectural inspiration as the building of a vaulted cathedral in the Middle Ages, but, surely, for no less of courage and science, and, in providing for the safe, swift and harmonious adjustment of every part of its complicated organism, for a far wider range of knowledge. The one required a century of deliberate and patient toil to complete it; the other must be finished, equipped, and occupied in a year of strenuous and carefully ordered labor; no part of its complex being overlooked, all the details of its manifold functions being provided for in the laying of the first foundation stone, and the whole satisfying the eye as a work of art as well as a work of convenience and strength. Whether one compares a modern building of this sort with a cathedral of the first class, with one of the imperial baths or villas of Rome, or with the Flavian Amphitheatre itself, it must hold equal rank as a production of human genius and energy, not only in the skillful economy of its structure and in its defiance of fire and the other vicissitudes of time, but as a work of fine art developed among practical considerations which seem fundamentally opposed to expressions of architectural beauty."

It was the Chicago office-buildings of 1893 which forced upon M. Paul Bourget, classically trained Frenchman though he is, the recognition of "the simple force of need as a principle of beauty;" which won from him the highest praise that may be accorded to works of the human mind — the praise which recognizes the artist as an unconscious instrument of vast forces, the inspired mouth-piece of a civilization. He writes: "There is so

little caprice and fancy in these monuments and these streets, that they seem the work of some impersonal power, irresistible, unconscious like a force of nature, in the service of which man has been but a docile instrument." It is this expression of the overpowering immensity of modern commerce "which gives to the city something of tragedy, and, to my feeling, a poetry." He finds in these temples of trade "the sketch of a new kind of art, an art of democracy, made by the crowd and for the crowd, an art of science in which the infallibility of natural laws gives to audacity apparently the most unbridled the tranquillity of a geometrical figure." [1]

Root met the conditions of this new art without scorn and with perfect sincerity. In fulfilling them he preferred the simplest materials and was sparing of ornament. One of the most troublesome requirements was the necessity for open shop-fronts at the base of these buildings, the point where a massive expression of structure is an artistic necessity. He met this by various devices: in the Rookery by mounting the building upon heavy granite columns and piers, behind which the large windows are recessed; in the Woman's Temple, the Insurance Exchange, the Phœnix and other buildings, by thickening the base, and cutting low square windows through the heavy walls without moulding or ornament; in the Mills Building (San Francisco) by designing the piers low in proportion to their thickness, and heavily accentuating the horizontal lines. In many of these instances and in general the massiveness of the lower stories is emphasized by the use of a heavier material than that used for the superstructure.

The entrances of these buildings are always large and generous, never mere holes in the wall. Here, with the

[1] *Outre-Mer*, by Paul Bourget; vol. i. ch. v.

suggestion of hospitality, comes a demand for grace of decoration, for greater delicacy and charm. Accordingly these wide portals usually invite the wayfarer by a wealth of happy ornament, spontaneously conceived and fittingly in place. The great archway of the Phœnix (now the Western Union Building) is confessedly one of its author's masterpieces. In the smaller granite arches of the "Rookery" entrances, the history and name of the building are commemorated by rooks at the capitals — for here stood formerly a temporary court-house, erected immediately after the Fire and degenerating shabbily into a "rookery," which lingered beyond its rightful date. The balconied porch of the Insurance Exchange with its archway and flanking tourettes, and the imposing granite gateway of the Temple, in front of its exterior court, may be mentioned as further evidence of the beauty and amplitude of Root's entrances.

Project for San Francisco Examiner Building

I will present a few details descriptive of the six or eight office-buildings which, by common consent, represent the best work of their designer in this direction. The first of these in the order of time, the Insurance Exchange, is a ten-storied edifice, composed in five architectural stories, the lowest of gray stone, the others of red brick, with a temperate use of ornament in carved and moulded brick and terra-cotta. The porch, which is admirably planned, is flanked at its second story by round tourettes corbelled at points level with the top of the low archway of the entrance, and conically finialed above the line of a narrow projecting balcony. Similar tourettes at the upper corners of the building emphasize the sky-line, with its corbelled brick cornice. The proportions of this façade, strongly accentuated horizontally, are rhythmical and satisfying, and the whole composition is expressive of dignity and reserve.

In the Rialto the massing is in strong vertical lines. Two tall pavilions are separated by a recessed court and gateway; and the piers which divide the fenestration are carried straight to the roof and finished with finials. These fret the sky-line too much, and the design has other defects; but it is a bold and striking architectural essay; its faults are not those of weakness.

The Rookery stands upon a plot of ground nearly square, giving the designer the advantage of depth which the narrow lots of the Insurance Exchange and the Phœnix denied him. Here there are eleven stories, and the material is brown brick, with a massive colonnade of granite at the basement. At the angles of piers the bricks are rounded, and there is much moulded brick and terra-cotta decoration suggestive of Arabic motives. Mr. Van Brunt objects to the equal value of horizontal and vertical divisions in this building, and finds in its adventurous detail "an absence of subordination and repose;" and Root himself always doubted whether its wealth of ornament would endure the test of time. But the people have set upon it the seal of their approval, and perhaps their verdict will prove the final one. In this case I stand with the people, for this building always charms me, affects me like a strain of music which fortunately combines delicacy with strength. Doubtless this arises partly from the spontaneity and lavishness of thought which it evinces — a prodigality of inspiration which is nobly carried off, without waste of strength. The effectiveness of one feature — the interior court with its audaciously planned stairway — has never been called in question.

The Phœnix or Western Union Building is notable chiefly for its noble entrance, already referred to. Before the recent addition of one story, this building was a composition in eleven stories, the two-story basement being of brown stone, and the superstructure of red brick with terra-cotta ornamentation. This building contains many interesting experiments, some of which were followed up afterwards, and others, such as the use of oriels, were abandoned. On the whole, the design, though brilliant and audacious, and standing well in the line of development, may be said to lack repose and unity.

The Masonic Temple was a problem which Root chafed under, but to which he attempted to give the most direct solution possible. "Sky-scrapers," elevated out of true proportion to their base, were not at all to his liking; and in this case, two stories were added to the design after he felt that its altitude was already too great. One does not feel sure of the strength of the base, which in most of the firm's buildings is wholly adequate. The thirteen undeviating stories which rise above it are a frank expression of an undeviating purpose, but the eye waits for its reward until it reaches the strong lines of the gables, supporting the steep roof with its dormers.

MILLS BUILDING, STUDY OF ELEVATION

Facsimile Reduction of Mr. Root's Sketch

The Monadnock — "Jumbo," Root used to call it — was the last of the tall buildings to show walls of solid masonry. For this building Mr. Aldis, who controlled the investment, kept urging upon his architects extreme simplicity, rejecting one or two of Root's sketches as too ornate. During Root's absence of a fortnight at the seashore, Mr. Burnham ordered from one of the draughtsmen a design of a straight-up-and-down, uncompromising, unornamented façade. When Root returned, he was indignant at first over this project of a brick box. Gradually, however, he threw himself into the spirit of the thing, and one day he told Mr. Aldis that the heavy sloping lines of an Egyptian pylon had gotten into his mind as the basis of this design, and that he thought he would "throw the thing up without a single ornament." At last, with a gesture whose pretense of disgust concealed a shy experimental interest, he threw on the drawing-table of Mr. Dutton, then foreman of the office, "a design," says this gentleman, "shaped something like a capital I — a perfectly plain building, curving outward at base and cornice." This was the germ of the final design, and it provoked much discussion and study in the office. Mr. Dutton and others suggested modifications; the projecting base was carried up through two stories instead of one, the cornice modified, the lines of the bays carefully studied. Mr. Wegman tells of standing over Root's drawing-board when he was at work on this elevation, and watching him draw in the Egyptian cornice; and many persons remember his desire to grade the color of the building from brown bricks at the bottom to yellow at the top — a project which only lack of time for the manufacture prevented. Critics are divided as to the value of this design, some declaring it not architecture at all, and others — Mr. Montgomery Schuyler, for example —

pronouncing it the best of all tall office-buildings. To my mind there is grandeur in the simplicity of its lines, and refinement in the delicacy of its gradations. From the great outward sweep at the base, the eye rises without weariness to the gentler slope of the cornice and wins a sense of vastness, of dignity and repose.

The two parallel façades of the Rand-McNally building, executed wholly in brown terra-cotta, use this material frankly and with grace. The entrances, placed at the ends of each front, are especially fortunate. The Equitable Building in Atlanta is an admirable composition — a free rendering of French Gothic, strongly massed in horizontal divisions. A narrow façade, never erected, for the Weber Piano Company, is interesting as one of Root's rare experiments with Renaissance motives. The design is very effective.

The Mills building of San Francisco is the last to be considered of those buildings in which the commercial idea alone demanded expression; and it is one of the most successful of all. Root himself, in a letter to his wife dated September 14th, 1890, says: — "This Mills building is to be a great success — I am very well pleased with it." Like the two Temples, and many other buildings which were unfinished when he died, it was designed at a time of tremendous strain, when the World's Fair work was added to labors already excessive. In the same letter he writes: — "You may guess something of the nature of the crush when I tell you that of the $2900 pay-roll of yesterday (two weeks) over $400 was for over-time." It is said that the plans and elevations of this building were completed in two days. Four or five of Root's preliminary pencil drawings of elevations in various styles remain to attest the study he gave it.

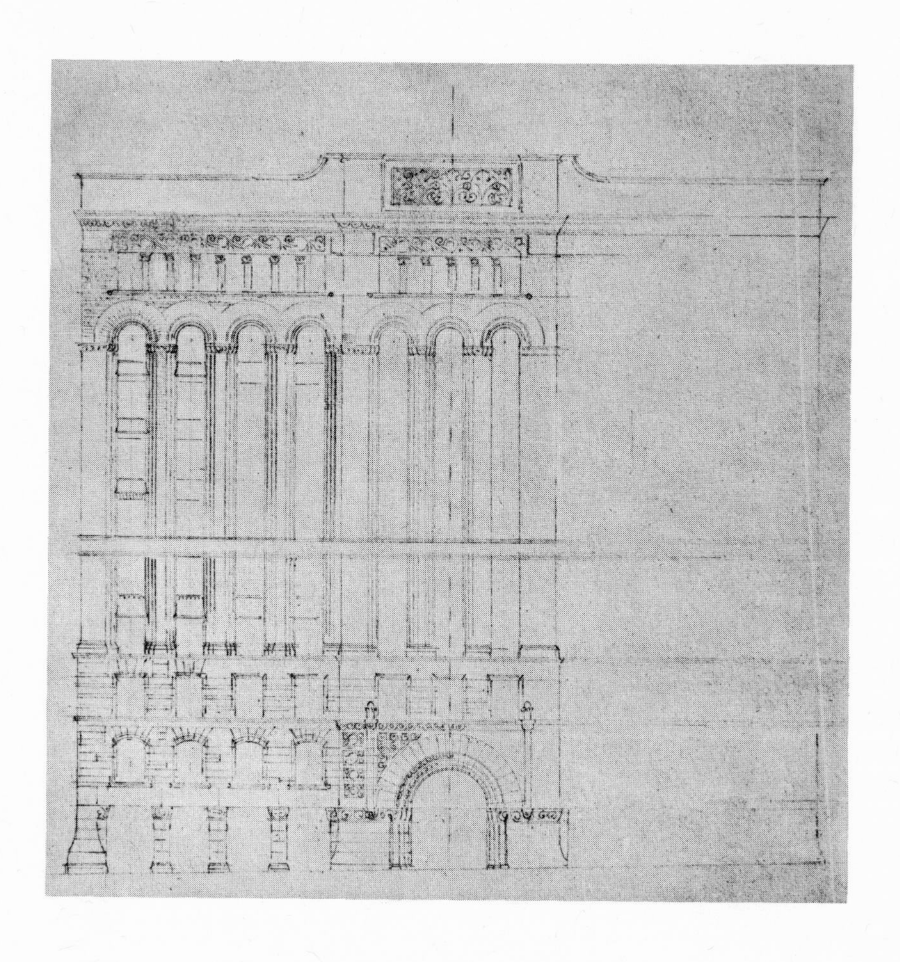

MILLS BUILDING, STUDY OF ELEVATION

Facsimile Reduction of Mr. Root's Sketch

The atmospheric conditions in San Francisco permitted the use of a creamy marble for the lower stories, and cream brick and terra-cotta for the superstructure. The three stone stories, pierced by oblong windows, and divided by strong horizontal lines, form the base of the design, the wide arched entrance embracing two of them. On this base massive fenestrated piers arise at each corner of the building to a light secondary cornice six stories above; and between them, on each façade, is a lofty arched colonnade of pilasters supporting another fenestrated story, and graced, along and above the arches, with profuse decoration in terra-cotta. The whole composition is crowned by an attic story — a light arcade supporting a strongly projecting cornice. The effect is one of athletic dignity and power, with the supple grace of perfect poise.

In the Temple designed for the Woman's Christian Temperance Union, the problem presented to the architect contained a motive of sentiment and aspiration, which demanded expression in a building chiefly commercial. The triumphant fulfillment of these two elements of the equation makes this structure perhaps the most beautiful building of its kind yet erected. "As an expression of strength and dignity," says Mr. Van Brunt, "crowned worthily by beauty and grace, no nobler example has been given in modern times." "It is the only one of the tall buildings," said an architect recently, "which succeeds in carrying a roof."

The first design for this structure, intended for a site of a size, shape and outlook different from the one finally selected, is interesting for the beautiful Romanesque tower which rises at the corner to a height of 230 feet — one of the best towers, for the strength of its base, the grace of its upward sweep, and the beauty of its crown, which Root ever designed.

As erected, the Temple consists of twelve stories, having a two-story granite basement, and a superstructure of red brick with terra-cotta ornament. The design is powerfully massed. Its two great pavilions are connected behind a recessed court, in front of which the main entrance pierces a curtain wall continuous with the two-story rock-faced basement. The pavilions have great round fenestrated towers at the angles, starting from corbels at the second story, and between them the groups of windows are arched under the cornice which, with terra-cotta ornament in bas-relief, finishes the second architectural division of seven stories. Above this the third architectural division consists of a story uniformly pierced by low arched windows, supporting a low attic story, through which, at the centre of each pavilion and along the sides and centre of the building, are steep gables; and behind them and the conical roofs which crown the towers, rises loftily the tiled hip-roof with its dormers. A slender and beautiful flèche near the centre (not yet erected) completes the design.

The style of the royal châteaux of the Loire in its earlier and more severe phases is suggested by the treatment of roofs in this design, although, in its seriousness and stability, in its majestic grouping of large masses, the building confesses a fundamental Romanesque sentiment. The strength of its base, the harmony of its proportions, the grace of its sky-line, give one a sense of power and fitness, poetically, rhythmically expressed. Its many stories rise in their place by right, without heaviness or strain. It achieves completeness, appeals to one's feeling as inevitable.

Other buildings in which the commercial purpose is imbued with something of loftier aspiration, are the Kansas City Board of Trade, the competitive design (never erected) for the Cincinnati Board of Trade, the Herald Building in Chicago, the design (never erected) for the "Examiner" in San Francisco, and one (also unfulfilled) for the Boatmen's Savings Bank in St. Louis. This group includes some of Root's most interesting and varied work.

The competition for the Kansas City Board of Trade, which occurred in 1886, was conducted more sanely than the one in Chicago. Like the other, it was a general competition, including a few designs from prominent firms invited and paid to compete; but the committee, under the rules of the American Institute of Architects, was assisted

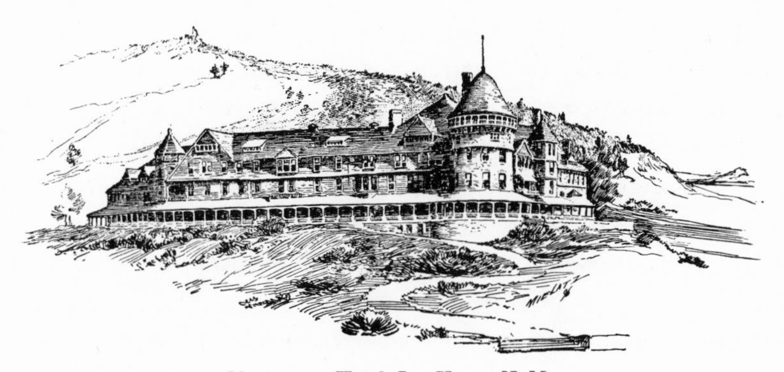

Montezuma Hotel, Las Vegas, N. M.

by experts, unaware of the authorship of the designs they examined. From the first Burnham and Root disliked competitions, feeling that they were rarely productive of the best results. After their first years they never entered one except upon invitation and payment, and their experience with the Chicago Board of Trade made them extremely careful about the terms, methods of award, etc., in any competition which they consented thereafter to enter. In Kansas City, their design being one of five approved by the experts, the committee awarded the commission to them, and it led to a number of important buildings — the

Midland Hotel, the American Bank Building, and others, including dwellings. The Exchange Building is a strong, spontaneous essay in civic architecture. The material, above the brown-stone base, is red brick, with terra-cotta ornamentation of the same color. The design confesses frankly a Romanesque inspiration, — the great tower, which rises abruptly behind the recessed court, from between the mighty wings of the structure, being a triumphant proof of the adaptability of the style to modern meanings. The two large pavilions which it unites differ somewhat in design; the one on the left, which contains the great trading-hall on the fourth story, bearing a low pediment with sculpture in bas-relief, and a narrow balcony at the base of the hall's lofty round-arched windows. The pavilions are strongly divided horizontally into three architectural stories, and are united in front by a screen containing the massive gateway — a round arch springing from low massed columns, which leads into a glass-covered court or chamber. The tower is broad and low, very beautiful in its grouping of windows and roofs, the semi-circular front, with its roof of steep conical slope, being particularly effective. This building is a noble monumental structure, which will speak to the future for this age as eloquently as monuments of the past declare to us the spirit of epochs.

In the competitive design for the Cincinnati Chamber of Commerce, the initial idea was that of a large Flemish guild-hall — a motive dear to its author, and remote from the Romanesque. A spirited, luxuriant rendering of this idea gives us a central story of lofty elliptically arched windows resting on two strong sub-stories, and crowned with an attic story flowering richly into dormers and corner towers with conical spires, and supporting a steep hipped roof. This design seems most joyously inspired; it is full of color and exuberant charm.

ENTRANCE TO MILLS BUILDING, SAN FRANCISCO

The Boatmen's Savings Bank, if erected, would have been one of the most original of Root's works. Its design was suggested by the uncommercial demand of the directors for a single lofty banking-chamber, unaccompanied by offices for rental — a demand which gave a rare opportunity for strong massing. The design is extremely simple — a Romanesque conception of a great modern hall of commerce. A wide and lofty arched entrance at the centre, with a group of small windows above, is flanked on either side by a single immense window rising above a low square barred window in the basement. The solid stone structure is surrounded by a steep tiled hip-roof. The design has a massive dignity which yet shows no trace of heaviness — a fault extremely rare in Root's work, in spite of the temptation to it in Romanesque design.

Of the newspaper buildings, the façade erected for the Chicago "Herald" is beautiful in its masses and proportions. Three wide elliptical arches for windows and entrance in the first story support three groups of windows, whose three stories form the second architectural division. The last consists of another fenestrated story, above which a lofty gable projects from a tiled hip-roof with small dormers. This façade, which is executed in brown stone, is one of the most charming of Root's smaller studies. He seized with delight the opportunity it offered for emblematic sculpture, placing a bronze "herald," modeled by Mr. Gelert, at the gable, and bas-reliefs under the arches of the crowning tier of windows. He was always endeavoring to make architectural use of sculpture and painting, believing that the arts develop most healthily when in alliance, and that the modern tendency to separate them from each other makes them exotic, and removes them from the sympathy of the people.

The eighteen-story structure designed for the San Francisco "Examiner" would have proved, if erected, a noble monument. The shape of the corner-lot — an elongated hexagon — suggested to Mr. Burnham during one of his Western journeys the idea of a great hexagonal commercial tower. Root's treatment of this idea suggests the Woman's Temple by its fenestration, by its corner towers ending in conical roofs, and by its strong lofty gables supporting a steep hip-roof with dormers. The wide segmental arch of the entrance springs from corner towers thickening massively downward; yet it seems not quite adequate to the vast weight imposed upon it, and I always feel that the designer would have strengthened this feature if the building had been erected. Otherwise, the lines and proportions of this tower, and especially the crown of it, are beyond praise for beauty and power.

The Davidson Theatre in Milwaukee, whose interior was afterwards burned and rebuilt from designs by Mr. Atwood, was the only one Root ever designed, though he was eager for such work. In the association of capitalists which was formed for the erection of the Auditorium, Burnham and Root had loyal partisans, but these awoke to their desire too late, when the great opportunity had been so far promised to Messrs. Adler and Sullivan that the other firm promptly vetoed the efforts of their friends. I remember asking Root about this time what would be his idea of this building, and his reply may be quoted as showing what he would have tried to do. "One would have to provide for a great hotel and an office-building," he said, "which should have a perfectly simple and frank expression. The problem would be to unite these elements with a tower which should bloom like a rose. It is in the tower, and there alone, that the exterior can show the central artistic purpose of the building."

He longed to build churches, but in his few slight experiments in this direction he was much hampered by lack of money. He felt the lifelessness and overstrain in modern applications of the Gothic to church architecture, and usually preferred the Romanesque. Rev. Maurice J. Dorney, for whom he designed St. Gabriel's Church at Forty-fifth and Wallace streets, remembers that Root, in talking over the problem with him, said that people too often attempted to

Fragment, House of William B. Hale

build "little cathedrals," instead of being content with parish churches. He thought that the Gothic style demanded heroic treatment in precious materials, and that the Romanesque was more suitable to a simple home of the people.

St. Gabriel's Church is treated on large simple lines, and is one of the most characteristic designs which Root ever put forth, as personal as the clasp of his hand. The material is a warm brown brick, shading from red almost to black. The broad gable over the archway of the entrance, springs, at the right, from a campanile very noble in its proportions. This tower is square, with round tourettes at the angles, ending in conical roofs, the one at the corner of the building being a turret larger than the others. The corbelled belfry, with its pyramidal roof, imparts to the tower a lofty grace. The façade of the transept repeats the lines of the main façade, apart from the tower, with a triple window in place of the entrance.

The interior is fine in the sweep of its strong lines. The choir is large, easily accommodating two hundred persons, and a round-arched colonnade in the apse gives it an effective background. Root's beautiful design for altar, screen, reredos, etc., has not yet been carried out. Father Dorney praises the church for its perfect fitness to the needs of his parish and for its admirable acoustics.

The first design for this church, which was too expensive to be executed, is considered by some judges Root's finest ecclesiastical work. This shows a large Romanesque church in brown stone, with equal transepts and a beautiful square central tower, low in proportion to its width. Both these churches give one that impression of spontaneity, of inevitableness, of commanding power, which prove a mind possessed by its inspiration. Their towers rise as lyrically as some of the belfries in villages of central France.

The Presbyterian Church of the Covenant, on Belden Avenue, is a free translation of the Byzantine to modern purposes, but it still waits for its tower. Another of Root's essays in the Byzantine was the design offered by invitation in competition for the Soldiers' and Sailors' Monument of Indiana. Root's idea of this monument — an idea in which the committee, preferring a shaft, did not acquiesce — was a memorial building, constructed of precious materials, and containing niches for statues, panels for paintings, and room for archives, flags and other mementoes. An octagonal pavilion, surmounted by a lofty octagonal dome, is his interpretation of his idea — a singularly fortunate and delicate essay in monumental architecture.

Root's best buildings have a way of "singing to the blue sky," which proves the genius of the man. A poet once remarked this rhythmic quality in the little Art Institute, at Michigan Avenue and Van Buren Street, which is now occupied by the Chicago Club, and whose fine entrance has been sadly marred by its new occupant. Here the designer could not pay tribute to art alone; on a corner lot of moderate size, space must be provided for rental as well as for galleries, necessitating an edifice of four stories instead of the conventional two. Yet the building is dedicated to the Muses by every line and ornament, by the grace and aspiration in it. The design, which is executed in hewn brown-stone, is emphatically in the Romanesque spirit. It is admirably massed, having three horizontal divisions: a story showing a generous entrance archway and two groups of two windows each over a low basement; two stories, each with three groups of three windows each, separated horizontally by carved screens and surmounted by round arches; and lastly, in front, an evenly fenestrated story supporting a high gable; and, on the north façade, four dormers projecting from the slope of the roof. Round tourettes at the corners, rising from corbels in the central division and crowned with conical finials, support the gable and roof and emphasize the sky-line. I will defer to a later chapter the description of Root's design for a Fine Arts Museum pure and simple, which, though never fulfilled, remains as his last and crowning work.

Of hotels and apartment houses he designed many, most of them tall city structures, planned as rigorously for space and light as an office-building, like the Great Northern in Chicago, the Midland in Kansas City, and the St. Louis in Duluth. Sometimes, notably in the last, he contrived to give a singularly habitable and inviting look to his design, in spite of stern limitations. A more attractive study than these was the Montezuma Hotel at Las Vegas, built for the Santa Fé Railroad Company, far away among the mountains of New Mexico. Here the long low building seems to grow out of the very rocks from which its wide projecting roof slants upward. The generous welcome it offers, the sense of shelter from invading storms, the absolute fitness of every line and feature of it, make this far-away inn one of the most exquisite idyls its author ever dreamed.

Other commissions from railroad companies were for stations in various towns. One of these is the Grand Avenue Station in Kansas City, another is in Des Moines, another in Galesburg, Illinois, and smaller ones are in Buena Park, a Chicago suburb, in Clinton and Ottumwa, Iowa, in Fort Scott, Kansas, and elsewhere. The firm erected pavilions and other structures in various parks, among them a charming one on the lake shore in Jackson Park, a casino in Garfield Park, and an open-air sanitarium in Lincoln Park.

And now the course of this review brings me to his dwellings. Of these one may find more than a hundred examples in Chicago alone, so varied in motive and style that it would be hopeless to attempt to suggest even remotely the charm of those which attain beauty, or to criticise those which fall short of it. The more conspicuous of them are listed with their locations in the appendix among the other works of Burnham & Root, and the student of architecture may judge for himself. In many of them, especially the earlier ones, the designer was obliged to concede much ; the list includes a great deal of pioneer work which did not represent his best thought. The long series gives striking evidence of his versatility, and of his readiness to experiment with new materials. Various architectural styles supply widely contrasting motives; and, in addition to the commoner varieties of brick and stone, less tractable materials are used, such as green stone, broken boulders, Georgia marble, etc. Some of these experiments are successful, others fail of enduring charm.

The variety of motive shown in these dwellings repre-

Kansas City Board of Trade

sents partly the mood of the architect, and partly the character and taste of the owner. The client, his aspect and habits, were always, with Root, a large element in the inspiration of a dwelling. When some one complained that a certain house was not pretty, "They are not pretty people," he retorted with entire seriousness; and a closer view showed that the house had a solidity and sobriety which fitted its occupants. Interiors, even more than exteriors, were affected by the owners' customs, and a further inducement to variety in both lay in the practice, commoner in the West than in the East, of separating a house from its neighbors — a practice which enlarges opportunity for unity of design. In his paper on "City Homes in the West," published in 1893 by Charles Scribner's Sons in a volume entitled "Homes in City and Country," Root refers to the suburban aspect of residence streets in Western cities. He traces the development of taste in dwellings, from the old "balloon-frame" wooden house, through the period of "Queen Anne" patches and that of rock-faced Romanesque heaviness, to the growing preference for greater simplicity and grace. He studies also the interior plans, more varied in the West than in the East because of the greater openness to light, and more expressive of the owner's insistence upon comfort — a trait which takes the best room in the house for the family living-room, instead of reserving it for occasional visitors. The interiors of Burnham & Root's houses show a charming variety of arrangement and detail, but it is impossible to consider them in this review.

From the large number of houses designed by Root, I shall speak of only five or six, selected because they are characteristic of phases of his thought, landmarks in his progress; and because, with all their variety, each has distinction and repose.

The house built in 1874 for Mr. John Sherman, at 2100 Prairie Avenue, scarcely stands among these, but deserves mention as the firm's first important commission. Many features of the design were revolutionary at the time, especially the high-pitched roof. Strong slanting roofs Root felt to be almost a necessity in storm-beaten

Chicago — "in this climate no house standing alone," he wrote once, "can be good without a visible roof;" and the roof became an important element in his designs. The entrance porch or recessed loggia he felt to be another essential of a Chicago dwelling, as a means of protecting the in-comer from hot or inclement weather.

House of Mrs. Max Meyer

The house in gray cut-stone erected in 1882 for Mr. Augustus Byram, at 2909 Michigan Avenue, is an admirable design, the north façade, now unfortunately obscured by another residence, being especially interesting. A large red brick house erected the same year for Mr. S. A. Kent at 2944 Michigan Avenue has more of French Renaissance feeling than is common with Root, and its façades show a great deal of beautiful bas-relief ornament in terra-cotta. This design has beauty of proportion and great delicacy, but it has been criticised by the purists for certain defects of ungrammatical detail.

A narrower house erected for the late Mr. Max Meyer, at 2009 Prairie Avenue, is beyond criticism, for a more perfect little composition can scarcely be found. The motive here is French Gothic, and the material is red-brown chipped brick, with brown-stone basement, copings, mouldings, etc. The first story shows an elliptically arched doorway and two windows. Above these windows a group of three curves outward very slightly in the second story, their centres on a line with small a window over the door. In the third story two large windows are grouped under a beautifully finialed coping; and on the level of their centre springs a curved gable containing two tiny attic windows. The detail is very delicate, and the general effect most humane and lovely.

Another beautiful narrow façade, erected at 65 Bellevue Place for Mr. Reginald de Koven, is a charming example of strictly urban architecture, and the interior plan is equally inviting. The material is reddish-brown brick, rough-faced in the first story, smooth above. Large copper bays at the second and third stories lead to a steep gable at the fourth, projecting from a sloping roof. This design, which has something of Flemish Gothic feeling, is graceful in proportions and rich in color.

A more pretentious house is that erected for Mr. John V. Farwell at the corner of Pearson Street and the Lake Shore Drive. Here the motive is Romanesque and the material is rock-faced black and gray mottled stone. This

PROJECT FOR A CHAMBER OF COMMERCE, CINCINNATI

is a good substantial house, well massed and planned, but it yields in beauty and originality to another Romanesque design further up the Drive — a house built in 1889 for Mr. Voluntine C. Turner at number 112. This is probably the best of Root's dwellings in this style. The material is a beautiful granite-like gray stone of rather straight cleavage. It is difficult to work, and such carving as it accepts must be strongly modeled. At the left is a round tower with a conical roof, and the entrance is at the side, behind this tower. At the right of the lower story is a hexagonal bay, with balcony above, and a low stone balcony carries the basement wall out to a line level with the tower and bay. In the third story is a beautiful curved gable, supporting a steep roof. Similar gables far back at the sides carry another roof across. The grouping of these dark-red tiled roofs with their chimneys is most happily conceived. The admirable grotesques, which form almost the only decoration, are delightfully in keeping with the mediæval style of the design. This house, unquestionably, seems born to live. "It will be as fine a century hence as it is to-day," said a critic recently.

Two houses in Goethe Street were among Root's last and most successful works, and their beauty illustrates his versatility. One, at the corner of Astor Street, erected for the late Mr. William E. Goudy, derives special interest from the fact that the design was intended originally for the architect's own residence. It is committed to the style of the French châteaux, and executed in gray cut stone, with a gray slate hip-roof. The wide, elliptically arched porch is near the centre of the longer façade, and above it, at the third story, rise a gable and tall chimney. In the narrower façade on Astor Street, the corners, with the sloping roof, are curved, and a small gable with windows projects from the roof above the copper cornice. This design is admirable for dignity and refinement.

The other of the two, and the last dwelling to be mentioned, is Mr. E. H. Valentine's residence on the corner of North State Street. This house is strongly colonial in feeling, its designer's only important work in this style. It does not follow servilely any given colonial type, but it confesses plainly the simplicity and dignity, even the severity, of the style. It is a large residence of two stories and basement, with an additional story of gables and dormers projecting from steep roofs that cross each other. The brownstone porch, with its triple archway, is admirably handled, and the warm red and brown of the Roman bricks give a rich tone to the structure. The success of this design shows the hospitality of Root's mind to the suggestions of a style altogether new to him, and makes credible the assertion that he might have gone far in experiment with motives derived from the classic.

Hall, House of Mrs. Max Meyer

Any reviewer of Root's work must emphasize the fact that it was merely preparatory. He had just gotten his materials well in hand, he was just beginning to win commissions for the kind of work he preferred, when fate deprived us of the ripened fruit of his genius. The large commercial structures, which must be pronounced his most important contribution to architecture, in a certain way do violence to his memory. He was deeply an artist, a poet; profoundly a lover of his kind, a dreamer of God. Temples of art, of music, of religion, were what he chiefly longed to do; but along with the opportunity for these came the higher opportunity of death.

VI

LIFE AND THOUGHT

T was in the spring of 1882 that we began to be intimate with John Root. At that time he was re-awakening to the joy of life. He had accepted engrossing work two years before as a refuge from sorrow, and this had restored the sanity of his temper, his sensitive consciousness of the beauty of the world. He was of a genus rare in the West at that time, one which until then we had scarcely encountered. To call it the artistic type would be hackneyed and not fairly descriptive, for this phrase has come to imply a complete give-and-take of emotion and expression in a nature which has no reserves. I would describe him rather, without reference to types, as a creature devoted to beauty by every instinct of his soul, one whose imagination instinctively rounded out the rhythms and unities of this inscrutable world of sense and spirit. Thus he was hospitable to the music of life and impermeable to its dissonance. Pain and evil he apprehended philosophically from afar — a basic undersong in the universal pæan; but their notes were not strident to his consciousness — they did not reach him as discord. Perhaps the special quality of the man is best described by the word *musical*. He was deeply, instinctively musical. All nature, all life he apprehended as harmony — harmonies of line, of color, of sound, of spirit. And underlying this sensuous consciousness in his mind lay that intuition of mathematical law which is the basis of all harmony. His sense of law was inherent in his sense of beauty, and it was in the symmetrical union of these two — the mathematical and the artistic apprehension — that his genius for architecture lay. For architecture, for music also; and most of all, for life. Life is the highest art, and he was a master in it; for to a soul thus complete in itself every day is a new joy. Thus there was an atmosphere about him — a certain freshness and radiancy drawn from the light and music in which he moved; and the most casual passer-by, unless he were a blind materialist, shared the buoyancy and perfume of it.

At this time he was indulging one of his idealistic friendships. The object of it was a great tenor in embryo, whose studies he lavishly assisted. Time was when they walked out the night together, Root filling his friend's mind with new ideals of Faust and Siegfried and Lohengrin, dreaming of enriching the stage with a new star. But the loves of the imagination were losing their power over him, for he was yielding now to a feeling more vital than he had ever known — a love strong enough to hold him more and more closely to the end of his life. It was an idyllic season with him — this summer of 1882 when we learned to know him well.

His face had lost nothing of sensitiveness during these three years since I first met him; in fact it never lost this trait, or hardened, as it grew in power, from the mobility of youth. Emotion played easily upon his features, curling his lips, expanding his nostrils, flushing his cheeks, lighting his dark blue eyes. The lines of his face were fairly regular: a high forehead, narrowing upward; a straight nose, a trifle shorter than the average; a fine mouth, its changing outline visible under the thin, light moustache; a firm, strong chin and jaws; and very small, delicate ears, set low and close to the head. His head was well rounded and compact in shape, his neck short, his chest broad and full, and his frame powerful. At this time he was in good athletic trim, but in his later years, unfortunately, he used his brain too much and his muscles too little, so that he became too heavy. The streak of laziness in him prevented his enjoying the hardier kinds of exercise, such as shooting, tramping, horse-back riding; but water-sports gave him keen joy. A swim on the border of the lake, or a sail over its sparkling waves — these were rapture to him; and nothing thrilled him with more delight than to be caught in a squall and blown almost over on the tossing waters. He was entirely fearless, accepting risks without thinking of them; feeling, with Robert Louis Stevenson, that "it is a far finer thing to be in love or to risk a danger than to paint the finest picture or write the noblest book."

With him music was not only the food of love, but its voice — a voice more direct than speech. He used to sing much at that time, having a clear tenor voice, which he used artistically until it was silenced, a few years later, by a slight but persistent hoarseness. And he would play by the hour, improvising or rambling among remembered themes. He scoffed at his music: it served him as cigars served other men, he said, for rest and soothing after the work of the day; he no longer had time for honest study of it — the ear and the memory must be his guides. I suppose it was because of the surroundings that I used to enjoy his music more than that of many famous performers. The ordinary concert hall, with its stiff chairs, its lights, its crowd, its programmes, is the last place in the world to listen to music. But given a couch and cushions and a dark corner, with a born musician at the instrument, and one may follow the great dreamers to their most sublimated ecstasies. "There is no thought," says a recent writer, "only mood." And yet we impede the mood by hostile influences when we invoke the most elusive of all the Muses.

We were kept laughing in those days by a wit kindly or merciless, according to the temptation, for he could not resist such temptations. He could tell good stories in three or four dialects, and his puns were shameless. I remember that one of my first talks with him drifted to the subject of puns, and he amused me by heaping whimsical maledictions upon the head of the punster and setting forth his depravity and insolence — a tirade straight from a burdened conscience. Few of his bits of repartee have escaped the oblivion which overtakes talk; and these linger in memory by mere chance, not by a survival of the fittest. But some of them may bear citing, though the zest of such things lies chiefly in the occasion.

"I'll give twopence for your thoughts," said some one.

"Am I looking too pensive?"

Again — a lady asked him to dine, saying, "We want your talk as a sauce for our dinner."

"But my talk is not saucy," he retorted.

One of his draughtsmen asked to be congratulated on his birthday. "How old are you?" said Root.

"Forty-two."

"You bear it with fortitude."

And one fine summer day, when an affectionate damsel in the park seemed more intent upon her companion than upon the flowers, he explained that her occupation was "not horticulture, but husbandry."

"A protective tariff," he said one day when politics

were under discussion, "is like damming a river to keep it to yourself. You have to keep raising the dam *ad infinitum*."

Again, "The artist has only lungs; the public is the atmosphere he breathes."

It was difficult for his wit to spare people, especially in his youth. Of a rather vapid young lady he remarked, "Her father is a lumberman, and her face looks as though it had been carved out of soft pine." A certain gentleman's mouth looked "like the ruins of a forest fire." Another man, who always kept his mouth open, "ought to have a hook and eye on his lips." When we called his attention to the fact that a lugubrious gentleman was becoming animated, he objected: "He can never be animated until he puts hinges on his ears; when so large a part of his anatomy is in repose, he can scarcely be lively."

A forgetful woman explained a lapse of memory by saying, "You have improved so much since I last saw you that I should never have known you." "I devoutly hope," Root answered, "that I won't improve so much before the next time you see me that you won't know me again."

A lady who was much given to flattery he always managed to out-flatter. At last she said, "You are so sarcastic, Mr. Root." And he answered resentfully, "I can be sarcastic about Niagara, or the Himalayas, or the pyramids of Egypt, but never about you, Mrs. X."

Mrs. Matilda B. Carse, whose ardor and ability in the service of the Woman's Christian Temperance Union have never spoiled her appreciation of a joke, asked him once if his three-year old son would not like to lay the cornerstone of the Temple. Root replied, "Why yes, and we'll have him show his appreciation of the honor by singing to the crowd his favorite song:

'Charley has good beer and wine,
Charley has good brandy.'"

It was on the cold damp morning of this "dry" ceremony, after many tongues had moved eloquently in praise of temperance, that Root turned to the business men who had sat solemnly through it with him, saying, "Let's go and get a drink."

When a callow youth at a wedding asked him if he did not pity the bridegroom, he answered, "Yes, Joseph; I pity any man who has not married my wife."

But I am anticipating his history. On the twelfth of December, 1882, he married Dora Louise, the eldest daughter of Henry Stanton Monroe, a lawyer of Chicago, and Martha Mitchell, his wife. For their honeymoon journey, Root led his bride back to his own South, to the family in Atlanta, and to the sunny lands and seas beyond. She traced home to his youth certain traits of her husband; discovered, for example, his feeling for negroes, his sympathy with their sunny amplitude in doing nothing. "Whad ye do with this quahtah if I give 't ye?" he demands of the ever-present picaninny. And the boy makes a solemn face and vows he "won't use it fo' no foolishness." "Then you won't get it," says the tempter, while the boy's jaw drops; "promise me you'll use it for foolishness." And wide is the responsive grin.

Even the honeymoon journey was shortened by new commissions, new projects which were crowding into the office. So Root took up the old work with a new inspiration, and thenceforward to the end of his life his labors were strengthened by unbroken happiness. Fortunately was it so ordered, for, with natures like his, happiness is a prerequisite of growth. Such men need sunshine, like the flowers and bees, and cannot fulfill themselves without it. Under its influence he systematized his life and followed closely a routine, never carrying his work into

Stairway, House of V. C. Turner

the social hours. He loved order, system, all the friction-conquering forms. He liked to have friends about him, to give them good dinners, good wine and good talk. He liked to watch the game of life and get into the moods of people, for he understood men and women intuitively, especially women. He was as prone as George Meredith himself to take the woman's point of view; always gave her the benefit of the doubt — against, for example, that common household tyrant who likes to be cajoled and wheedled, or that other who dares not risk his egotism by frank equality in marriage. I remember the wholesome energy with which he declared, "He would make a woman miserable!" of a paragon of a man, a model among Philistines. His wife supplemented him admirably, but they were not alike. She had been an omnivorous reader from childhood; he never was. He got suggestions from books and his imagination roamed away with them; but the amount he could learn and remember about an author from a sip or two was astonishing to us, for indeed the vigor and accuracy of his memory were exceptional. Her instinct was for realism; his was always in search of the spiritual essence, aware of the supernatural. She was rational, he imaginative, and both had the love of art.

A letter written to his brother not long after the latter's engagement is interesting as throwing light on his own experience. Referring to the lady, he says: "You should marry her just as soon as you can. No man will be more helped by a wife than you. She will unhorse you from lots of your hobbies and free you from much of your own self view. But as a compensation she will give you a broad human view of life, especially of its beauty and pathos, that will make you wonder how you could have ever thought you knew anything about it. And this will be a thousand times accented when you see her and you mixed up and reflected in your children, the same which heaven send to you with other good fortune."

His own children came to satisfy an old longing, for from boyhood he was always establishing intimacies with little people. In one of his early letters, which he wrote at twenty-three to congratulate his sister upon her first-born, he showed an intimate comprehension of the prejudices of earliest babyhood, for he had been boarding with a family which produced numerous specimens for study. "My prophetic soul!" he exclaims, "an uncle! Eight and a half pounds passes words, particularly *this* eight and a half pounds, — particularly when I reflect that before this letter reaches you the Eight And A Half pounds may become Ten — Ten pounds sterling. And this is one of the troubles technically called A Little One! So interested am I that my soul becomes indeed prophetic. Shall I describe my *nevvy?*

"*Item:* Head round like an ostrich egg, and tinged with pink; covered with as much hair as a cocoa-nut has. *Item:* Eyes blue (for lack of a better color). *Item:* Nose not yet grown out, but at present hopelessly in eclipse. *Item:* Mouth round like the top of an organ diapason, which comparison is further carried out by the fact that he works his pedals when it sounds. (*Mem.:* Therefore his pedals are constantly at work.) *Item:* Smiles when he is asleep. (*Mem. Medicine for Colic.*) *Item:* Hands, when doubled, of a size to exactly fit into his mouth or eyes." And so the enumeration goes on.

His elder daughter appealed to him by many a trait from his own character, and I used to think some of his best talk was given to her. He invented a string of queer fairy stories and animal stories for her, and when she was three years old he taught her thirty or forty songs, which she used to sing to his accompaniment in a little clear true voice which sifted sunnily through her shock of red curls.

HOUSE OF VOLUNTINE C. TURNER

Some of these songs he composed himself: one of them — a dreamy air for Mr. Eugene Field's "Dutch Lullaby," is the only one of his countless improvisations which we have remembered and preserved.

In the summer of 1886 he took his wife and little daughter abroad for two or three months in England and France — the first time he had crossed the ocean since his boyhood. In England, Chester, London, Oxford, Canterbury were the principal stopping-places; in France, Amiens, Rouen, Paris. His wife noted how inevitably he took the architectural point of view; buildings interested him most. In London he growled much over the street vistas. The new Gothic annoyed him, also the Renaissance according to Sir Christopher Wren. The old Gothic, the true Gothic, was always a joy to him. In England he was delighted by its surprises, its rambling irregularity; in France, by its splendor and power — the majestic unity of design in the great cathedrals. He felt less foreign in France than in England, although unfamiliar with the language. He liked the streets better — the harmony of architectural effect; though here the monotonous repetition of unvarying details wearied him.

He had letters of introduction to certain English architects, whose insular ignorance of American work and slavery to petty traditions tried his soul. One evening he came back to his wife much excited after a session with them, in which he had succeeded in talking them down, and shaking them, for the moment at least, out of their contempt of all new-world thought, and of all progress in architecture. He had to brave himself for such an encounter with new people in a new place, for he was naturally shy and extremely reserved — not one of those ready travelers who pick up acquaintances in steamer and railway-carriage and hotel, thereby enriching their experience. He was not so enthusiastic a traveler as those whose imaginations are less pictorial. He enjoyed it, but he could get along quite happily without it. His mind's eye was as potent as the eye of the flesh.

He permitted his wife to attend to the family correspondence during this trip, but I find one letter in his hand, addressed to her father, which is rather amusing. It is dated "Paris, June 22d, 1886." "My dear Governor," it reads; "it is with great difficulty that I write in English, and if it were to Harriet that this note was addressed I should word it in the choicest Parisian French. Paris, as well as the pension, is a great place! Louise has so fully written to the family all the news that I will forbear in that direction; but I cannot forbear to write a word of the pension itself. When you first go down to breakfast, your impression is that you have struck a home for incurables. The old maid who sits at the foot of the table has no use of her legs, the reason being that she uses her tongue so much as to give her legs no show. Then there is a 'Baronne' who sits opposite us — looks like a superannuated camel — who can't use her legs; reason, she uses her jaw so much that her legs don't get a show. Of the other five persons besides ourselves, two are far gone with consumption — these last leave to-day. So you see that our party is doing the robustuousness for the pension.

"At meals the conversation is very enlivening. Everyone talks French, except Louise and me, who at rare intervals talk English between ourselves. Our French we are reserving to call each other hard names by in case of a family row. Occasionally Louise launches out with great momentum, and I blush with pride at the accomplishments of the family. But she generally balks about mid-way the journey, and I feel more assured and natural. As for me, I reply to all long French sentences with one equally long and much more involved in English.

"My own impressions of our stay in England and France are now in a very cloudy state. I suppose, by the date

House of Edward Valentine

of our arrival in Chicago, they will have settled somewhat, and then I may be able to see something in them. . . ."

After the short rest he returned quite willingly to the young West, which, after all, he loved the best, and to the work which gave his faculties the keenest joy. It was at about this time that he wrote somewhere of the "greater openness of mind, greater leaning toward new things as such, which characterize the typical Western mind;" and he did not feel comfortably at home in a society of fixed intellectual traditions and conventions. Under softening influences, his character deepened during these years, his wit became less merciless and more humane, and from being dreaded he grew to be loved, with a certain enthusiasm and fervor, in the city whose finer aspirations he divined and led. He believed in a great artistic future for the West, and believed that it was near; and he never lost an opportunity to hasten its coming. Thus his influence, founded upon strong faith and high enthusiasm, became not only a power among men of affairs, but a profound inspiration to other artists, saving them from discouragement and winning from them the best work of which they were capable. "I have never seen his equal as an inspiring force in art," said a painter recently; "he made anything seem possible." The various architectural journals, the societies of students of art and architecture, were always appealing to him, and his papers show how often he prepared essays and lectures for them in addition to talks less formal — often at times when he was accomplishing an amount of work which would have overwhelmed three ordinary men. Everything was so easy for him, he was so strong physically and intellectually, that he never appreciated the limits of human capacity. Thus when his first illness struck him its mortal blow it found him enfeebled by over-work, conscious of fatigue for the first time in his life.

The social demands upon him became excessive, and there was a convivial streak in him which responded gaily to such calls. The number of art clubs he helped to found, of which he was president or executive committee or both — are they not written for woe or weal in the chronicles of Bohemia? For one of these, I remember, an evening was arranged, for which short papers were to be written by an architect, a decorator, a painter, a sculptor, a musician — papers which were to prod the public and hit off delicately the respective professions. It ended by Root's writing all of them except that of the musician, and swearing off from further reliance upon fallible artists. It was largely by his initiative that the Western Association of Architects was formed, and finally merged into the older American Institute of Architects. He saw in this Association a means of strengthening and elevating his profession in the West, of educating the artistic sense of its members, exalting their ideals of professional honor, and regulating their conduct toward each other and the public. He read papers at its conventions, accepted its offices and thoroughly fulfilled the duties of leadership. His office letter-book affords many proofs of unselfish work in this field. In July, 1887, he wrote to a fellow architect: —

"I am very sorry that men are kept from joining by considerations such as you mention. The Association cannot assume perfection in its members. If the individual members were perfect there would be no need for the Association. Its object is to create a certain *esprit* by means of which each member shall be elevated in his aims and practices, and so long as men hold aloof because of their own disapproval of certain things in the practice of others you will never have an organization of vital efficacy. The whole question resolves itself into the subordination of personal prejudices to the general good."

On another occasion, however, he showed care for the character of members. "It would seem better," he wrote, "for the good of the Association that it should free itself from the encumbrance of each individual member guilty of such conduct, than allow within its membership the widespread apathy towards it or dissatisfaction with it which the action of one such member occasions."

In September of that year occurred the first mention of a project for uniting the new Association with the older and prouder Institute, which had hitherto been inhospitable to Western men. Root's letter-book, at this date, is full of the plan. October tenth he wrote as follows to ten leading Eastern architects urging their coöperation: —

"The next convention of the American Institute of Architects as well as that of the Western Association will probably be of unusual significance. There seems to be a growing sentiment among members of both organizations that all members of the entire profession of the country should in some way unite their influence so as practically to form one general American Association. This may be brought about in several ways. By the union of the two existing associations, by the formation of a sort of confederacy between the two, or by the organization of a higher association comprising the best men from both of the existing institutions.

"It seems peculiarly desirable that at both the coming conventions there should be representation in some form of the best men from each association. It would be a very great advantage to the profession throughout the country if you could make a personal effort to see that your own work is represented. . . ."

The two societies were merged soon after under the title of the elder one, and to the end of his life Root devoted much time to its affairs, holding the office of secretary when he died.

He used to attend the conventions both before and after this union, often with papers and speeches as well as drawings. Even in the autumn of 1890, when overburdened with work for the World's Fair and for many large buildings, he went to one of these reunions in Washington; and his last journey was undertaken to attend a meeting of the Institute's executive committee. At the banquets his after-dinner talks were relied on to relieve the monotony of solemn harangues. Sometimes the newspapers preserved for us these frothy utterances. For a banquet of architects in Cincinnati in 1889, he formulated a "code for the guidance of persons practicing the profession of architecture," which hits off very neatly the frailties of the profession. On another occasion, talking on the subject of "Putty" to a convivial company of architects and builders, he whimsically reminded the builders of "a thousand uses for putty which are not recognized in the trade." "Not only do you use putty to fill in flaws in your carpentry, your masonry, your plastering and plumbing, but you also take in the too confiding architect, who is suspicious of no guile, by that moral putty with which you fill in the cracks in your moral characters. At first thought this seems hard to say, but you know as well as we that there are gross defects in every building in Chicago; and you also know that, like the king, the architect can do no wrong. Therefore they must come from you. We architects confess this great fact every day of our lives, and now is the time — this occasion of festivity, to own up to your deviltries. Don't you know that if a fireplace fails to draw it is because you masons filled up the flue; that if the house settles it is because you failed to use good cement in the foundations, and not because the architect designed them too small? And as for the rest of you, take the putty out of your own cracks and own up like men. Don't you plumbers know that diphtheria and scarlet fever were unknown until you and the doctors formed an alliance with the undertakers? Whether you carpenters confess it or not, we architects know that the only way to keep woodwork from shrinking all to pieces is to catch and kiln-dry the carpenter — poor shrinking thing."

Again, at another of these feasts of art he responded to the toast "The Lady of the House." After paying tribute to the matrons of the classic past, he proceeds: —

"To-day the architect of a dwelling-house meets a problem rendered more complex by the voice of the lady of the house. Unless all of the ancients, except Xantippe's husband, were dreadful liars, Madame, the wife, had but little to say in the planning of the ancient house. To-day she has, and that by a large and increasing majority. We all remember, as it were yesterday, when the unblooming monotony of our office was first broken by the sudden frou-frou of silk, the odor of patchouli, and Madame. We were in the midst of designs for a great cathedral which (if ever built) would surpass Cologne; for in those days pure idealism was very prominent in our practice. Upon the advent of this unwonted visitor we became painfully conscious that we were not in reception costume, and that access to the wash-basin was covered by the chair Madame was seated in. Do you not all remember that little plan on scented note-paper she had studied out at home? In this plan the stairs occupied a space eighteen inches wide and four feet long. The average size of the rooms was 20 by 20 feet. There were seven of these in the first story. The outside dimensions of the house could not be more than thirty feet square. There were to be oriels and bay windows till you could not rest, with ingle-nooks and stained glass, and all sorts of frills; and executed in cut stone, the total cost was not under any circumstances to exceed $4000. After days of labor, after much cold sweating, the house was planned, was figured, came preposterously high, was refigured and built, oh, so simply, and with such abandonment of lovely accessories! And with this little episode our gallantry as architects received a blow well nigh deadly. . . .

"Perhaps the best way for us to arrive at a just con-

Hall, House of Edward Valentine

ception of what our duties are in the premises would be to say what a dwelling-house is not, and then what it is.

"It is not a band-wagon, though you might sometimes think so, nor is it a circus tent.

"It is not intended to suggest having been struck by an earthquake.

"It is not intended for dolls or children, but for grown people.

"It should not seem to be built from the top down, nor to be hung up by the chimneys.

"As to what it is: —

"It is to live in, and therefore should keep out cold weather and water, but not whiskey.

"Its windows are meant to look out of.

"Its bay windows should be where by means of a not too long ladder you can get into them.

"Whatever the first intent of the house, the second purpose is to connect a series of large and convenient closets by dependent rooms."

And so he goes on with his list of essentials.

On one occasion, when the "Queen Anne" fever was passing away with its shreds and patches of architecture, and the "Romanesque" fever was inflicting upon us mountainous ebullitions of hewn stone, Root seized the opportunity of a convention of architects to lance these monstrosities with satire. He used to remark upon the tendency of houses in the former style to "suddenly jump up and down and howl" as one looks at them; and once he characterized an eccentricity of the latter — columns made of blocks of rock-faced stone — as "feather bolsters tied up with a string." Root entitled his speech "Architectural Freedom," and gave it at a dinner of the Western Association of Architects November 18th, 1886, at the Union League Club House in Chicago. The "Inland Architect" reported it as follows:

"No thoughtful student of architectural history can fail to congratulate the profession and the public at large that the day of architectural freedom has at last fully dawned. The night has been long and cheerless, heavy with the groans of weary watchers. Ages have passed since the first faint glow upon the hilltops told that morning was nigh. But now from every rock and crag, from every hill and housetop, from every face and in every glad voice is reflected the brightness of the newly risen sun.

"To us, basking in the glory of this new day, the darkness and danger of the night just passed seems almost a fiction, but when at rare intervals we realize that it was not, our hearts are wrung with pity for the vast throng whose lives flared up and flickered out in vain endeavor to pierce the gloom. It seems unutterably pathetic that in these dismal dungeons of night so many great men should have beaten out their souls, bowing their necks meanwhile to yokes the most intolerable; yokes of tradition, of precedent, of arbitrary and iron law. To us who stand free and upright it seems impossible to estimate the vast change that has come; and yet we cannot fully realize the greatness of our own good fortune without striving to feel something of their misery, shedding, as we pass by, a tear of sympathy upon their hapless graves.

"Let us, therefore, go back into the dim past and there search out a few of our professional brothers who spent their lives beneath these cruel tyrannies. In all other ages than our own, the architect has been unable freely to follow his own judgment or inclination, because of a vast number of purely arbitrary laws which met him at every turn. These, like the traditions of the Pharisees, came from darker ages, and, growing with each year, they, vine-like, encircled and choked the fair tree of true architecture.

"Some of these laws were of almost inconceivable severity and impertinence. Think of a law which compelled the architect to design all columns with a fixed relation of height to diameter; all entablatures with a fixed height in terms of the columns beneath them.

Among the Greeks the columns must moreover have certain well-defined peculiarities of form, and the entablature certain equally well-defined adjustments of its three parts. No Greek architect was allowed to place the cornice at the bottom of the entablature and the architrave at the top ; nor to group the cornice and architrave beneath the frieze. Nor was he permitted to place the columns above the entablature, nor to erect the columns with their capitals at the bottom and their bases in the air. Greek tradition was so exacting as this.

"Greek historians narrate that when the Parthenon was done, there was in Athens a man named Apollodorus, whose chief work was the designing of smaller habitations for the people. This Apollodorus, being one of the most enthusiastic admirers of the Parthenon, proceeded to build all over Athens a hundred little houses just like it. He built them of wood; he built them of clay and of cement; he made them of green stone, of blue and of red. The metopes contained 'ornaments,' sometimes of beasts and birds, sometimes of flowers, but most generally of mere things. Just ornamental 'ornaments.'

"Ictinus and Phidias bore this sort of thing for some time, because it seemed undignified to complain to Pericles. But one day, emboldened by past success, Apollodorus built a new house on which he erected the two end pediments after the Parthenon, but put a flat roof of tar and gravel between them. This, not only Ictinus and Phidias, but also Pericles himself, and all the people of Athens so resented, that Apollodorus was banished the city, and all his goods confiscated to erect a temple to the god Hermes.

"The Romans, though in general much more tolerant than the Greeks, were scarcely less tolerant in relation to their architects. It is stated that so humane a prince as Augustus ordered a Græco-Roman architect to be swathed in cloths saturated in pitch, and to be then burned, because he had built in Brundisium a house, all of whose windows had their arches at the bottom and their sills at the top.

"So also you remember the scroll found at Herculaneum, which narrates the sad fate of the architect, Tuticus, who built the house of Pomponius, the board-of-trade man. Tuticus designed this house so that all the windows upon the front were shaped like large keyholes — an effect which must have been striking, though difficult for us to realize. When the house was completed, all the art critics of the day arose and made a great ado, and for some time the architect's life seemed in danger. At last the tumult subsided and all seemed over, when, one stormy night, Pomponius, the board-of-trade man, came home from the weekly meeting of the Knights Templar, and mistaking a window near the ground for the keyhole of the door, tried to let himself into the house by jabbing his key into the window. Then the infuriated populace rose to a man, and tore the unfortunate architect limb from limb.

"In later days, in mediæval Europe, we find the same absurd laws and prejudices. One incident, handed down to us in an old missal now at Vienna, shows that as late as 1266 it was insisted that so absurd a law as that which placed the battlements of the house at the top should be vigorously enforced.

"The Count Walter of Limburg had commissioned Otto von Sweitzercase to build for him an addition to his castle, in the shape of a great round tower. Now Otto had been a draughtsman in the office of Gerard de Von Trond, and also Wenzel of Klosterneuberg, and, according to his statements (draughtsmen being much the same in all ages), had designed all the 'essential' parts of the Cologne and St. Stephen's cathedrals; so, by the time he got ready to 'start for himself,' he had, in his mind, been emancipated from the thraldom of all the traditions to which Gerard de Von Trond had so servilely bowed. He therefore conceived the notion that the new tower would look 'real nice' if a very richly carved and machicolated cornice were put about its base, like embroidery about the things which by the vulgar are called 'pants.'

"Walter of Limburg, being a wise prince, had not bothered the architect much, and had not decided, as so many people do now, to live in the castle while the improvements were going on, so off he went, having lots of fun drinking and fighting, and swearing when the architect's certificates reached him, till Otto told him the tower was done. Then he got unusually drunk, and came back. One glance at the tower, and the haughty prince fell back shrieking in the choicest Latin: 'I've got 'em again!'

"Next morning the great Otto Von Sweitzercase laid his head on the block.

"Later still, in France, architects as clever as Otto fell victims to the prejudice of the time. In an able paper published in 1884, Monsieur Jules Délibes shows that the notorious man in the iron mask was an architect, a certain François D'Erehomme. To him Louis XIV. intrusted the designing of a wing to Grand Trianon. Poor Monsieur D'Erehomme was puzzling over the design, worried by the fancied necessity of creating something entirely new for Le Grand Monarque, when the pencil he was using slipped, thus accidentally producing a form which, for a window, Monsieur thought quite too enchanting. This window he used with great freedom on the water front of the château. But alas! the capricious monarch was not pleased, and the iron mask was the end of it all — the iron mask and one high window. As Louis cruelly said, 'He shall see during his life but one window, and that window he shall not be able to see through.'

"Passing backward to England at an earlier time, we find in Samuel Pepys' diary a charmingly told story of Nell Gwyn and Hugh May, the architect:

September 20.

"The king seeing me this morning at Whitehall, whither Sir W. Coventry and myself had gone for a game of pêle-mêle, spoke to me of the new garden house he had built for himself. But, Lord, I did know by his smile that it was for that pretty, witty Mistress Gwyn to live in. His majesty said that to Lord Teviott he had intrusted that he should plan a fair fête champêtre for the day when the house should be complete, and his majesty bespoke both Sir W. Coventry and me that we should attend upon that day, at which I was exceedingly glad.

September 22.

"By water to Kew, and thence to Hampton Court, singing many catches and glees most merrily; and, Lord, how foxed Sir W. Cateret did get, and only eleven of the morning.

"Arrived at the court, we did find my fair Mrs. Batelier, to whom I made many pretty speeches, and whom I kissed many times — may the Lord forgive me!

"Mistress Nell Gwyn went with the king, and all of us following, with Sir W. Batten and Sir W. Pen, and a most merry party.

"The king had not seen the new house, nor had Mistress Gwyn, and when we came in sight of it, there was Mr. Hugh May who did plan it.

"Then Mrs. Gwyn, when she saw it, fell a-laughing and crying till we all thought she had a fit; and at last she says to Mr. Hugh May: 'What aileth the house? Some evil hath, perhaps, befallen it! It seemeth all twisted and awry.'

"Then said Mr. Hugh May, very soberly: 'No evil hath befallen it. It is well and soundly built.' 'Aye,' replied Mrs. Gwyn, 'But of what style is the architecture of the house?'

"'Queen Anne, your ladyship,' says Mr. May. Then we all fell a-laughing most heartily, but Sir W. Cateret, being well foxed, was exceedingly wroth, and beat Mr. May most soundly till we all did interfere lest the man be grievously hurt.

"Where Hugh May got the name of Queen Anne I don't know myself. Perhaps he got it from the 'Inland Architect.'

"One more instance from our own country will show that even so late as 1794 architecture had not yet become free in that perfect sense in which we understand freedom. In a letter from President Washington to his agent, dated April 16, he writes:

"By post of yesterday I am in receipt from you of plans prepared by Mr. Stevens for the renovation of my house at Mount Vernon. You will express to him my unqualified surprise that he should have supposed me capable of accepting designs so indecorous. That I who have endeavored to live free from blame in the eyes of my fellow men, and with the approval of my own conscience, should be thus considered by a man in my own employ is beyond my comprehension.

"From the drawings before me, the pillars of the portico seem to be connected by a device of curving and irregular form, each side of which is different, the whole being filled in with small balusters like the stair railing within the house. The end gables also of the house seem to be adorned with all kinds of fragments of wood, cut into strange and meaningless designs.

"I cannot fully comprehend the divers curious forms in which he has cast the windows. They seem to be in all respects different from such as are shown in the established works upon architecture.

"Pray tell Mr. Stevens for me that after my retirement from the cares of the high office I now hold I expect to return to the privacy of my home and to reside at Mount Vernon. Therefore I do not wish to deserve the anger and just contempt of all my neighbors, nor to be in the state of Virginia a perpetual derision and by-word.

"I will neither accept his work nor pay him a dollar for the drawings which you have sent me, and if in any respects the works upon the house have been executed, he must remove the same, under penalty of legal process against him for damage."

"Thus you see how many and how painful were the

restrictions laid upon architects in all these different ages, and what ignominy it must have been to be an architect, a practitioner in this noblest of high arts, when every step was taken with the feet thus clogged by galling chains.

"We, living in the full light of the nineteenth century, freed from the thraldom of even our less fortunate brothers across the seas, — we men of the Western Association of Architects can do what we please. For us no Jove thunders on high Olympus; for us no bloody despot wields autocratic power; for us no ignorant peoples grovel in the beaten paths of their own superstition. This is the age, and this the country of the great architectural go-as-you-please. I know of but one grave difficulty which besets us. This is the answering of the question, so constantly asked, 'What is the style of that house?'

"All of the old styles known in the books are obsolete or obsolescent, and yet we still use their names. Why should we not frankly accept the actual condition of things and name our own styles? No one man may hope perfectly to do this; but I trust you will pardon a single, if only a feeble attempt, provided it be in the right direction.

"Looking then back over the last twenty years of architectural development (for it is in the short space of twenty years that we have burst the last bonds of slaves), the first style to rise up and demand a name will be what we may call the Victorian Cathartic. This you will all readily recognize. You can see it in full flower in the London law courts. It came upon us all in the time of our virgin innocence when architecture seemed the vale of pure Arcadia, and Ruskin was its prophet. Seduced by the blandishments of this new Renaissance, we yielded ourselves easy victims to its sway, and since that fateful day what crimes against Beauty and Truth and Power and the rest of the seven lamps has it not led us to commit!

"The Victorian Cathartic was too true to be good, and too good to be true. As long as its method of production remained secret (in the category of other patent medicines) it had a great and ready sale. But when some too trustful architectural chemist or some too inquisitive lay patient found out the formula, the sales ran down to nothing.

"Then came the Tubercular Style, sometimes called by the facetious Queen Anne. This style is characterized by two sorts of eruptions, external and internal. It has for a long time held us in more or less complete control. Sometimes, when it looks as though we had got it out of our systems, it breaks out with new violence; and the troublesome thing about it is that no man can say where or in what fresh form it will manifest itself. Viewed externally, you will recognize this style by its varied and highly colored eruptive features. Generally the affected house is red as to the scalp, with a complexion of all colors, from cobalt blue to saffron yellow. Its eruptive tendencies manifest themselves in all sorts of things, from wens to carbuncles and ringworms.

"In its interior manifestations the Tubercular Style often takes still stranger and more alarming forms. The house becomes, in its various functions, most strangely disarranged, and the various organs undergo the most extraordinary enlargements and contractions. I have seen Tubercular houses in which the heart and liver were so changed from their normal sizes that the hall was big enough for a castle, and the attending servant could n't pass around the table when the family were at dinner. Yet it is singular that the history of medicine records the case of no man who ever died of a Queen Anne or Tubercular house.

"Then there is the Cataleptic Style. This is supposed to have originated in New England in the last century. It can be recognized by the careful suppression in its external aspect of all that would indicate life. In general the house looks like a hard-featured Puritan at Meetin', — only more so. Viewed internally, it is so white and bloodless as to be strongly suggestive of a prolonged cold-water diet.

"A style of work now in very common use and called the Romanesque might often be more properly called the Dropsical. Here you note a general enlargement of all the members. The roof especially becomes greatly distended and very heavy, and the whole middle of the house is so swollen as to indicate plainly the nature of the disease. In detail each member partakes of the generally enlarged type, and as a natural consequence of this enlargement, there is a tendency to obliterate all angles and corners, creating instead rounded and protuberant surfaces.

"Many other names applicable to styles of architecture now in vogue will suggest themselves to all of us, and under each of the general names I have suggested, many minor classifications might be named. It is also true that where such wide freedom exists, the difficulties of general classification are greatly augmented. All that I can hope to do in a sketch like this is to convey a hint, which I am confident you will be swift to act upon. A committee of architectural nomenclature might do much. I devoutly hope that by conference between ourselves and the American Institute we may in some way bring about the revision of this question. As it stands, architectural nomenclature is a delusion and a snare."

His talk was often more seriously suggestive. I used to

wish sometimes for a phonograph, and now and then I would attempt to atone for the lack of it with the note-book in which, at this time, I used to jot down impressions of persons and bits of conversation, although my memory was always too weak to reproduce talk without stiffening it. "Ah, these men!" he exclaimed one day, apropos of some unhappy love-affair. "One of them goes about seeking an ideal. He looks into a woman's eyes, and if he sees reflected there a little god — lo! his ideal is realized. But if he sees nothing but a puny conceited little man — away with her! she 's no ideal for him."

He took always the rational point of view — even to hardness, rather than the sentimental. Discussing capital punishment, he referred to "the popular misconception of the value of human life," and said, "Human life has no inherent value; its value should be judged by its relations to the community; when it becomes obnoxious, the community has a right to protect itself by destroying it."

One evening we were discussing famous men, and he remarked, "Men of genius often remind me of those artificial hills in our parks, which are made by scooping out room for lakes alongside. The lofty qualities of their minds generally loom up near some hollow filled with waters which it is n't safe to disturb."

In noting the fact that intellectual progress does not include moral progress, he thought them sometimes even antagonistic. "In some minds the entire absence of character seems to go toward the strengthening of the intellect; at least it removes hindrances — witness the career of Napoleon and others less notable." He touched on the fallacy of the modern idea that universal education will raise the masses morally, and believed that the school system should be changed in favor of more practical training.

THE HERALD BUILDING, CHICAGO

On another occasion this subject was pursued further, apropos of some one's disparagement of the intellectual power of Washington. Root thought that the man who was the soul of a great nation in a crisis could hardly be lacking in intellect. "Washington's blows," he said, "were always straight from the whole man — he was well poised, complete; and that is the final test of the supremely great man. The moment you can dissociate intellect and moral force in a man you relegate him to the second rank."

Then Napoleon was inevitably brought into the field, another talker finding it strange that such a mind should not have foreseen the inevitable ruin, and stopped short of it. In Napoleon, Root found the supreme development of the intellect, — that marvelously trained brain, with its miraculous intuitions; in his history the utmost that intellect, unbalanced by moral force, can accomplish. He attempted to compare Napoleon's career and tactics with those of a bold speculator, — a "plunger," and when the comparison was resented, he defended it, declared it just. "It is strange," he thought, "that men do not more keenly realize that the man who lives giving out always from himself to others is the great man, and he who draws all things inward toward himself the little one. The latter is legitimately comparable to small things — often strikingly resembles them. The former is primeval; he is one with the forces of nature, and nothing petty can be mentioned with him."

One day, in the summer of 1890, three or four persons were discussing schools of art, and he was consoling us for the absence of the longed-for "American school." My report becomes unrighteously a monologue, and much conventionalized at that, for it was written for a newspaper. His point of view shows certain reminiscences of that summer of travel in '86, and reminds us, by a few touches, — the mention of Bouguereau as a typical French artist, for example, — that less than a decade is already long ago. "There is no question," the article credits him with saying, "that a great school of art, enthroned on the traditions of the past and dealing out oracles for the future, is, on the whole, a good thing. It begets reverence for the correct, compels artists to be scholarly and dignified in their work, and, so long as the school does not go astray, certifies the production of works which will not be positively bad, even though they may not be emphatically good. Yet, as Viollet le Duc acknowledged, a man born and reared in the traditions of a great school of art is absolutely prevented from looking at nature *de novo*, from taking a fresh point of view. His eyes are inherited from countless generations, and their preconceptions color what he sees. He is overburdened with learning, and he cannot stand erect and walk freely. The modern French artist is so involved with tradition that simplicity is lost to him. He tries to paint Madonnas, and gives us unsophisticated young women with gold rings around their heads, as Bouguereau did in his series on the life of the Virgin. He models a nude woman of perfect figure, as Falguière did with his 'Femme au Paon' in this year's Salon, and his compeers and critics pronounce it Greek, when, after all, if we may believe the photographs, we have nothing but a model with a fine form and inane smile posing in a self-conscious attitude in front of a peacock; also, in the handicrafts, one finds the French workman the most skillful in the world in his specialty, yet incapable of deviating a hair's-breadth from the prescribed formulæ. How beautiful, for example, are those cartouches, palm branches, and other devices which one finds carved in the stone of half the buildings in Paris!

Yet each cartouche is exactly like all the others, the leaves of all the palm branches fall in exactly the same order, one crossing the others with the same tiresome, unalterable

State Street, showing Masonic Temple

grace. An architect may draw careful designs of new cartouches for his building, yet when the façade is finished he will find the imperishable old ones reproduced in every line and curve. It is simply impossible to drag the French workman away from his traditions. The American workman, though untrained, is instinctively an artist. Alert, responsive, and intelligent, one can get anything out of him under proper teaching.

"Now, in America, we are free of artistic traditions. Our freedom begets license, it is true. We do shocking things; we produce works of architecture, sculpture, and painting which are wholly, irremediably bad; we try crude experiments which result in disaster. Yet somewhere in this mass of ungoverned energies lies the principle of life. A new spirit of beauty is being developed and perfected, and even now its first achievements are beginning to delight us. This is not the old thing made over; it is new. It springs out of the past, but it is not tied to it; it studies the traditions, but it is not enslaved by them. It is doing original work, and it will do more.

"Compare the best of our recent architecture — some of Richardson's designs, for example — with the most pretentious buildings recently erected in Europe. In the American works we find strength and fitness and a certain spontaneity and freshness, as of stately music or a song in green woods. They carry a message; they appeal to the heart. In the noblest sense they are works of art. Contrast with them the London law courts or the New Sorbonne. The English building is a barbarous mass of machine-made Gothic, absurdly inexpressive of its purposes, a travesty on the significance of true Gothic architecture, an affectation and an eye-sore. As for the French structure, it is the same old French Renaissance which Louis XIV. delighted in, and which has been worked over and over until its inspiration has died away.

"Then in sculpture. Where, in the older nations, will you find an angel like that bas-relief by Mr. St. Gaudens, that divine creature who stands straight as a caryatid, her high wings rounding into a scroll? She speaks with her own voice, with no weak echo of Greece or Italy. And the 'Farragut'—of all the sailors who were ever modeled, he is the first whose statue stands in sailor's attitude—legs apart yet evenly balanced, as though the moving deck were beneath them. It seems to have taken a pair of fresh American eyes to get outside of art to nature, and discover that thus an admiral stands on the quarter-deck.

"In painting we have not gone so far on our own road, yet it is by no means true that we are altogether French. We are learning the French technique, which is the only technique worth learning, but already we are using it for our own purposes. We call our painters French, but Frenchmen do not. A common phrase in the Salon is, 'How American that picture is!' and this phrase seems to mean ardor, freshness, joyousness, and several other desirable qualities of youth. American painters are making their impression,—not only individually but collectively, nationally,—and we may trust to time to strengthen it."

Some one spoke that day of a recent disheartening exhibition at the Royal Academy, and Root characterized the present English school as "a calf tied to a pole, who is forever winding her rope around the pole until finally she has no ground at all to graze on." "It was Sir Joshua Reynolds, with his reverence for classicism," he thought, "who tethered her; he was free enough himself, but he did not preach freedom."

But it is futile to try to preserve talk. The best of it is ephemeral as the froth of champagne, which continues only in the stimulus it gives. In intercourse with Root, all kinds of people felt this stimulus,—workmen, artists, men of affairs. "No other man," says Mr. Owen F. Aldis, "ever impressed me so quickly and so deeply. I met him first at a reception, and we went off into a little room and talked until one o'clock. He did not know I had any special interest in architects, but from that night I knew he was a genius, and the next day I brought him a building." This was the first of many commissions, and Mr. Aldis has never lost that first keen sense of the man's personal charm.

It was exciting to watch his imagination play with a subject, shift the lights and colors upon it, turn it back and forth in unexpected relations. He was not a monopolist, claimed no more than his share, joyed in thrust and parry with a good opponent. At one time, before his marriage, there was a brilliant little handful of men who used to have nights of talk and revelry now and then. His disposition was lavish: whatever he had, whether in his mind or his pocket, he was ready and eager to give away. He did not reserve himself for the intellectual and the elect, but bestowed his gifts broadcast. Weakness appealed to him, the weakness of the poor, the forlorn, the old — the sort of weakness which has no stateliness, but is crossed by humor for the greater pathos. For such ill-starred kindly beings he always had a word or a laugh. I remember a dull neglected old gentleman whom he befriended thus one summer at the seashore, and who afterward sent a message of remembrance to "the clever young man who put himself out to entertain an old stranger." In those days a certain aged lady was childish and deaf and difficult to talk to; and he was one of the joys of her life. They had an enduring joke between them which he never lost the thread of, and the new phases of which gave her keen delight.

He liked men and women for character, for social adaptability, for qualities of sympathy and open-mindedness and good breeding, rather than for the amount of their mental endowment. Certain kinds of persons bored him into absolute silence — an utter incapacity for speech, resulting,

East Entrance, Rand-McNally Building

he used to say for excuse, from temporary vacancy of mind; and the intellectually vain bored him much more unmercifully than the fools. Of fools he could be tolerant — from a distance; indeed, he could reason himself into tolerance at closer range, but he could not keep his mind from wandering away from them into odd fancies which would sometimes take speech in spite of him. The Pharisee and the Philistine were a sore trial to him, and he often avenged himself by stamping one of them upon some coin of speech which would pass current for years. His shafts of sarcasm or direct rebuke were keenly pointed and unerringly aimed. When he felt that such weapons were salutary, he used them without pity or remorse.

Life was so interesting to him from many sides that he responded to men of contrasting types, and doubtless he gave too much to the lighter sort whose appeal was to his vivacity and conviviality, — in many cases to his generosity. The publicans and sinners claimed his kindliness by many a human trait; of them he was perhaps too tolerant. I doubt if he ever even tried to refuse an appeal for help after his success began. An old friend of his was exclaiming the other day upon this trait. He told one story in which the bounty was finally justified, though at great risk. A man, once well employed in one of the decorative arts, had been going rapidly down-hill with drink. Root had known him long, and helped him from time to time, though he was considered a hopeless case. At last he appeared at the office one day, utterly bedraggled, and asked for money enough to get to Cleveland, where he had been offered employment. Root looked him over, marched him to a tailor-shop, fitted him out with new clothes and plenty of money, and urged him to keep up in the new place. "And that very night," said my informant, "he was in a saloon dead drunk, rolling those new clothes on the floor." Yet, strange to say, he pulled himself together, went to Cleve-

CINCINNATI CHAMBER OF COMMERCE, PERSPECTIVE STUDY
Facsimile Reduction of Mr. Root's Sketch

land the next day, and succeeded in conquering his habit. Before Root died, he had become once more a reputable citizen and a good designer in his specialty, besides giving evidence of that rarest of the virtues — gratitude.

Other similar stories might be told, not always so happy in the dénouement. Many I O U's from members of the artistic fraternity, found among his papers after he died, gave proof of his liberality; but the unrecorded loans, the words of sympathy or appreciation, the dinners given, the orders for work secured — many kinds of service to those less fortunate than himself — are registered only in their memories. Qualities of sympathy and responsiveness were so patent in his character as scarcely to need mentioning, and there was an obvious danger in them against which his partner's strength and firmness were always a wholesome influence both as a check and a spur. Mr. Burnham was not less generous, but he was more judicious. The two complemented each other admirably, in points of adaptability, not only to their profession, but to life as well. The elder partner was more serious, more strenuous. He had a large-hearted belief in men which impelled them to live up to it, which enabled him to get the best work out of people — a power which achieved great results when he was Director of Works at the World's Fair. Root had the more logical sense of values, an imagination whose feet were on earth, though its head might be in the clouds. Though he was prodigal in his own affairs, and rarely made good investments, his judgment of business matters connected with his work was good; in estimates and advice to clients he was systematic, economical, precise. "It is curious," writes his brother, "that one so liberal and so artistic personally should have inaugurated a style of business building, the essence of which is its great capacity to pay."

It interested him to work out a problem from exact premises. He was more ready than his partner to study details, to accept facts and limitations. The two minds dovetailed well; both had the love of order and magnetic power over men. In the office the influence of both trained the large force of draughtsmen to the accurate discipline and harmony of an orchestra. An architect who worked four years in their office says that this fine result was accomplished without severity. "No fault was ever found with our work by either Mr. Burnham or Mr. Root. I cannot imagine how they accomplished it. They must have gone into a closet for a private swear now and then. The men were treated invariably like gentlemen."

When the firm moved into a large suite of offices on the top floor of the newly finished "Rookery," in 1888, Root possessed for the first time a private office, having hitherto worked with his draughtsmen. There he found an electric contrivance by which he could summon any employee. However, the men noticed no change in his habits — when he wanted a man, he went and spoke to him as before. Finally one of them asked why he did not use his bell. "I 've cut the wire," Root answered; "didn't want to get into the nasty habit." And to this day the useless instrument hangs in its place with the severed wire.

This story illustrates the firm's attitude toward employees, which was one of confidence and courtesy. Mr. Burnham's fine belief in the integrity of a man's intention, and Root's sure knowledge and swift sympathy were strong incentives. Both of them held very high the standard of their profession, careful always, in matters small as well as great, to avoid all occasion for suspicion. Root's letter-book gives many evidences of this care. "There is so much dirty work done in our profession," he writes, "that I don't want to risk even a chance of suspicion." Again, he refuses to interest himself in a patent whose use would partly depend

Vestibule, Mills Building

upon its being specified in the office. Numerous presents are declined; in one such case he writes: "This is one of the calamities of our profession, that not even from our friends, if they are related to us in business, may we accept courtesies like this." A commercial community found him singularly sane for an artist. His clients discovered that he never tried to dodge an issue or a question, and that he could always make his points clear to them. Indeed, among hard-headed men of business, trained to swift accuracy, he won high repute for precision and correctness, and in the heated discussions with such men which gave the World's Fair its brave initiative he was until his death the effective spokesman for art. From first to last the firm held to the highest ideals of professional honor, thus winning respect for their æsthetic ideals. Gradually, as the community became acquainted with these men, and perceived the swift efficiency of their work, it began to recognize the new force which they stood for — a force unfamiliar, hitherto somewhat disdained, but destined for great achievements. In many ways, John Root, sensitive, impressionable, creative, concentrated and expressed the sense of beauty and love of art latent in the strenuous, ambitious, imaginative city where he had cast his fortunes. The people responded generously to this recognition of their higher hopes, bringing tributes of love to him during his later years as to some young hero who carries upward his country's flag. His trustworthiness in ordinary matters made men credit his enthusiasms. He was a dreamer, but with that added power which distinguishes the prophet from the visionary — the power of making men follow him to his dream.

He was a dreamer; and if the conditions of his profession confined him, or compelled him to move more slowly than his desire, he could always escape with his dream in music. To him music was a necessity of life, not a decorative incident. In an early letter he speaks of the "half-starved, pinched feeling which attends deprivation from music."

It was the background of thought with him, the ever-present principle which kept the world in tune. If there are elemental rhythms which move the planets and change the seasons and govern the moods of men, he was one of the few mortals so keenly poised as to be conscious of the vibratory song; and his personality passed it on to others by delicate effluence. To the various expressions of this harmony in art, in thought, in religion, he was necessarily responsive, and music appealed to him as the closest expression — not for humanity at large, not the highest aspiration of the race, but for him individually the nearest and dearest of the great voices. I once heard him say that he never felt so keenly alive as in listening to the third Leonora overture. For him, apparently, that was the supreme triumph of man in art; Greek sculpture, Italian painting, Elizabethan poetry appealed more remotely to him. I think he would have confessed that architecture also made a remoter appeal. Architecture, he would have said, is earth-bound by all its conditions and materials. The architect, at best, can but reach out for his vision from afar off, struggling with hard unyielding stone against hard unyielding limitations of time and cost and man's desire. His heart was in the struggle; these very limitations allured him. A musical career might have isolated him too much from life, and suppressed his development on certain sides. Yet it may be true, as a famous pianist once said, that "a great musician was lost when John Root took to architecture."

He slighted this accomplishment, yet it was based on thorough musical scholarship and good training. He was proficient in harmony and counterpoint, and familiar with the development and history of music. He would sit in his easy-chair of an evening, and enjoy a musical score just as others enjoy a poem or a novel. Even among professionals one rarely encounters a musical memory so richly stored, so ready and available. To get the best of his music, it was necessary either to catch him in a high companionable humor, or to give him free rein and few listeners, let him work himself into the mood. Then he would improvise for awhile, or wander about among German songs — Raff, Schumann, Schubert; or sketch out the orchestral harmonies of certain beloved movements of Beethoven's symphonies, or interpret the strife of the spirit in Wagner's operas. It was always a special joy to us if the mood led him to Schubert's "Erl-king," for all the wild spirits of the air obeyed this invocation, and chased our shuddering senses through the night and wind. Yet if one asked him in cold blood for this song, he would play it but dumbly. The great sailor's song in the "Flying Dutchman" also thrilled us with vastness as he gave it; and I can never forget the orchestral splendor which he sometimes managed to impart to a piano sketch of the "Ride of the Valkyries." One winter we used to go occasionally of a Sunday afternoon for an impromptu organ recital in Central Music Hall, where the emptiness, the loneliness, the spacious shadows swayed by a remote dim light — all deepened the spell of art.

Captain Horace G. H. Tarr, of New York, tells a story illustrating the persuasiveness of Root's music. "The great power of the man," says the Captain, "was in expression. He could express his thought on the instant in whatever happened to be the most convenient medium, — architecture, music, writing, speech; and he could express your thought quicker and better than yourself. I remember how he captured 'The Lambs' one night in January, 1889, when he and I invaded the Bohemian headquarters for supper after going the rounds of the theatres. There were ten or twelve artists of various kinds in the room, and others in the supper-room beyond. Some of them recognized us and asked what we had been doing. 'We have been to every reputable theatre in New York,' said Root, 'seeing the good, bad, and indifferent — an act of this, five minutes of that.' 'And what was the worst?' some one asked. 'It was the worst I ever saw on any stage,' he answered, laughing; 'it was Mrs. Potter and Kyrle Bellew as Antony and Cleopatra.'

"We hushed him up by showing that Mr. Bellew himself was at the piano, trying to pick out some unattainable theme which seemed beyond his reach. Root was horrified at his indiscretion, but it was too late to amend it. Soon the actor went into the supper-room, and after a moment Root swung over to the piano and took up unconsciously the strain which Mr. Bellew had been searching for. In another minute that audience of artists in both rooms was hushed and attentive — and I assure you it took a master to hush them. Mr. Bellew and others drifted forward from the dining-room to listen. The music rolled on — the house seemed too small for the stature of it; and when it closed with a great bang! bang! there was a stormy outburst of bravos.

"Mr. Bellew asked to be presented to my friend. 'It is an honor to meet you,' he said most gracefully as he shook Root's hand, 'and to tell you how much more I have enjoyed your performance than you seem to have enjoyed mine.'

"It was the only time I ever saw John Root at a loss for a repartee. But he soon recovered with a delicate compliment for Mr. Bellew's work in characters less robust than the Roman warrior."

Music translated itself into color to his imagination;

symphonies flashed themselves out to his eye as well as his ear. He wrote somewhere of "the reds and yellows of brasses, the greens of oboes and flageolets, the violets of cellos, and the blues of violins." He looked forward to the development of color as a great art of the future. In an essay on "The Art of Pure Color," he presents the phases of this future development, which has been a favorite dream of other minds sensitive to beauty. "Music begins as a mere setting to words," he reasons; "its very scale originates in the inflections of the human voice in speaking. Yet, little by little, words contribute less to it, until it finally takes upon itself forms which words cannot express, and gives utterance to emotions but for it voiceless. . . . Is there not an art which stands to painting as the music of an oratorio stands to its words; which, as music shakes off the needless help of words and finally becomes symphonic, will free itself of all incumbrances of line, and vindicate its right to separate existence?" In this art of the future "the arrangements of color will be written upon a score, like the notes of music, and we shall sit enchanted while the performer plays for us this symphony. As in the great 'Im Walde' symphony by Raff we hear the twitter of birds, the sighing of trees, and all mysterious music of the forest, so in this color-symphony we shall see the lifting of gray clouds, the first rosy streaks of dawn, the molten gold poured from the sky into lakes and brooks, and the final coming of Apollo. In another symphony we shall see, as in Beethoven's 'Eroica,' the struggle of the human soul through mists of doubt, through darks of despair, into fullness of day, into the greenness of fields and the bloom of flowers."

He speaks of the debt which the new art, and indeed the older arts as well, will owe to science, which "follows the search of truth for truth's own sake, and in the search finds vast treasures with which art may decorate the world. . . . To Science will Art turn, that she may have her semi-paralyzed optic nerve galvanized into new and truer vision, and that she may gain from the laboratory instruments for the expression of her own thought."

The light cast by science upon the principles of beauty was always an alluring subject of thought with him. He had scientific friends, whose experiments he shared or followed closely, winning suggestions for his imagination at every forward step. And he kept informed of the progress of research and discovery. He felt no antagonism between science and art; everywhere he reiterates the sympathy between them. In one of his papers he writes: "Between science and art has of late grown up a strange hostility, marked by frequent contempt on the part of scientists and constant neglect on the part of artists. Meanwhile science has been steadily persisting in a course which art would do well to follow — the faithful pursuit of truth wherever it may lead. Never before in the history of the world have men of science been so devoted to the very refinement of truth as now. . . . In this faithful search for truth science has not only set an admirable example, but has also thrown a thousand side-lights on art. Will the artist use them? All nature has been manifested in a new revelation: every simple phenomenon has been shown to possess a significance hitherto unsuspected. Shall not artists awake to what is about them? It is useless to say that science deals with that which is, art with that which seems to be. Every man knows how far from truth this is, for the actual vision has been expanded a thousand-fold, and is still expanding through the influences of greater knowledge. In nearly every art career in the world, on the other hand, has been seen the slow obscuration of pure vision, and the substitution of perverted judgment; and thus the artist finally fails to see truly that which is. It is here, as elsewhere, that science may be helpful. To know what is, will help us to maintain that purer vision which is too often thus overclouded. From this scientific love of the inexorable truth, art may draw an inspiration which, while it may begin in the lower plane of homely yet true representation, shall ultimately soar among the stars."

In an essay entitled "A Utilitarian Theory of Beauty" he elaborates still further his ideas of the true relationship between art and science, as "parts of a co-related whole, complements of each other, standing to each other as the intellect to the affections, as the thought to the act." By utility he desires to express "the idea of use, of fitness — in a sense, of goodness itself; by beauty all those pleasure-giving qualities we define by words, from 'exquisite' to 'majestic.' Beauty is a utility, but not always an obvious utility." He considers it under three heads: "as a Utility of the Present, of the Past, and of the Future."

Under the first head he traces to fitness the beauty of natural forms, — man, animals, plants, and the larger aspects of nature. He follows the development of the arts, and of each individual artist, through three periods: "First, the more or less symbolic type is manifest, in which nature is represented by partially arbitrary signs. . . . In the second period the race or artist studies more directly the methods of nature, and begins to copy her work with some degree of accuracy. But in this literal copy of nature much is reproduced which, being peculiar to the individual alone, detracts from the perfect expression of the type. The artist therefore systematically conventionalizes; that

HOUSE OF MRS. WILLIAM J. GOUDY

is, makes more prominent than in nature the essential character of the object copied. Art has now reached its climax. Hitherto nature has been studied, and into man's reproduction of natural objects have been infused nature's methods. Now sets in the third period and the process of decay; the artist begins to substitute his system for nature's; the eternal fitness of things gives way to vagaries and whims; fashion grasps at the novel, losing the underlying causes of novelty, and then come final imbecility and death. The period when art attains its fullest and most perfect expression comes when artists, by a careful analysis and synthesis of nature's methods, make nature's purposes clearer.

"Art attains its best expression," he insists, "only by following the natural law of utility or fitness. . . . It is a law of nature that she never makes in one material what she can make better in another. . . . This law of pure fitness is also a law of art, marking all the highest art the world has ever known." He traces the operation of this law in architecture, exemplifying with much detail "the only two completed and perfect styles of architecture, the Greek and the Gothic," and concluding that "in every art beauty is in direct proportion to fitness."

To maintain the truth of this proposition in the arts more remote from use, he considers Past Utility, looking "to an earlier age, or (which is the same) to lower organisms, for the utility. . . . Man is an epitome of all previous life. . . . Each form of life through which the human family has developed has contributed its share to that vast fund of treasured experience known as man. And each race of men through which our ancestry might be traced have brought their lives as an offering to ours. . . . Our mental and physical structure is built up very much like the geological formations under our feet. First and nearest us are the shifting sand and the alluvial soil, so to speak, of our own conscious acquirement. These mark the individual, and with the individual partially disappear. Then we find these temporary characteristics fixed by transmission from father to son into family traits, which we may compare to the close and firm clay, resisting to some extent the action of the elements. Next, as generations go by, these family tendencies are solidified into the underlying sandstones of national life. In the fierce heat of internecine strife, national traits are fused into a more enduring form, constituting the granites which extend under vast sections of the earth's surface. But below these lie the primitive formations and the great seething mass of the Master Workman's furnace, — the multitudinous life preceding us and surrounding us, out of which have come the fundamental elements of our own mental structure.

"It is through this process that we have acquired the many intuitions which are in no sense conscious cognitions. We have simply learned lessons ceaselessly reiterated to our ancestors through countless ages. To them nature told truths face to face, and by a thousand forms of daily experience, while we simply inherit what they have so laboriously acquired. Among all things that we are affected by without knowing why, none move our emotional nature to such a degree as Sound and Color. Why music appeals so deeply to us we cannot, from our own history, ascertain; nor can we tell what events of our life or of our fathers' made abstract color a source to us of such endless pleasure. What direct utility there is to us in color, we have but lately begun to ascertain; while as yet we can only speculate in the dark as to the immediate utility of music."

So he traces this utility back to "the vast underlying

strata of preceding animal life," showing that the utility of color began in the interdependence of insect and plant life, of music in the love-cries and war-cries of animals, and increased through higher animal life by countless facts

Dining-Room, House of Mrs. William J. Goudy

of daily experience. "From these lower lives we get our mental bias, so to speak; and what was to them a thing of common experience and of the highest personal utility has become to us a source of delight — a thing of beauty. These phenomena of sound and color have been passing down through the strata of the world's structure, until now they permeate the very foundation elements of all life. For this reason, because they have been and still are so useful, they have a profoundly recognized beauty. . . ."

After considering in detail the historic development of these fundamental instincts into arts, he passes from the Utility of the Past to the Utility of the Future. "Art has at all times suffered from two things — lack of knowledge and lack of aim: is there not in a utilitarian theory of beauty the possibility of both? In past times, as in the Italian Renaissance, art has had definite aims and lofty inspiration, but was hampered by lack of knowledge. At the present time our knowledge has increased, but we lack motive — inspiration. This fact is commonly attributed to the growth of a scientific spirit which opposes flights of the imagination. . . . Inspiration artists certainly do need; but if they have it not, they must blame themselves, not science. They endeavor to portray the beauty of nature while they refuse to learn from nature's methods in what that beauty consists. They sigh for inspiration, and scorn inspiration that science has placed at their very doors. Not such will be the artist of the future. He will gladly welcome every new fact of science as an aid to his work, and from the revelations made to him in the laboratory of nature he will gain fresh insight into the true principles of art. Is science dry and unimaginative? Does science crush the rising fancies of the poet or the painter? How grossly is he misled who thinks so!

"Let him, so deceived, pass but one hour considering, from an art standpoint, such magnificent scientific theories as La Place's 'Nebular Hypothesis' or Darwin's 'Development of Species,' and then ask if his poetic imagination need look further.

"When artists thus faithfully study nature by the light

of science, we shall no longer be in doubt as to the value of the arts. Portraying in forms of idealized beauty the natural principle of eternal fitness, each work of art becomes a lesson for better living. Based upon uses, art becomes useful. Artists will be then, as now, priests of the temple of natural beauty. But from that temple will then be lifted the veil of mystery, and men will see their goddess face to face — a deity surpassingly fair, because divinely good."

Thus in many lectures, as well as in talk less formal, he dwelt upon the sympathy between science and art, and urged upon artists that frank acceptance of the spirit of the age which has wrought such miracles for science. He did not despair over the preference of his time for the more exact forms of truth. He felt that art is vital only when it accepts and frankly expresses the spirit of its environment; and he marveled at the pessimism of certain scholarly lovers of the past who see no opportunity for art in the stress and thrill of the modern movement, who shut their hearts against the passion for beauty, for truth, for the happiness of others, which underlie its commercialism and skepticism. If the people of the great West had not yet been given an art which they could recognize, he knew that they were ready to welcome their own when it should come.

And he never lost an opportunity to hasten its coming; upon artist and patron he urged loyalty and sincerity. "There never was a picture that people loved," he told them, "nor a building that they went out of their way to see, which was not essentially local. Michelangelo did not paint Spanish beggars; nor did Jean François Millet paint Alpine mountains. So thoroughly have all great artists been permeated by the spirit of almost their very city that this spirit has often swept them away from a single art.

Thus Leonardo, or Giotto, or Angelo, or a dozen others of the Renaissance were engineers, architects, men of science, men of letters, critics, all in one — compendia of all things about them.

"For artists, thus surcharged by the spirit of the people and the aspect of things immediately about them, there has always been success and fame; and for artists here similarly imbued, await similar success and fame. What have we of inspiration to offer artists intent on thus bringing themselves into harmony with us? What inspired Teniers, or Rembrandt, or Cuyp? What the Ostades or Frans Hals? They had themselves alone, and Holland. What had Millet? Peasants and harvests, and sunlight and mist, and the sound of the Angelus.

"Here we are content that artists should sit under a north skylight and paint for us memories of Dutch peasants and Picardy apple blossoms, or even pictures of landscapes they have never seen. Can they do nothing better for us? Let them come down to us and try. Eternal thanks and deepest love to him who shall open our heavy eyes to the beauty about us!"

He would have religion also yield itself heartily to the spirit of the age, accept science as its most powerful assistant and minister in the long search for truth. His keen spiritual intuitions looked, not backward to dogma, but forward toward a symbolic interpretation of nature and life as divine harmony, toward the gradual release of the human soul from its crudities of materialistic thought. Thus his sympathies at all points were intensely modern, or more than modern — tending toward the future rather than the past. He never felt that he was too good for his place and hour, never sighed for atmosphere, for the classic past, or for any of the foreign and unattainable conditions which many American artists demand for the development of their genius. He was singularly free from egotism: scarcely suspected his powers until they were called into play, and heavily discounted all praise. I have noted often the incredulous smile with which he banished compliments of his

Fireplace, House of Mrs. William J. Goudy

work; to him each last achievement was imperfect, useful merely in suggesting the better things which might be done. His standard in life was not one of intellectual values. Intellect was to his feeling a faculty, to be taken as a matter of course and developed to the limit of power, but it was the last thing in the world for us mortals to be proud of; indeed, the best of us accomplish so much less than we might, that it behooves us to be humble in proportion to our endowment. He cared little whether his work was credited to him or not, and felt many more twinges for what was wrong in it than thrills for its triumphs. He suspected the opinion of the moment, felt that time alone could pronounce a verdict on any man or on any work of art. And in the mean time his own essays were merely on trial — nowhere more severely than in his own consciousness.

At every side the world, as time went on, was demanding and receiving more and more from him. And yet — how can I show it? — there was something in him which withdrew more and more behind an impenetrable reserve. One had to divine the life of his spirit, follow it by vague hints — cold thoughts which serve to veil emotion. Yet every one who knew him well felt a large background behind his life and work. "Beyond the world of superficial appearance," he wrote, "lies one of surpassing beauty, from which the happiness of life is greatly derived. The constant effort to find under rough exteriors this underlying beauty is in itself a pleasure. In this higher world the explorer meets no disappointment. The discoveries that reward the patient laborer are endless." He looked not at things, but through them, with a vivid sense of their unreality, of the inexplicable mystery. He strove at the mystery with theories and dreams, potent to charm for a time, but one after the other inadequate. The consciousness of the infinite possessed him with increasing power, and made the issues of life intangible, uncertain. Even when he was most absorbed in his work, that sense of aloofness would sweep over him, and charm him away on wings. I used to wonder often where his soul would lead him, and I do not yet feel sure that art would have held him to the end of a long life, with life's average of sorrows. The mystic in him might have threatened his joy in art and its manifold claims, diverting his love of beauty into other channels. Yet such vague surmises become too definite as one states them — lose themselves at once in improbability. I wish to indicate merely that under this man's joy in life and all its issues lay a deeper joy in the eternal glory and harmony, and that his search for the beauty which men may reach was inspired by a keen vision of the ineffable beauty which lies beyond desire. If we had been wise as oracles in those days, many a trait and circumstance would have offered us premonitions of his early death. But we went on blindly wondering why all was joy with him, incredulous of the fate decreed to those whom the gods love.

VII

THE WORLD'S COLUMBIAN EXPOSITION

LATE in the eighties the militant young metropolis became possessed of a new ambition. The French exposition came and passed, the four hundredth anniversary of the landing of Columbus drew near, and projects for the commemoration of the great discovery crystallized into a demand upon the United States government for an international exposition. In the contest which followed between the different cities, Chicago had from the beginning the advantage of faith. It was no idle faith, however; not that easy sense of security by which New York lost the honor. The enthusiasm of the city was set on its mettle; an aggressive campaign was organized, and five million dollars pledged by private subscription, before other cities had begun to act. In the winter of 1889–90 Chicago sent to Washington a committee of her foremost citizens, fully equipped with large promises, and prepared to assure Congress that the great prize, once in their hands, would not "get into politics." New York could not offer such assurances, neither was she so richly provided with available sites. Other cities contesting were manifestly unfit. Thus

Root's Study for Central Pavilion of Main Building at Washington Park

on the twenty-fourth of February, 1890, the House of Representatives passed the bill locating the Columbian Exposition at Chicago, fixing the four-hundredth anniversary in October, 1892, for the dedication of buildings, and May to November, 1893, for the six months' festival. This bill soon passed the Senate, and became a law in April by the signature of the President.

No true Chicagoan ever doubted the ability of his city to win the prize and to wear it with honor. While Eastern newspapers were predicting "a cattle-show on the shore of Lake Michigan," Chicago business men brought all their executive experience to this novel enterprise, organized its great stock-company, appointed capable directors and officers, who in turn allotted the numerous committees and commenced the work. One of the surprises of the fair was the success of these business men in their new rôles. Bankers and merchants were appointed to committees on grounds and buildings, music, ceremonies, were called upon to decide delicate questions of taste and diplomacy, and as a rule proved intelligently equal to the new demands. From the first their fellow-citizens trusted them; perceived that they appreciated the magnitude of their task. Even men who, like John Root, were possessed by visions of beauty, doubted little that the opportunity would be given for fulfilling them.

From the moment Congress awarded the prize, Root took high ground in regard to the fair. At that time few hoped to rival Paris; the artistic capacity and experience of the French made us distrustful of ourselves. We should have a great American fair, but in points of grouping and design we must expect inferiority to French taste. To such doubts Root opposed his ardent energy. "We have more space, more money," he would say; "and we have the lake; why should we not surpass Paris?" He had not seen the *Exposition Universelle,* but he absorbed it now through figures and photographs. The minutest details of design, arrangement, and dimensions were ready for reference in his serviceable memory, and his faculty of architectural clairvoyance made the French exposition a reality to his vision, so that he astonished persons who were familiar with it by the accuracy and completeness of his superior knowledge. His first idea was to place the Chicago fair on the Lake Front — the strip of public land east of Michigan Avenue and between Lake and Twelfth Streets. The Illinois Central tracks were to be depressed and covered, and a wide area of land eastward reclaimed from the lake, inside the government breakwater, by filling for the grounds and piling under buildings. Root saw here an opportunity for a lasting public improvement in the heart of the city, which should make a beautiful park, adorned with an art museum, a music hall, and perhaps one or two other permanent buildings, out of a worn and unsightly strip of sward and a few hundred feet of the lake — a project which, though not carried out for the Fair, is now (1896) being promoted, with good prospect of success, by leading citizens for the advantage and beauty of the town. The Lake Front location had other advantages, notably that of accessibility, which caused it to be favored at first by the directors. At the first meeting of the Grounds and Buildings Committee, May 9, 1890, the Lake Front was chosen as the site for the Fair, and a committee of three appointed to investigate the legal difficulties which lay in the way of securing it. Doubts soon began to assail the committee, however, for on May 15 we find it advertising for proposals of an available site, embracing at least 250 acres unbroken. (The area finally covered embraced 686 acres, of which 189 were under roof.) During the following three months many sites were proposed and discussed. Jackson Park, then a forlorn waste of sand and bogs just redeemed from long litigation, was offered by the South Park Commissioners. The entire West Side park system — three improved parks connected by boulevards — was tendered from the west. A "northwest site" near the north branch of the Chicago

River, and a "north-shore site" — wooded lands on the lake shore near Buena Park — were offered by private capitalists. Each of these sites was strenuously urged upon the committee, whose gloom deepened as the tangle became more complicated. On August 10th Mr. Frederick Law Olmsted, the distinguished landscape architect, came to Chicago at the invitation of the committee. Burnham and Root offered him the hospitality of their large offices, and he states that from this time he and Root, renewing an old acquaintance, were continually in conference.

Mr. Olmsted's first reports were not auspicious for Jackson Park. He doubted if enough land could be reclaimed from the morass, and preferred the north-shore site, which was high and well wooded, in case railroad communication could be secured. This expert opinion only increased the uncertainty, and the contest waxed warm during these August days. The heat of it absorbs me even now, as I glance over a book of newspaper clippings, with their contradictory head-lines.

Aug. 12. "Fair may all go to Lake Front."
Aug. 13. "Can Midway be secured?"
Aug. 14. "Site in a tangle; directors in deep gloom."
Aug. 15. "Lake Front is lost; not to be reconsidered."
Aug. 18. "Practically settled for Jackson Park alone."
Aug. 20. "North shore in favor."

And thus for weeks opinion veered back and forth before a committee anxious for the best results, but uncertain where to find them. On August 20 this Grounds and Buildings Committee appointed Messrs. F. L. Olmsted and Co. consulting landscape architects. "There is no more eminent artist living than Mr. Olmsted," said Root to some of the directors. "His appointment means much for the Fair — is an omen of highest promise. He is a genius."

The next day John Root was made consulting architect, an appointment amended on September 4, at Root's request, so as to include his partner. On that day, having recently returned to town from the seashore, he had a two hours' session with the committee, explaining his ideas for the great show, so far as they had taken form.

His study of this alluring problem had begun even before Chicago received the award. While the rival cities were pressing their claims, the subject was under discussion one evening at the Root dinner-table. An Eastern girl who was visiting the family remarked: "If Uncle Sam decides to have an exposition, I wonder what it will be like." The host's eyes twinkled at this, and he drew a paper from his pocket, saying, "Since it 's all between ourselves — *if* Uncle Sam has a Fair, and *if* it comes to Chicago, and *if* B. and R. are appointed its architects, it will be something like this:" and he spread the paper on the table. "But where will you get your water?" asked my informant, remarking lagoons and water-ways in the plan. "Lake Michigan is large enough to furnish it," Root answered; and indicating a pivotal point in the plan, he added, "The principal building — the building for offices — will stand there."

Capt. Horace G. H. Tarr describes a similar incident. At about the same time he remarked to Root that he was sure Chicago would secure the Fair, because there was no enthusiasm in New York, and congratulated his friend upon his chances of becoming architect-in-chief. Thereupon Root confessed that he had been thinking how he should like to treat the problem. "He went on to describe his idea," writes the Captain, "called for some paper, and sketched a plan of the buildings, inlets, and grounds to illustrate it. And I saw then a vision of beauty and grandeur which was not surpassed over three years later, when I stood in the White City thinking of his hope and witnessing its fulfillment."

Soon after his appointment as consulting architect, Root telegraphed to his friend and employee, Mr. Jules Wegman, to shorten his vacation and come home. Mr. Wegman came down at once from Wisconsin and reported at the office. Root told him he wanted his help in the World's Fair work, asked him to bring out the data Mr. Wegman had gathered at the Paris exposition, and then fell to work over a layout five times as large for Jackson Park. "He mapped out the lagoons, the island, the principal buildings, etc., essentially on the lines finally laid down," says Mr. Wegman, "I helping him with draughting and calculations. He called it the shirt plan, because the central basin was shaped like a shirt — sleeves, neck, rounded end and all." Mr. Aldis, of the Grounds and Buildings Committee, recalls his first view of the plan. "Before he presented it to the committee, he brought me the sheet of brown paper, one day, and with much enthusiasm, his eyes flashing, he pointed out the lagoons and the island, the locations of buildings, the axes of groups — all the essential features of the final plan."

On September 10, Root wrote to his wife, then ill at the seashore: "At last we have a *site;* and the only wonder seems to be that all of this talk has been inflicted upon us, when there seems to have been no reason to doubt that the site originally presented by the directors would be finally confirmed. Last night I laid out Jackson Park in a preliminary way, making large use of the lake and of interior lagoons, etc.; and I am satisfied that there can be obtained a most picturesque and novel effect, — barges, gondolas, flags, and flutter, and 'all such.'"

Two days later he wrote: "The World's Fair fares slowly, but with infinite pains of labor. Standing by its bedside as I am, and holding its hand, I wait for the result with clammy brow and parched lips. Yesterday Codman and I (very nice fellow — Olmsted's partner) faced the Building Committee for a fight and got it, coming off victorious all along the line. I don't think we will have much trouble, and that a very good part of the Fair will go on the Lake Front — say Art Building, Liberal Arts, Electrical displays and appliances, and perhaps Government Building, together with some villages.

"A conflict may come about between our directors and Uncle Sam's commissioners, but let us hope not, and meanwhile refrain from saying that we ever thought the thing possible."

Thus Jackson Park and the Lake Front gradually loomed with some definiteness out of the chaos, the latter not to be much enlarged, to have four or five buildings only, and to serve as the "gateway of the Fair," connecting by rail and boat with the main portion six miles away. This was the "double site" selected by the Grounds and Buildings Committee of the Chicago Directory, to be offered by that body for the approval of the National Commission at its first meeting in November, in accordance with the provisions of the act of Congress.

It is impossible to conceive to-day the confusion which the artists of the Fair were expected to reduce to order. In September, 1890, nothing had been determined and everything was demanded. The designers repeatedly tried without success to induce the local and national officials to state the number, sizes, and purposes of the buildings required. When the first "classification list" was finally made out by a committee of the National Commission, it did not indicate what or how many buildings were to be erected. Being compelled to work in the dark, the artists took the initiative and settled the problems for themselves on lines which were afterwards ratified by the acceptance of their general plan.

Lagoons were inevitable in Jackson Park. As early as 1870, when this reedy waste of bogs and marshes was first reserved for a public pleasure-ground, Mr. Olmsted had called it the Lagoon Park, and later he suggested a plan for its improvement which showed water-ways and a large island, in a form somewhat similar, in the northern part, to that shown at the Fair, and widening at the south into an irregular basin. The planning of these water-ways and the grouping of buildings around them was the problem now before the designers of landscape and architecture. Mr. Henry Sargent Codman, the capable young partner of Mr. Olmsted, came on from the East early in September, made careful studies of the grounds with sketches showing their adaptability to the purposes of the Exposition, and took part in the discussions on the subject of the ground-plan. During these talks it was always Root's hand which held the pencil, but every feature of his large brown-paper drawings was sharply discussed by the four men who composed the Eastern and Western firms, each one of them potent in suggestion and criticism. Root's incredible intuition and facility would sketch out an idea in the most effective possible way before it was fairly conceived in the brain. In addition to this readiness he brought to the task his swift inventiveness in design, and that vigorous pictorial imagination which could foresee the ultimate result; and, moreover, a most persuasive tongue. Mr. Olmsted brought to it that genius for the evolution of out-door effects of beauty upon which, through a lifetime of fine experience, he has built up his original and colossal art — an art which uses mountains, rivers, and prairies for its instruments as familiarly as the other arts use clay, or pigments, or brick and stone. Mr. Burnham contributed a large faith and enthusiasm for beauty which gave force and magnetism to his good taste and judgment. Codman brought to the study of the problem a closer academic training than any of the others. Scarcely twenty-seven years of age, he had recently made, in the schools of Paris, a study of large out-door schemes in the grouping of architectural monuments in landscape. Destined, like Root, to die before their dream should be embodied, he already showed commanding talent in his chosen profession — a profession peculiarly adapted to the dreamy spaciousness of his mind. He had eyes which saw into the distance and the future, and a heart which divined nature and aided her finest aspirations. In his death, which occurred January 13, 1893, his country lost a highly endowed and accomplished artist, one who would have developed and carried forward the principles and traditions of the majestic art which the genius of his partner had introduced to the American people.

Now that both Root and Codman are silent, it is difficult to define the share of each in suggesting the ground-plan of the Fair. Mr. Wegman's testimony, quoted above, would seem to indicate that the main conception was Root's, his plan adapting as far as possible Mr. Olmsted's old suggestion of a Lagoon Park, with its island and lagoons. It is said that from Codman came the idea of formalizing the great central court — surrounding its water-basin with balustrades, parks and buildings in formal lines. Mr. Olmsted suggested that the most imposing building should stand at the head of this court. Root set the court at right angles with the lake in the broad southern portion of the park, and connected it, near its western end, with the long lagoon running northwestward parallel with the lake, and widening to enclose the wooded island. Even the first tentative sketch described by Mr. Aldis and mentioned by Root in the letter of September 10, already

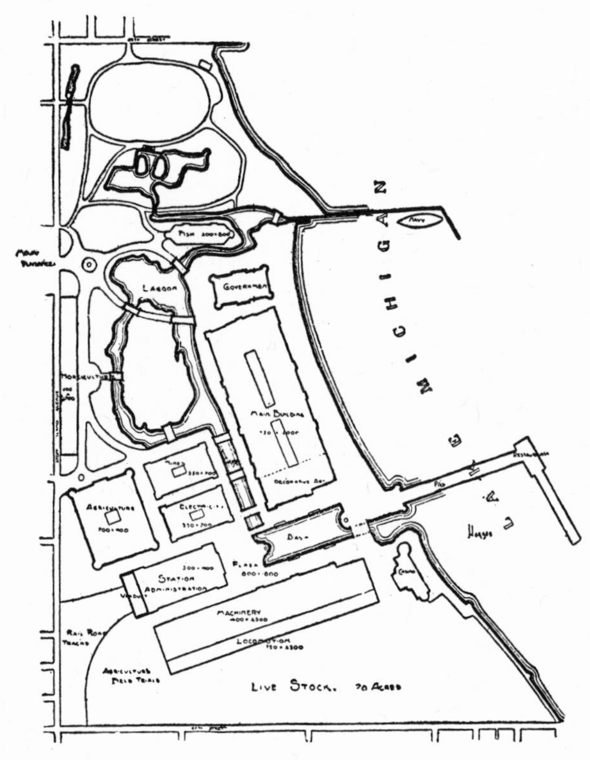

Root's Sketch of World's Fair Ground-plan. (From the " New York Tribune " of December 21, 1890)

quoted, shows the germ of this arrangement and of the final grouping of buildings about the court, though the waterways are smaller than those planned afterwards. Mr. Olmsted pointed out that this ground-plan experiment did not adequately meet the problem of entrances, and he suggested improvements at various points. The water-ways were now enlarged and changed somewhat in shape, and around them Root tried various groupings of buildings, of which the diagram shows the last one.

From the time of the first sketch, Root called the scheme the "shirt plan," though the southern sleeve to the shirt

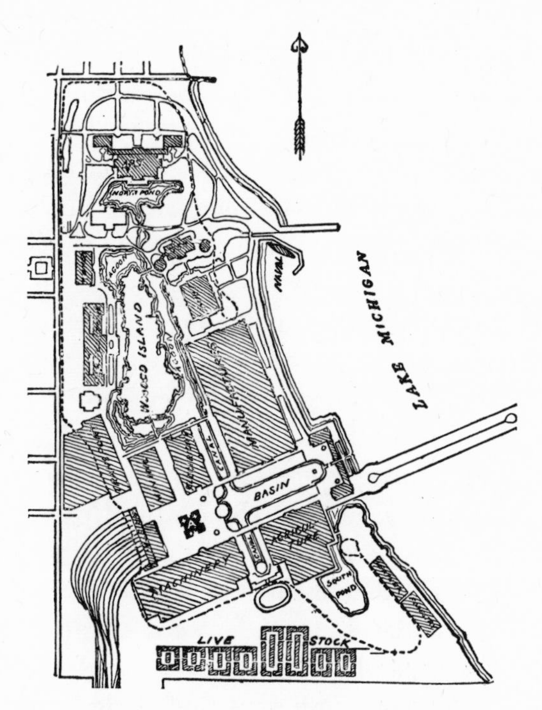

Final Ground-plan of Columbian Exposition

was endangered afterward when he offered to Machinery Hall the whole space south of the central court. "Well, Codman, the shirt plan goes," he said one day after a long study of possibilities, and both of them had many sessions over it with the Grounds and Buildings Committee. His word was fulfilled — the shirt plan "went" to the end. By comparison of Root's diagram with the final map of the

Fair, it will be seen that the variations were changes of detail, not fundamental in the general scheme. In the offices of F. L. Olmsted & Co., in Brookline, the Chicago drawings were carefully studied, and certain modifications suggested, chiefly by Mr. John C. Olmsted. The plan was then submitted to the Board of Architects, the leading designers of the country, at their first session during the days of Root's fatal illness, and by them subjected to searching criticism. They tried other arrangements only to reject them, and at last approved the scheme almost exactly as it was presented to them. The changes made in the Brookline office from the plan which Root drew were chiefly as follows: Two buildings instead of one were placed south of the Court of Honor, thus restoring a south lagoon, which was included in the September sketches, but afterwards cut off. Thus the long lagoon vista was extended southward, the great central fountain being moved back a little out of the line of it. The buildings for Electricity and Mining were turned around so that both should give to the Court of Honor, the Government and Fisheries Buildings were shifted to the axis of the central group, and a few other details were altered. Afterwards the Obelisk and the Colonnade were suggested by Mr. Peabody to complete the southern vista, and the beautiful Peristyle Mr. Atwood suggested and designed, instead of the thirteen columns in honor of the original States, which had been Mr. St. Gaudens' first idea of a lakeward finish for the Court of Honor. But in its essential lines the Columbian Exposition was built on the plan evolved in Chicago by the happy collaboration of gifted minds, and sketched out by Root's hand on that famous sheet of brown paper over which many battles were fought with many committees, and which was formally adopted at last by the National Commission.

STUDY FOR EXPOSITION BUILDINGS, JACKSON PARK

Facsimile Reduction of Mr. Root's Sketch

The Lake Front, also, was the subject of much study and experiment during these weeks. Day after day Root was summoned to suggest and define, and the swift rush of this labor, added to his regular office work, strained even his strength of body and brain. At this time, the middle of October, it was proposed to place five buildings on the Lake Front — Fine Arts, Electricity, Decorative Arts, the Music Hall, and the fabulous Water Palace. The rest of the Fair was to go to Jackson Park, and "complete plans and specifications" were ordered, with characteristic Chicago intrepidity, to be ready in twenty-four hours in accordance with this division of exhibits — a labor for which, in Paris, a full architectural corps had been allowed one year. But by this time the finished beauty of Washington Park, a mile inland, had begun to allure some of the Exposition officials, whose minds, untrained to the preconception of architectural effects, grew doleful at sight of the morass on the shore. Root was called upon, October 27, to present in hot haste a plan for Washington Park. He responded promptly to the demand, placed on the great meadow a vast ⊔-shaped building for the main exhibits, and grouped the smaller structures in as close conformity as possible to the finished roads and groves of the park. A large water-color perspective was made of this plan, which shows a most effective composition, centring in a superb Romanesque tower which rises from the middle section of the main building. The plan was attractive, in its way, but the South Park board refused to assent to it, declaring it too destructive of their expensive improvements. Root also opposed it, and placed against it the most recent studies of Jackson Park, explaining the manifold advantages of the lake and its connecting lagoons. And when the National Commission, an unwieldy body of three or four hundred politicians and men of affairs appointed by the President and the Governors of the States, came together for its first meeting in November, it was still "Jackson Park and the Lake Front" which the Chicago directors offered for their ratification.

And now the great battle for a site, which had been settled and unsettled so many times, had to be fought all over again. Some of the Commissioners drove to the parks, and recited among their colleagues their disgust with the swampy wilderness where Chicago proposed to receive the world. They made loud demands upon the South Park Board for the unconditional surrender of Washington Park, whose broad grassy meadow offered a more promising welcome. When that body stood out firmly against the demolition of its roads and groves and ponds, granting the use of the park only under restrictions, the Commissioners and Directors were plunged into hot war, the former threatening to compel Congress to remove the Fair from Chicago, and the latter defying them. The city newspapers, in the mean time, were urging any surrender to save the Fair; and those of other cities were jeering at Chicago's inability to find a site. This was the situation at the sessions of Saturday, November 15; threats were thrown back and forth between the rival bodies, and on each side the law was laid down in forcible language. It was the first heat in the long contest which finally established the supremacy of the Chicago Directory and the redundancy of the National Commission. Before adjournment a conference was arranged for Monday, when committees from both bodies, and another from the visiting Congressional committee, should meet and discuss the vexed question.

At this meeting the consulting architects were invited to report. Root felt that it was "now or never" for Jackson

Park, and that the decision must be wrested from passion to reason. He felt that the National Commissioners were not imaginative — they judged blindly from present conditions. The artists must reveal to their mind's eye the completed work, lest that dream of stately palaces mirrored in clear waters should disappear forever. They had until Monday to avert the threatened calamity and make peace between the rival bodies — a Sunday in which to plan their victory for art. On that day the enemy had never been stronger. The Sunday "Herald" published an interview with the Chairman of the Committee appointed by the National Commission for the morrow's conference, which reported him as saying: "If the directors do not abandon their position a deadlock will ensue, and in that event no presidential proclamation, calling for foreign exhibits and state coöperation, will be issued." War clouds hung heavily over the rival bodies which divided the government of the Fair, and the city was in despair.

But Messrs. Olmsted, Codman, and Root had their heads together in council. Codman wrote a brief in favor of the lake-shore site; but, as it was deemed expedient to take the attitude of an impartial judge instead of that of a special pleader, this brief was not presented. Root embodied the ideas and researches of the two landscape architects with his own, and formulated the whole into a long report which both firms signed, the original rough manuscript of which exists in his handwriting, except the three closing paragraphs, which may be lost from the manuscript, or which Mr. Olmsted may have contributed. This report is a good example of Root's exact and logical style when writing for business men of business matters. It considered impartially the advantages and disadvantages of each of the two sites from the six points of view of accessibility, relationship of parks to each other, cost of preparation, cost of maintenance, disposition of buildings, and cost of restoration. It presented figures and estimates, strictly tabulated so as to appeal to men of business, which showed a net advantage of $59,000 in favor of Jackson Park. It showed that if Washington Park were chosen, hardly a square yard of its surface could remain undemolished: piles would have to be driven for heavy buildings; groves destroyed to afford avenues and vistas; soil turned up everywhere for water-pipes and drains; surface levels modified; and the beautiful meadow, which had seemed to the Commissioners an ideal site for the Fair, utterly wiped out by buildings too large for it. And, with all these sacrifices, adequate space could not be obtained for the effective grouping of buildings. Thus the apparent advantages of this inland site gradually disappeared under his logic; and when, in reviewing Jackson Park, he showed the value of the lake and lagoons for decoration and transportation, the advantage its wild spaces offered to the designer as "virgin soil to be modeled at will to a large purpose," no reasonable man could hesitate. Having presented the claims of each park, he concluded: —

"It is difficult for one not experienced in technical consideration of such matters to rightly view this subject. In one case, a park now finished and beautiful is almost totally undone, presenting, during its temporary occupancy by the exposition, scarcely a charm not equally possessed by any piece of wooded prairie, and after its restoration retaining such scars and mutilations as may still, after so many years, be witnessed in Fairmount Park as relics of the Exposition of 1876.

"In the other case, a piece of ground is presented, like clay to the hand of a sculptor, with which anything within the artist's capacity may be accomplished. Its natural advantages are those which are most characteristic of Chicago — its proximity to Lake Michigan and its free use, not only of the rare beauty of this great sheet of water, but of such festive and Venice-like lagoons as may be supplied from it, imparting to the whole Fair grouped about them double enchantment.

"Upon the subject of the grandeur, beauty, and impressiveness of the central group of buildings, . . . their influence upon the imagination, we are required to give an opinion for which we shall be responsible before the world as artists. That opinion is that the capabilities of Jackson Park for the purposes of the Fair are of a much higher order than those of Washington Park.

"We have many reasons for this opinion, which cannot be presented under the conditions prescribed for this report. But there is one reason so simple that no tangible fact can be more open to immediate and general apprehension. It is that this location will associate the Fair with the grandeur and beauty of the one distinguishing natural, historical, and poetic feature of this part of the American continent, — its great inland seas.

"Let the central buildings of the Fair be placed, with all possible exercise of architectural and landscape art, upon Washington Park, and the result will be no better than could be obtained with equal art on any flat plain anywhere in the world. Let them be placed on Jackson Park, in such relation with Lake Michigan as is easily practicable, and the result will have a grandeur that no World's Fair hitherto has ever possessed."

This report was printed in pamphlet form and distributed among the Commissioners on Monday morning. At the conference meeting of the three committees, Root took the floor, and, with the aid of maps and plans, explained and amplified the report. Mr. Harlow N. Higinbotham, afterwards President of the Exposition, in describing the scene, says: "There was no resisting the clearness and force of his reasoning. The Commissioners, who had been so violent on Saturday, threw up their hands and had nothing more to say. Washington Park was saved from destruction, and the Fair went where it belonged." The newspapers also gave to this report the credit of settling the troublesome question of site. A few days later the very Commissioner, whose strenuous opposition to Jackson Park has been quoted above from the "Herald," as Chairman of the Conference Committee recommended that the Commission accept the report and approve the ground plans; and his recommendation was adopted without opposition. I remember how Root laughed over the capitulation of this gentleman, who learned a wholesome lesson of respect for artists, and frankly became their champion.

Mr. Charles L. Hutchinson, who was one of the members of the Executive Committee of the Exposition Directory, and who was in frequent conference with Root before and after his appointment as Consulting Architect, said recently: "You cannot overstate John Root's services to the Exposition. He wanted Jackson Park when the landscape gardeners and nearly every member of the Committee were opposed to it. In the very beginning of the enterprise, he saw very clearly, more clearly than all others, how beautiful would be the effect of combining land and water in this park; and he persisted until every one else came around to his opinion. It was his mind, more than any other, which was felt in the initiative of the great enterprise, and to him is due more praise than he will ever receive in this world." Mr. Owen F. Aldis, and other members of the Grounds and Buildings Committee, are willing also to be quoted on the subject of the Consulting Architect's services. "John Root made the Fair until he died," says Mr. Aldis; "or no, I must modify that, because Mr. Olmsted had a share in it; I don't know how great. From these two men came the artistic impetus of the Columbian Exposition, and it was carried out on the large lines they laid down."

Root looked upon the Columbian Exposition as a great opportunity for his profession, and he accepted the post of consulting architect with the avowed purpose of concentrating upon this work the best American talent, and of making it an object-lesson to the people in the management of great building enterprises. His appointment gave him wide discretion. Though the Grounds and Buildings Committee intended to invite the collaboration of other architects, it did not assume the initiative in this matter, but permitted Root to formulate his own scheme for an architectural corps. It was taken for granted, meanwhile, by the majority of directors, by the press and the public, that he would be the designer of the principal buildings. His professional confrères expected this also; Eastern architects had no hope of participating in the work, and those in Chicago were bitterly suspicious of exclusion. I remember how Root came home one evening, soon after his appointment, cut to the quick because one of these, always hitherto a friend, had apparently refused to recognize Mr. Burnham when they met at a club. "I suppose he thinks we are going to hog it all!" he exclaimed, disheartened.

Soon, against all persuasion, he announced his intention of designing none of the chief buildings in Jackson Park. To preserve the impartiality of a judge would be impossible, he insisted, if he should assume a rôle. Both he and Mr.

Burnham wished to give the great enterprise a national character by inviting the leading architects in the country to take part in it, and to this end they now directed their energies before the Committee on Grounds and Buildings. December 8 Root presented a memorial to this committee, describing impartially four possible methods of procedure. It reads as follows in the original manuscript in his handwriting: —

"Preliminary work in locating buildings, in determining their general areas, and in other elementary directions necessary to proper progress in the design and erection of the structures of the Columbian Exposition has now reached a point where it becomes necessary to determine the method by which designs for these buildings shall be obtained. We recognize that your action in this matter will be of great importance not only in its direct effect upon the artistic and commercial successes of the Exposition, but, scarcely less, upon the aspect presented by America to the world, and also as a precedent for future procedure in this country by the government, by corporations and individuals.

"In our advisory capacity we wish to recommend such action to you as will be productive of the best results, and will at the same time be in accord with the expressed sentiments of the architectural societies of America. Whatever suggestions are here made relate to the main buildings located in Jackson Park. That these buildings should, in their designs, relationship, and arrangement, be of the highest possible architectural merit is of importance scarcely less than the variety, richness, and comprehensiveness of the various displays within them. Such success is not so much dependent upon the expenditure of money as upon the expenditure of thought, knowledge, and enthusiasm by men known to be in every way endowed with these qualities. And the results achieved by them will be the measure by which America, and especially Chicago, must expect to be judged by the world.

"Several methods of procedure suggest themselves: —

"1st. The selection of one man to whom the designing of the entire work should be entrusted.

"2d. Competition made free to the whole architectural profession.

"3d. Competition among a selected few.

"4th. Direct selection.

"1st. The first method would possess some advantages in the coherent and logical result which would be attained. But the objections are, that time for preparation of designs is so short that no one man could hope to do the subject justice even were he broad enough to avoid, in work of such varied and colossal character, monotonous repetition of ideas.

"2d. The second method named has been employed in France and other European countries with success, and it would probably result in the production of a certain number of plans possessing more or less merit and novelty.

"But in such a competition much time, even now most valuable, would be wasted, and the result would be a mass of irrelevant and almost irreconcilable material which would demand great and extended labor to bring into coherence. It is greatly to be feared that from such a heterogeneous competition the best men of the profession would refrain, not only because the uncertainties involved in it are too great, and their time too valuable, but because the societies to which they almost universally belong have so strongly pronounced its futility.

"3d. A limited and paid competition would present fewer

embarrassments; but even in this case the question of time is presented, and it is most unlikely that any result derived through this means, coming, as it would, from necessarily partial acquaintance with the subject and hasty, ill-considered presentation of it, could be satisfactory.

"Far better than any of these methods seems to be the last.

"4th. This is to select a certain number of architects because of their eminence in the profession, choosing each man for such work as would be most parallel with his best achievements; these architects to meet in conference, become masters of all the elements of the problems to be solved, and agree upon some general scheme of procedure; the preliminary studies resulting from this to be freely discussed in a subsequent conference, and, with the assistance of such suggestions as your advisers might make, to be brought into a harmonious whole.

"The precise relationship between the directory and these architects might safely be left to a general conference, at which all questions of detail could be agreed upon. The honor conferred upon any man thus selected would create in his mind a disposition to place the artistic quality of his work in advance of the mere question of emolument; while the emulation begotten in a rivalry so dignified and friendly could not fail to be productive of a result which would stand before the world as the best fruit of American civilization."

This memorial was emphasized by oral argument, and its recommendations were adopted by the Grounds and Buildings Committee. Burnham and Root had determined, weeks before, upon their board of architects, and now five representative firms from other States were nominated, confirmed, and notified of their appointment, viz.: Richard M.

Hunt, McKim, Mead & White, and George B. Post, of New York; Peabody & Stearns, of Boston; and Van Brunt & Howe, of Kansas City. It was intended that these gentlemen should design the main group of buildings around the Court of Honor, leaving the other buildings for Chicago architects. But they were no sooner appointed than strong opposition to the employment of outsiders began to impede the action of the committee. It was said that Chicago was paying for the Fair, and Chicago men should have the designing of it; and that, moreover, professional talent in this city, compared with that in the East, was fully as competent and more progressive. Under pressure from local architects and their friends in the directory, and from the spirit of local patriotism in general, there was danger, in spite of the firmness of certain members of the committee, that the appointment of the five firms might be rescinded. Both the consulting architect and his partner, who, late in October, had been appointed chief of the newly organized Department of Construction, thus becoming the executive captain of the great enterprise, were forced to fight many wordy battles, both in and out of committee rooms, to sustain the national character of the exposition. On Saturday, December 27, Root was before the Grounds and Buildings Committee to present, on the part of the Construction Department, a report stating, among other matters, that the Eastern architects would accept their appointments. At this meeting, with his usual quiet marshaling of facts and arguments, he persuasively defended the appointment of these men on broad grounds of public policy, and urged the committee to hold its ground. On December 30, members of the committee spoke strongly in the same vein, holding that they were in honor bound to stand by their action; and the matter was so decided on January 5.

In the report presented by Root on December 27, the committee was requested, "as the above reported action covers all that may be expected by this committee as to its outside designers," to confirm the nomination of ten specified Chicago firms for the designing of other structures. On January 5 the committee divided the list of ten by two, authorized Mr. Burnham to notify the five firms, fixed January 10, 1891, as the date of the first Conference of the Board of Architects, and gave to the Chief of Construction absolute freedom in the assignment of work to the various designers. The committee never passed upon any design after its acceptance of the ground-plan, wisely leaving all questions of art to the artists.

Thus the great work of designing and constructing the Columbian Exposition began in a spirit of friendliness and high emulation. The magnanimity of Burnham and Root, the largeness of their point of view, could not but conciliate their rivals and extinguish jealousy. So it was with universal approbation that the Grounds and Buildings Committee, in conjunction with the Art Institute, requested this firm to present designs for the Fine Arts Building, which was then assigned to the Lake Front, and which was to become after the Fair the city's permanent Museum of Fine Arts. This commission Root accepted as a great opportunity, and it was his favorite study during the last months of his last year. Too long had his muse been claimed by commerce; now at last she was winning for the poet-architect tasks after his own heart. These Columbian honors promised to open a new era in his art, and his spirit responded gladly to the inspiration. Dimly the people for whom he wrought were beginning to recognize in this man a leader; one aware of beauty, persuasive to make them long for it, strong to make it real for them. Though scarcely conscious of their allegiance, they were yet bearing him on their shoulders during these weeks of heroic exertion, and he felt behind his creative force that mighty force of public sympathy which alone can nerve great souls to put forth their utmost power.

VIII

LAST DAYS

JOHN ROOT'S conception of the Fair differed much from the White City of memory. If he had lived and his ideas had prevailed, the Columbian Exposition would have been a City of Color; a queen arrayed in robes not saintly, as for a bridal, but gorgeous, for a festival. These two ideals are both worthy of honor. One was embodied in delicate beauty, to win the praises of the world; the other vanished when a great man died. For the first I do not need to speak: its noble stateliness made its own appeal. We lived for half a year in the awe and wonder of it, and it lingers in memory, under the sunshine of that gracious summer, as a glimpse into realms unearthly, the chosen abode of perfect souls. For the second I must say my feeble word, remembering the enthusiasm and strength of purpose which this unrealized dream concentrated. That word will be unconvincing, perhaps; because no architectural scheme can be fairly judged until it is completed before men's eyes, and because any disturbance of our memories of the White City will seem a desecration. But the beauty of the lily is no reason why the rose should not also be beautiful. And all the flowers of memory cannot make it impossible that one unrecorded should be as lovely as these. The difficulty lies in the proving. What eye can behold the perished flower, however marvelous? What hand can delineate the Columbian City as its first architect saw it? Mine is powerless to offer more than a few hints showing the rough outline of his conception.

The fundamental point in Root's creed as an architect was sincerity: a building should frankly express its purpose and its material. Thus it would have been impossible for him to design, as the chief buildings of the Fair, imitations in staff of marble palaces: these could not express their material; or to adopt a classic motive: this could not express the purpose of a modern American exposition. He wished to admit frankly in the architectural scheme the temporary character of the Fair: it should be a great, joyous, luxuriant midsummer efflorescence, born to bloom for an hour and perish — a splendid buoyant thing, flaunting its gay colors between the shifting blues of sky and lake exultantly, prodigally. Edifices built in pursuance of this idea should not give the illusion of weight and permanence: they should be lighter, gayer, more decorative than the solid structures along our streets. To his mind the dominant note in our civilization was its youth, its newness, crudeness: manifestly things were beginning here, — beginning with a swift rush and turmoil of creative energies. He wished to show its affluence, its sumptuous conquering enthusiasm. He wished to offer to the older nations a proof of new forces, new ideals, not yet developed and completed, but full of power and prophetic of charm. He wished to express our militant democracy as he felt it, pausing after victory for a song of triumph before taking up its onward march.

Manifestly these turbulent awakening energies could not be presented through any formal and crystallized type of architecture. The classic type, Root was inclined to feel, had attained its ultimate perfection in Greece, and its motives had been restudied and developed through succeeding centuries until they were scarcely capable of a new vitalization which should express the modern purposes. It was a style for the open-air life and the fair blue skies of Athens, not for wind-swept and storm-beaten Chicago. Moreover, it was a monumental style, not suitable for holiday structures built of temporary materials. Among all the tentative sketches of the Fair, or portions of it, which Root threw off from day to day during these busy weeks, there is scarcely a trace of a classic motive. On the contrary, there is much that is unconventional or even bizarre, conceived in a lyric mood with delightful freshness and spontaneity. He was much pleased one day when an English artist, trained in the schools, but hospitable to new suggestions, recognized what he was striving for in one of these drawings: "You 've got an exuberant barbaric effect there — a kind of an American Kremlin," he said; "lots of color and noise and life."

A vigorous and masterful panorama of ephemeral magnificence — such was the ideal these sketches present. Kremlin and Nishni-Novgorod give suggestions of the turn his mind was taking with regard to form and splendor. This idea of a World's Fair would not have given the nations a Celestial City — it would not have been divine, but it would have been sympathetically and broadly human. Its appeal to the popular imagination would have been, perhaps, the more intimate, potent, and enduring. Root's sketches adopted usually the Romanesque type of arch and column as a form more pliable than the Greek, a form which admitted the use of American species of flower and leaf in ornamentation. The Fisheries Building, which was designed by Mr. Henry Ives Cobb, was the best example on the grounds of Root's ideas of Fair architecture. Its frankly playful use of staff, as a medium whose easy plasticity invited an endless variety of gay detail, would have struck him as honest and poetic; and the delicate, even humorous adaptation of sea-forms of animal and plant life would have appealed to his sense of fitness. Such happy imaginings, however, he would have vivified with color instead of freezing them in white. Color was, to his feeling, a necessity in any architectural expression of a great festival. In this opinion he was at one with the Greeks themselves, who added to the creamy translucency of their marble brilliant accents of color. He was outborne also by the instinct of the people, who loved the Court of Honor best, not when the noon sunshine glared on its façades of opaque white, but when the twilight made them luminous with pink and gold and purple, or the Night, flashing her million lamps, clothed them in mysteries of shimmer and shade.

I am convinced that the people would have responded with joy to an intelligent use of color in the treatment of buildings at the great festival, that it would have added a strong element of beauty and gayety, and emphasized the grandeur of noble façades. The Transportation Building, with its beautiful Golden Door, was an interesting experiment in this direction, although Mr. Sullivan's sumptuous orientalism was scarcely given a fair setting as the only strong note of color among many classic façades of changeless white. Problems of out-door decoration have been studied but little by our decorators, for the best of reasons.

Root had much confidence in Mr. William Pretyman's ideas on this subject, an enthusiast whose old-world studies did not make him reject new ideas. During these months they discussed somewhat this problem of out-door color, and afterwards, when Mr. Pretyman was appointed Chief of Color for the Fair, he experimented in the tinting of staff with thin washes of pure transparent oil-colors, believing that opaque paint of the ordinary kind would harden and artificialize the delicate material, and that white especially would destroy its creamy translucency. In these experiments beautiful results were obtained, but Mr. Pretyman resigned his post too early to carry out his ideas, the only example of them on the grounds being the little East India House, that delicate opal set in green. Any one who saw the Fisheries Building, for example, when it was first completed in 1892, and noted the lovely amber tones of the staff melting graciously into the sunlight, could not fail to feel a painful shock when this seductive bloom was hidden forever under the heavier white. Somehow the poetry of the building seemed to have gone out of it.

Root's possible decisions in points of detail are of course a mere matter of conjecture. While he lived all projects were still chaotic, and his mind, as usual, was open to all suggestions. We know only his initial preferences, not his ultimate choice. During these months the scale was still his dominant thought. "He was thinking of the bones as no one else did," says a gentleman familiar with him at this time. "He had dug up his mammoth and set it up while others were wondering how big such an animal could be, and when told of its existence, were opening their eyes without being able to measure its magnitude." Yet he did not neglect the sinews and integument of his giant. During these last weeks of his life he caused experiments with colored tiles and terra-cotta to be carried on at the terra-cotta works; and his accurate mind — a mind which, in the service of clients, hated extravagance and waste — was full of speculations in regard to the availability and cost of this material and of others, such as glass, wood, staff. Staff, which had been used extensively in Paris, was not his preference for large structures, though it might have been his choice eventually for a great deal of the work. He would never have used it in imitation of marble, but he would have appreciated its delightful temptations to gayety of modeling and coloring. Terra-cotta, in rather strong tones, he would undoubtedly have used as extensively as its price would admit. But, whatever the materials, his whole heart was centred upon his hope of an American Fair — an architectural scheme which should express exuberantly our young, crude, buoyant civilization, and strike our note at last in the world's art.

I have often wondered whether Root could have carried out his ideas of Fair architecture through the board of architects whom he appointed. Remembering his sanguine belief in these ideas, and the persuasive power of the man to inspire others with his own enthusiasm, I think it possible that he might have achieved the impossible with these men trained in the schools and bound by precedents. But it would have been much easier for his fertile mind to design the whole exposition than to get what he wanted out of others. We used to urge that he should strike the keynote of his scheme by taking the Administration Building, but the most magnanimous sense of duty to his profession made him reject the suggestion. The leading American architects should be invited to serve on the advisory board, and this invitation implied an extension of professional courtesy by which their senior member, whom Root recognized as Mr. Richard M. Hunt, should be requested to design the most important building. It implied, also, I suppose, a certain deference to the will of the majority of this board in regard to the type of architecture which should prevail. And so one may merely surmise what would have happened if Root's fixed purpose of a Fair which should express our national life and character, presented to these architects with all his exactness and persuasive power, had met their fixed resolve for the classic. Representatives of four out of the five outside firms came on together from the East for the first conference, appointed to begin on the twelfth of January. On the way they talked over the enterprise which summoned them, and fixed upon the classic type of architecture as the only one in which they could work together harmoniously. This plan the architect-in-chief could scarcely have ratified — could they have accepted his? It is probable that most of the five Chicago architects, judging from the character of their designs for the Fair, would have upheld Root. But the ideas he cherished so ardently were never presented to his fellow-laborers. On the morning when the first conference began, he was stricken with pneumonia; a day or two before it ended, he died. If he had lived, there would have been another battle of Chicago against the East, new methods against old, our own beauty against the beauty of the past. For my feeling that the progressive spirit would have conquered, I have only the precedent of the city's earlier victories, and my knowledge of Root's power in persuading men even against their training and preferences.

On the first day of the new year he went East, partly to attend, as Secretary of the American Institute, a meeting of its executive board; and partly to see the appointed architects, give them some ideas of the scope of the Fair, and of what would be demanded of them, and invite them to the conference. He was exhausted by the strain of the past few months, so that his spirit lacked something of its usual magnetic buoyancy. Thus he was somewhat depressed by the attitude of the Eastern men, whom he found singularly apathetic, utterly incredulous that any association of Western business men would give art a free hand in the manner he set forth. The dream was too extravagant ever to be realized, and they were extremely reluctant to undertake its realization against the hampering and tampering, the interferences petty and great, which they felt were certain to ensue. They shared at this time the general Eastern feeling that a Columbian Exposition in Chicago would be little more than a cattle-show. Root returned from his ten days' pilgrimage, tired and somewhat discouraged. He could not get these men interested, he said; he felt that this was the greatest opportunity ever offered to his profession in this country, and he could not make them appreciate it. They were coming to the conference, but reluctantly; their hearts were not in it. And the next evening I had an opportunity of verifying his words, when the visiting architects met socially at his house — the last of many revels there. In talking with them I was amazed at their listless and hopeless attitude toward the great undertaking which brought them to Chicago. Beautiful effects were scarcely to be expected in buildings so enormous and so cheaply constructed; the level monotony of ground surfaces in Chicago made effective grouping practically impossible; the time for preparation and construction was too short: these and other criticisms indicated a general feeling of disparagement. This was not to be wondered at, perhaps, in men new to an enterprise whose development we had watched with growing enthusiasm for months. Afterwards they felt the inspiration of it, and their rapture rose to a lyric pitch; but it was over the grave of the man who had summoned them.

So, with a precious oblation to the gods, the great festival moved on to its triumph. The partnership of a score of years dissolved by high decree, and the elder of the two enthusiasts for beauty assumed alone the grave responsibility to which both had dedicated their strength and hope. He gathered men of many gifts around him — artists, engineers, mechanics, laborers — and inspired them all with brave desire. Thus, under potent leadership, the arts and crafts moved onward swiftly in concord. The great task was achieved like a song; the city of love arose as by a miracle. And the world, which knew for a summer the joy of dwelling there, will make it forever the abode of dreams.

Among all the sketches and drawings which remain to show us Root's first tentative ideas of Fair architecture, perhaps the one for the main building at Washington Park is the most characteristic and suggestive. One or two of his drawings for it still exist (see page 217), and a large and accurate water-color perspective was made which gives an exact idea of its motive and details. It was this building which was dubbed the Kremlin. The design was made in hot haste at the behest of directors. Root laughed at it as a *tour de force*, knowing it too costly to carry out as it stands, the great central tower being five or six hundred feet high. But it was a superb dream, a magnificent outburst of poetic energy. The building surrounds three sides of an oblong court. The two wings and the corners are low — two stories high, under a succession of low hipped roofs. From the centre, at the end of the court, rises broadly an

SKETCHES FOR HABITATIONS AND OTHER WORLD'S-FAIR MOTIVES

immense octagonal tower, sweeping straight upward for more than half its height, the tiled roof thence sloping straight to a point. The wall-surfaces are golden brown — terra-cotta perhaps, with an exuberance of ornament in bas-relief. The effect of the grouping and massing is buoyant, simple, strong; a joyous wealth of power, like the athletic play of a young warrior. There is grace in it, courage, rhythm.

The early Jackson Park drawings are almost as interesting. A large water-color perspective, which must have been made in September or early in October, following the "preliminary" ground-plan mentioned in Root's letter of September 10, already quoted, shows lagoons and a large island in a form which is plainly the germ of the plan finally adopted, although the lagoon surface is much smaller. North and south of the central basin are two Romanesque buildings, their upper stories bridging the north and south lagoons over archways which, with their high sloping roofs and turrets, focalize the architectural composition of each structure. The larger and more imposing of the two extends back along the lake at the north. At the head of the central court rises the Administration Building, oblong instead of square, its high dome forming, then as afterwards, the chief architectural feature of the general scheme. This perspective is incomplete, showing buildings only around the central court, except for the historic habitations which are scattered among the trees on the island.

These sketches for a series of human habitations were done with Root's characteristic swiftness, and they show how the Fair interested him in detail as well as in mass. One of the gentlemen in the office caught him one day as he was starting for home, and asked him when he would give them this series. So he sat down and sketched off, one after another as they talked, fourteen motives for such an exhibit of dwellings — Græco-Egyptian, Greek, Roman, Chinese, Russian, Swiss, French, Flemish, Moorish, Norwegian, and others. They were the merest play, dashed off in less than an hour on the margins of sheets of drawing-paper before him, to be destroyed or preserved — he never cared which. But they remain to show his ready invention, the easy play of his mind in passing from one subject to another.

The scheme for a "Water Palace" on the Lake Front tempted him also, and he made a charming plan for it — a great dome sloping outward to rest on columns, and surmounted by the decorative form of a ship. The promoters intended to have an aërial river of water flowing over or under the dome, with the light shining through it. He made various ground-plans for the Lake Front, the first two or three reclaiming a large area from the lake so as to accommodate the whole Fair, and later studies using only the present strip of park. All of these included a permanent Fine Arts Museum at the head of Adams Street.

For this building, which was to be erected by the directors of the Art Institute and the Exposition company conjointly, Root left careful progressive studies and a beautiful final drawing, which remain to show the processes of his mind in thinking out a problem and solving it. The design was his last important work, and a work which interested him more than anything else he had ever undertaken, as it was to be a monumental structure erected for an artistic purpose. Moreover, the final design was singularly successful. The design was never carried out: the officers of the Art Institute found that, owing to the need of more light and other causes, they could not use it without such serious modifications as might be injurious, so they abandoned it altogether. If Root had lived, doubtless he

MUSEUM OF FINE ARTS, STUDY OF CENTRAL PAVILION

Facsimile Reduction of Mr. Root's Sketch

would have re-studied his idea many times before pronouncing it complete; but it is probable that he would have clung to the main lines of it.

He commenced his study of the problem in the summer. In a letter to his wife, dated August 10, 1890, he wrote: "I have just finished a very satisfactory day on the design for the World's Fair Art Building. I really think I've got a good thing of it. I've been keeping it in my mind for some time till I could get a long quiet day to get it out; and a long quiet beautiful day this has been." Two days later he wrote again: "I have spent the day on the Art Building, which I solemnly promise to make a joy. The only thing I dread about it is that, like some other things, it may be too good to be true."

The building was to be of pink granite, with a basement of reddish brown. The lower part of the sloping roof was

First Study for Fine Arts Museum

to be of brown Spanish tiles, and the upper two fifths of glass, for lighting purposes, vertically paned and crested with an ornamental ridge. The first study which remains shows a dome over the central section of the building, rising behind the low roof above the entrance. A large watercolor perspective was made of this, and one evening in the autumn, when it happened that I had stopped in for dinner, he brought this home and showed it to us; and we three — his wife and he and I — discussed it for some time and agreed upon a rather severe verdict. The same water-color is now before me, and I feel that we were right in

Façade of the Projected Art Museum

pronouncing the design, in spite of its good features, heavy and somewhat squatty, and in our feeling that it did not hang together, that the dome did not seem to be a part of it. After this he made one or two other trials at a dome; one sheet of brown paper shows one of these, and also the first hints of the final plan in two little sketches for the centre and an arm of the structure. He followed up this idea on another sheet, when he tried once more the central portion of the building, surmounting it this time with a rude sketch of the lower stories of a tower. But the tower, like the dome, was abandoned. This drawing is quite complete in detail; its two halves differ slightly, and the one on the left is canceled by two straight lines drawn swiftly across it — thus would he strike out an unsuccessful essay. The other side satisfied him better, though he had not yet reached his final idea. It shows the imposing round archway of the entrance, springing from groups of granite columns, supporting the upper story and roof, and flanked, without the intervening space which appeared later, by two strong gable ends. On this sketch Root wrote instructions in regard to materials, the placing of mosaics and bas-reliefs, and other details. The next step, aside from the study of floor-plans, was the final design. Every line of these various drawings was executed by Root, and the last one is complete, showing the entire west façade of the building. The central section is broadened a little, and the height of the hip roof increased, giving greater dignity and repose. It is flanked by two wings, which show a blind arcade ending in gable ends similar to those of the central section, but smaller. Another drawing gives a view of the south façade.

The most notable thing about this monumental design in the Romanesque is the grace, the lightness of it. It attains the dignity, the majesty which is recognizably within the scope of this style, but it attains as well an exquisite lyric beauty. The word "massive," which is descriptive of much of the most successful work in the Romanesque, would scarcely be applied to this building. It has great strength, but it has also a delicacy which is expressed, as a rule, only by the most successful designs in the classic. And the spontaneity of it, the power which it demonstrates, give one a sense of freedom, of largeness, a belief in great ideas. Manifestly the world is still young and the future is full of hope before us — since such a thing as this was done but yesterday.

One of the last of many nights of talk and music comes back to my memory as I recall these closing weeks of John Root's life. Six or eight friends — devotees of the arts — were gathered together in a place full of magic influences — a studio rich in the trophies of life and art. Over the great fireplace where heavy logs were blazing hung savage armor against the dark red wall — shields, corselets, helmets, double-pointed swords, won from remote

Maori islanders. Our eyes, passing along heavy mantel-shelf and wainscoting, beheld everywhere the blazoned heraldry of beauty: vases from China and old Japan, bronze bowls from Bagdad, encrusted green by time; great Persian trenchers of carven brass; symbols new and old of the splendid lineage of art. And above them the firelight flickered over rich old pictures — Rembrandt, Terburg, Lotto, and many another, inherited and brought over sea from the unprotesting past. Unearthly forces were awake that night; perhaps the deities of the hearth knew that we were there for farewell, and were kind.

We sat quietly in the firelight, among large swaying shadows. John Root was at the piano, yielding gradually to the inspiration of the place and hour. I listened to his wandering improvisations, and watched the train of "wise and foolish virgins," whose winged angels dealt them joy or doom so loftily above me, all in the compass of a gilded frame. A crowd of dreams beckoned me, led me onward, under banners that gleamed and flared. I passed beyond walls with them, beyond lands and waters, skies and stars; beyond sense and thought and life, into freedom of space and time. It was one of those rare hours when all influences conspire toward perfection and completeness of beauty, when art conquers the soul and bears it away.

The others felt the magic also, for we did not get back to the plane of earth that night. At last the music ascended the liquid silver notes of Lohengrin's farewell, and faded off into a long silence. And then talk took up the quest of beauty, and pursued her into strange places — into science, into democracy, into the future. And John Root's imagination swept over boundaries and barriers, and led our enthusiasm toward conquests which should dim the triumphs of the past, and restore to men their rights in art.

STUDIO OF WILLIAM PRETYMAN

We could see the dawn of the great day, and all of us would have vowed to hasten its coming, so contagious was the enthusiasm of the hour. Music, color, architecture — each enlarged its scope and purpose in that night of prophecy, and the arts united, confessed their dependence upon each other, and became one for the joy of man.

The watchword of the prophet was truth. Truth was the token which was to achieve these miracles. We must be true to our country and our time, true to the needs of our own people — their hopes and aspirations, as Greek artists were true to theirs. We must neglect no detail that will help us to know the truth, scorn no sympathy that will help us to feel the common life. And thus into imaginative souls will pass the universal strength from which alone great art can be evolved.

It is a joy to recall thus this man's enthusiasm, the activity of his mind, the power of his will. These were a force while he lived — a force which people were beginning to feel joyously, extravagantly. It was during the last month of his life that I talked with one of the city's typical business men, one of those large-headed, great-hearted leaders whom history at last will do justice to; one who, having employed Root, had gradually learned to love him. "Is n't John doing magnificent work now!" he exclaimed, his eyes on fire with enthusiasm, and his whole heart in his voice; "I tell you, I believe he is the greatest architect who ever lived!" "Phidias and Michel Angelo and the Goths are nowhere, I suppose," I protested, with a smile. "He will stand with them and men will acknowledge it some day," he insisted, and dwelt upon his reasons for thinking so. And the critics also were beginning to expect great things from him. On the evening of the fifteenth of January the late James W. Scott, editor of the Chicago "Herald," was dining in New York with a party of journalists, when one of them, Mr. W. M. Laffan, of the New York "Sun," speaking of art in the West, said: "You have a man of genius out there — from John Root we may expect anything." Mr. Scott's generous heart warmed at this praise of his friend, ignorant that he had died within the hour. Afterwards Mr. Henry Van Brunt called him "one of the most interesting personalities in the history of modern architecture;" and Mr. Montgomery Schuyler, at a banquet of builders in New York, spoke of the "true sincerity" of his work, and said: "I don't know any greater loss that could have happened to the architecture of this country and to the architecture of the future than that man dying before his prime."

The warmth of his personality went into his work; people felt it in the heart, as well as apprehended it in the head. It was perhaps his lack of egotism that made it impossible for men to be cold to him. They obeyed him and imagined they were but following their own desire. Practical men of business achieved his extravagances for beauty, thrilling with an enthusiasm they fancied all their own — an enthusiasm which he also credited to them rather than himself. And no one stopped to realize that he was the motive power behind many a fine enterprise until the sense of collapse came when he died.

Like all the leaders of the Exposition, he was constantly in demand during that autumn and winter of 1890, not only for the work that belonged to his office, but also for the more trying duties of entertainment. Distinguished persons from far and near, foreign commissioners and exhibitors — men upon whose good-will depended the success of the Fair, were coming to Chicago one after another; and the chiefs of the great enterprise had to receive them suitably and give them banquets. It is said that one high official resigned his post because of — not the work, but the dinners, which he could not escape, and which his health would not endure. Sometimes Root enjoyed this rôle of Columbian host, and sometimes he was unutterably bored by it; but he never discerned that these irregular hours, these crowds and talks and witty speeches, were exhausting his nervous energy. It was his instinct to respond to all demands, and no one connected with the Fair could do so much for it in this way as he. Many a traveler carried away a vivid impression of his power and charm, and mourned for him afterwards with a sorrow usually born only of long intercourse.

He had taken no rest for a number of years except a beggarly week or two each summer at the seashore, so we were rather glad of the little journey which opened the new year. Old friends who saw him in New York reported his high spirits. He returned by way of Atlanta, where one of the firm's buildings was being erected, and where his father resided with his sister and her family.

After a nine-days' absence, he reached home on his forty-first birthday, the morning of Saturday, the tenth of January. He went down to the office in a gay humor, and that very day received a commission for a large commercial building. It was a very polite gentleman who came in to offer it. "Now, Mr. Root," he said after their talk, "you will give me a beautiful building, won't you?"

"We shall try to, Mr. X.," replied the architect.

"Much of your work I like very much," continued the polite gentleman, "but — will you permit me to be quite frank?"

"I desire it above all things."

"Many of your buildings are remarkably successful; but — there are one or two I do not like quite so well."

"Very natural, I am sure," said Root.

"I suppose my taste is at fault, but — may I venture upon a criticism?"

"You could not do me a greater favor."

"Well, then, Mr. Root," — it was difficult for so polite a gentleman to confess his trouble, — "I like most of your buildings immensely, but — I do not like the Montauk Block."

Root put his hand on his critic's shoulder and shocked him black and blue by exclaiming, "My dear Mr. X., who in h—— does?"

That Saturday occurred an informal meeting of most of the members of the board of architects — those who lived in town and those who had just arrived for the Monday conference. This talk prepared the ground a little for the next week's work. When it was over, Root invited the visiting architects to come on Sunday evening to his house for an informal supper with a few friends. And then he left the office and went home.

He had confessed fatigue to a friend, but to his family he gave no hint of this, beyond telling of his relief in being at home once more. Labor, responsibility, weariness, made him conscious more keenly than ever of the joy of his life, and brought back his boyish preference for idleness. He longed to throw off all care, and talked to his wife of their wandering off somewhere in the summer for a long rest. "After the fifteenth I shall not be so busy," he said, as for weeks he had been saying it. After the fifteenth, when the conference would be adjourned and the work apportioned, he had long assured us that the heaviest strain would be over.

The next day — the last of his strength — passed quietly. A stroll to a sculptor's studio; a drive to the office for an

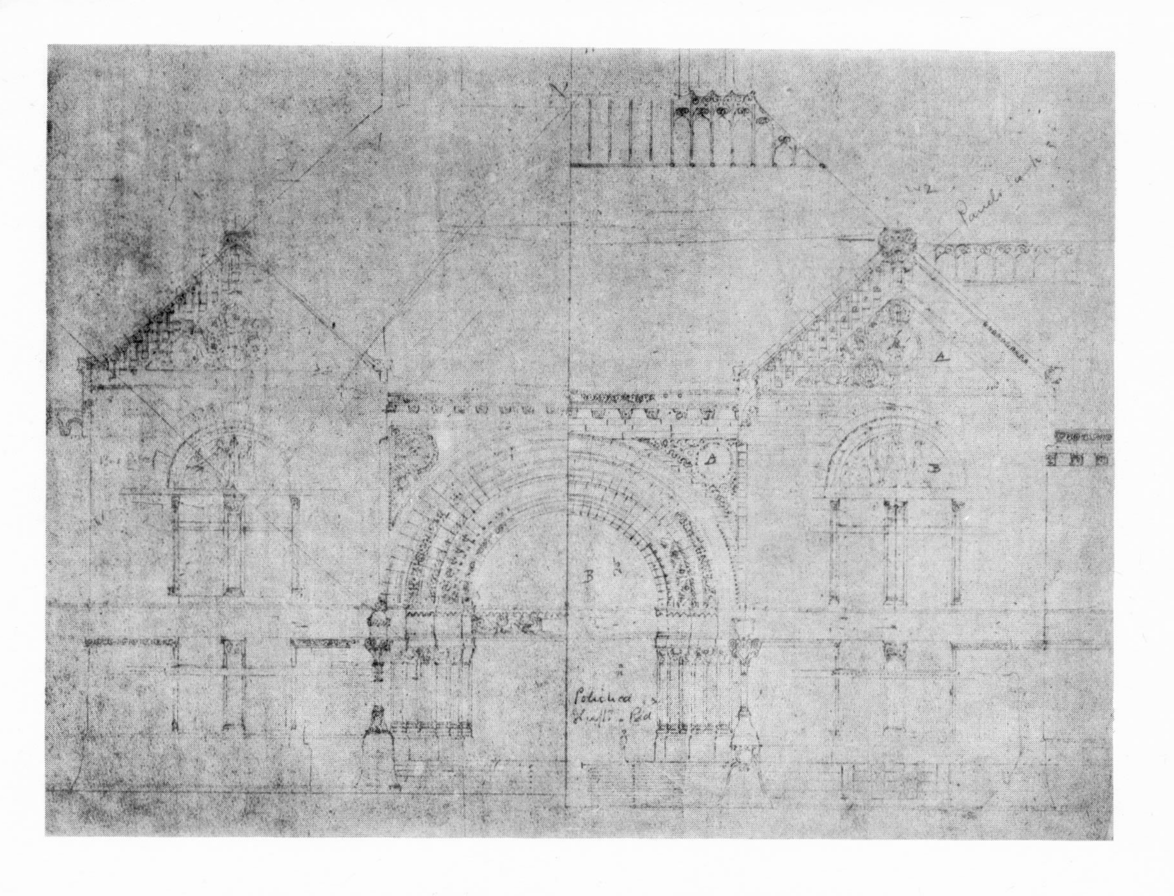

MUSEUM OF FINE ARTS, FINAL DESIGN OF CENTRAL PAVILION

Facsimile Reduction of Mr. Root's Sketch

hour or so of work on Mr. X.'s building, before he left his office and his work forever; an hour of singing with the children; and the evening with the architects and a few friends familiar to the house, meeting there together for the last night of its joy.

The next morning he awoke early with the fatal pain in his chest, and before many hours we knew that pneumonia was upon him — the one enemy against whom the physicians had always warned him as most dangerous to a man of his build. "I have n't escaped sickness all my life," he said, "to get off easily now. I knew, when my turn came, it would be a Tartar." But he took it very lightly, and in spite of the fierce pain inevitable in this malady, he never made a single complaint, or gave any sign of impatience. He kept the nurses laughing with merry speeches, and while all others were terrified, he was serene and gay.

Thus four days passed, he still incredulous of his illness. On the first he sent to the office for a drawing-board, intending to work in bed, like Richardson, on Mr. X.'s building; but gradually the thought of his work faded from his mind, which dwelt more and more tenderly with music. The last day was Thursday, the fifteenth of January, the day he had looked forward to so long as the beginning of rest.

Years before, in his early manhood, he wrote to his mother, after the early death of a friend: —

"In spite of one's philosophy, it seems hard that a young fellow should be called in the very hey-day of his life to leave it, before his powers are fully ripe, and before he has acquired control of himself to do much really effective labor. He seems to go into the other world unprepared — untutored, so to speak. His capacities for work are only just awake, so that he seems to enter on his great Life's labor like an apprentice. It is very difficult for the servants to see why the Master allots us all our places here as He does, much more why He allots to so many unskilled workmen places in His other workshop."

If he had thought of death during these four days, the coming change might have called forth something of this old wonder at his own incompleteness. But life beckoned everywhere; he could not see the veiled figure in the shadow. His power of instantaneous adjustment would have served him now as always, and one may regret that the opportunity was not given him of greeting death face to face, of hailing the "great Life" which had never seemed to him remote or cheerless. To his belief this mighty change was nothing — a mere transition from a world of incomplete conditions to one fit for the gradual purification and fulfillment of the soul's desire and energy. He would have achieved the new outlook in an instant, and died as he lived — gladly, without a murmur of reluctance, passing not into the dark, but toward the light. But the supernal herald came invisibly, and veiled his eyes with visions. The old dream of soaring through the air — a sensation long familiar to his sleep — came back to him often now. In the last hours, sweet illusions assailed his brain, and he talked of them to the women around him, calling these still by name. "Do you see that?" he said; "is n't it beautiful — all white and gold!" As the early night came on, he whispered huskily, "Do you hear that music?" And when they assured him it was lovely, his fingers played the celestial air, and his voice grew rich and deep once more for the last large words — "That 's what I call music — grand."

And so, into color and music, his soul passed out from

earth. The glowing eyes flamed up like a meteor, and then grew cold. He was dead.

It was said in the city that never before had so many strong men wept for the loss of one among them. Journalists could scarcely write of him for tears. Men whom he had aided sobbed like children when they heard the news. In the throng at his funeral, few tried to control emotion. Men high in the councils of the Fair despaired of it. "Any one in town might have died," said one of these, "lawyer, banker, minister — and his place could have been filled. But this loss is forever." And another compared this death to the fall of a general at the head of his army; "the rest of us will gather together and do the best we can, but the mind is gone."

"The wonderful thing about him," said one, "was the complete harmony of the man. He was equally developed at all points — a brain magnificently equipped, a character perfectly rounded; of how many could this be said, even among the great?" To his head draughtsman his name was a word of magic. "How do I know he was a great man?" he cried; "by the trouble I have in working out a bit of his detail — only so big." A fellow-artist spoke of his modesty, "in one so great the final proof of greatness." And another of the guild likened his career to Apollo's pursuit of Daphne: "He followed the spirit of beauty over hills and fields, and when his arms opened to clasp her she turned into the laurel."

Many tributes were brought to grace his memory — tributes of love, of praise, of sorrow. In the "Inter-Ocean" Mr. Elwyn A. Barron wrote: —

"Nothing is rarer than a many-sided mind equally fortified on every side; but this, so far as it was possible with a young man immersed in the manifold duties and responsibilities of an exact and exacting profession, was the character of mind that made John W. Root, at the age of forty years, one of the master spirits of the West and one of the foremost architects of the world."

The late Eugene Field, who was so soon to follow his brother artist, thus consecrated a long friendship : —

"The death of John W. Root removes from the midst of us the figure preëminently conspicuous among the young men of Chicago : in it we all recognize a grievous, irremediable public calamity. . . .

"His capacity for work was prodigious, and all that he did was done well and done quickly. Thorough intelligence characterized every performance of his. . . . He was essentially a social and a winsome man. His conversational powers were extraordinary : there seemed to be no subject which he had not investigated and in which he was not profoundly learned. Art, literature, history, politics, the sciences, philosophy — these things had been exhausted in his studies, and to the discussion of them and kindred topics he brought in charming reinforcement an immense fund of anecdote and an inexhaustible treasury of wit, conveyed always in the choicest of idiom. His humor was at all times refreshingly cordial, marked by exceptional delicacy ; he was a man of deep feeling, and he was easily moved ; he was keenly sensible to the influences of pathos and of mirth alike. . . .

"Successful to a remarkable degree and admired by all with whom he came in contact, his relations with all were tempered with singular modesty, thoughtfulness and benevolence ; he was charitable, kindly, liberal ; now that his strong brain and warm heart and willing hands are at rest, the stately edifices that bear witness to his genius, bespeak for him our reverential regard far less potently than does the memory of the brave, generous personality that shall gladden us no more on earth." *

And Mr. Williston Fish, knowing him little, but grieving sorely for the public loss, brought a white wreath to the tomb of one who "should have died hereafter."

"Beauty and strength, skill, learning and wisdom — these follow nature, and whence they rise, and how they grow and flourish, every man may know. But there is a thing above these, more beautiful than beauty, stronger than force, more cunning than skill, more learned than learning, wiser than wisdom; and whence it comes, what it is, whereon it flourishes, no man knows.

"Beyond all the secrets of study there is one last touch of nature, which is Life; and there is a last touch of humanity which is Genius. Philosophers can tell us truths, scholars can recount the world's learning, instructed artists can delight the eye, apt poets can please the ear, and apprehension can match praise to the work's excellence; but when genius has wrought there is creation; there are the smiles and tears of life, and the nearest understanding is only wonder at the dear mystery.

"Genius is rare. It comes but a few times in the careers of the oldest and noblest nations. Yet a man of genius we in our brief day have had with us. Has he been too close for us to perceive altogether what he was? We have seen him from day to day in the streets, in the clubs, in all the common walks of common men. And seeing him so he seemed but as others — the best of others — talking, jesting, sympathizing with his neighbors. We have seen him even in his workroom, and he was but making lines and figures and computations.

"He was one of us, yet he was not. We seem all in a common crowd and all alike, or differing but in a measura-

* From the *Chicago Morning News.*

ble degree : then we are tried by adversity, and one remains steadfast ; we are tried by war, and one rises to command our commanders ; and in the end we are tried by time, and one who sat with us is immortal. Others were heard in their day, but when their voices are silent, his still speaks on, and is forever listened to in the assemblies of the wise.

"John Wellborn Root is dead, and this city of triumphs and misfortunes, which had high triumph in his work, has suffered in his death profoundest misfortune. The city will still be great, powerful, prodigious ; but the hands — the two hands which could mould its ambition into beauty, its greatness into grandeur — are done with work.

"The city, the world, may well pause — they do pause — to consider their loss ; to recur to the past and the marvels achieved ; to regret, no matter how vainly, the future with its promise disappointed. There were beautiful forms ready to take enduring substance, and others in glorious procession would have followed, like towers upon towers, and palaces upon palaces in summer skies.

"What time does not destroy it cherishes, what it does not wear away it makes greater ; and the names of men great in art, cherished and made vast by time, weigh upon the senses of the present. Yet one may look over the earth and say that no builder of the ages wrought better from the dead stone his immortal monument than he who twenty years ago was a boy, and who now is dead.

> 'Till wasteful war shall statues overturn,
> And broils root out the work of masonry,'

he will be remembered. So long as one stone remains above another, those stones will have a tongue to proclaim his genius. For whatever remains will be right, just and beautiful beyond rules. The ruins will furnish examples for newer days." *

* From the *Chicago Morning News.*

If thou art fair, if thou art wise, if thou art fortunate; if men hearken to thy counsels and marvel at thy works; if flowers bestrew thy pathway and thy brow is wreathed with laurel; if children lift laughing eyes to thine, and the voice of thy beloved is rich like a harp with love; if thou hast followed with toil the climbing path, till the clouds are past and the summit shines golden in the sunlight; if thine eyes behold there the Vision, and thou alone canst reveal it to the children of men; if of all men thou art rarest and best beloved, till heaven can give thee nothing save time, save life: — then set thy house in order and prepare thy soul. The Lord has need of thee.

APPENDIX

APPENDIX A

JOHN WELLBORN ROOT

BY HENRY VAN BRUNT

From "The Inland Architect and News Record," January, 1891.

It is difficult, while yet our hearts are sore with a sense of bereavement, to review with eyes of cool judgment the unfinished life of a man professionally so conspicuous and personally so well beloved as John Wellborn Root. The stroke, which has deprived us suddenly of the gracious bodily presence and the active human sympathy forever, seems to throw over our memory a spell, through which the story of the bright career now closed is changed to poetry, and the voice now silent becomes a song. This pathos of death converts a memorial into a panegyric, unless the impulse of affection to gild and of admiration to extenuate is carefully corrected and chastened.

> "For it so falls out,
> That what we have we prize not to its worth,
> Whiles we enjoy it; but being lack'd and lost,
> Why, then we rack the value; then we find
> The virtue that possession would not shew us
> Whiles it was ours. . . .
> The idea of his life shall sweetly creep
> Into our study of imagination,
> And every lovely organ of his life
> Shall come appareled in more precious habit,
> More moving, delicate and full of life
> Into the eye and prospect of the soul
> Than when he liv'd indeed."

It is the fortune of every true artist to have the best, the essential part of himself made visible in his works. His mental development has a concrete, tangible expression, which can be studied and analyzed in the light of his achievements. He who would know Root as he really was — a man of genius and accomplishments, of generous impulse, of quick invention, of inexhaustible zeal — must look for him rather in what he accomplished professionally than in the accidents and incidents of his external career. [Here follows a sketch of his life.]

The peculiar alertness and openness of his mind, his hospitality to every form of intellectual appeal, his wide information, and his quick sympathy with art in all its forms, attracted to him the affectionate interest of the most advanced society of Chicago. He was an active member of its best organizations for the encouragement of literature and art. His clients became his friends, and he had the capacity of so impressing them with his force of character and with the generosity of his zeal in their service, that his work was to an unusual extent relieved from the interference of lay prejudice, and expressed, not a compromise, but the attitude of his mind at the moment of composition. He designed with marvelous rapidity and correctness of touch, reaching his conclusions at a bound. In his office he was the wise counselor and sympathetic friend of the draftsmen. His recognition by the profession as a leader is evident in the fact that he was the second secretary of the Western Association of Architects, its third president, and for six years a member of its advisory board. Upon the consolidation of the association with the American Institute of Architects, under the latter title, he was appointed to the especially responsible office of secretary, and was reëlected for the second term at the last annual convention. . . .

The work accomplished by the firm during the eighteen years of its existence is, numerically, of almost unprecedented magnitude, and in quality always interesting and scholarly, frequently brilliant and original, very rarely commonplace or merely conventional. It is generally understood that in the division of labor in the firm of Burnham & Root, the latter had charge of the department of design. But Burnham's influence throughout their whole joint career was undoubtedly very great and very salutary, not only as a restraint to exuberance, and as a power of especial sanity and force in the combination, but as an organizer, who made possible the efficient conduct of its large and complicated affairs, and brought its work into sympathy with the practical views of the commercial public.

A list of his works has been taken from the books of the firm, and represents, approximately, the order in which they were executed. These include forty-four structures of a public character, such as office buildings, hotels, churches, apartment buildings, schools, railway stations, etc., in Chicago; twenty-five of the same classes elsewhere; eight buildings to cost from $400,000 to $1,000,000 each, in course of erection, and one hundred and twenty residences of the first class.

I cannot review the more important of the many works enumerated without recognizing the fact that they touch, in importance and in quality, the highest points yet attained in the characteristic architecture of the West. Clearly, they differ essentially from any contemporaneous work in other countries, and exemplify, from the earliest to the latest, in their due order, a consistent progress toward some more or less remote point of ideal perfection. But we have yet to discover whether this point is attainable on the lines which he followed. There are fewer indications in this series of the forcing of structure into archæological or academic moulds than can be found in any modern European examples of corresponding buildings. Indeed, it seems evident that no architectural form has been imposed upon these monuments, but that their decorative character has, to an unusually large extent, grown out of their conditions of structure and use. At almost every point this healthy development has been protected from extravagance, affectation, caprice, or vagaries of invention by a fine spirit of discipline and self-restraint, and by a delicate feeling for purity of line. Like all the other characteristic work of the West, this is based distinctly on romantic, as opposed to classic motifs, and there are few indications in these examples of any aim to conserve the formulas of the schools in the matter of design, though Root had the true spirit of the Renaissance ever in his mind and on his lips. "No lasting success," he said, "comes to an architect who is not grounded in classics. Life is not long enough for one to himself discover those laws of beauty which thousands of years have evolved for architecture."

Root's mind was of studious habit, and though especially subject to artistic emotions and open to a quick appreciation of beautiful form in every style, he rarely suffered the enthusiasm of the moment to betray him into archæological masquerades. With a mind so thoroughly equipped with knowledge of the history of art, and a library so full of the most tempting precedents in other styles, he never fell into the student's error of eclecticism, but remained in all his conspicuous works loyal to that essential spirit and range of progress which had its roots in the archaic Romanesque of Southern France, and may have its flower, we venture to hope, in that illimitable country of the West which was a wilderness unknown when the craftsmen of Auvergne were carving the grotesques of the porches of Arles and Trophime eight hundred years ago.

If one were asked to define what constitutes a living art, I am mistaken if he would not recite conditions of practice in design not unlike those which I have outlined in this general view of the work executed under the impulse of this bright intelligence. It had opportunity and temptation to express itself in every mood of versatility, by reason of the incessant demands made upon its resources by the exigencies of a large practice. It would be a miracle indeed if, in this public exposition of an artist's inner life, illustrated by hundreds of buildings of every grade, we did not discover occasional evidences of carelessness and haste, of momentary caprice, of indifference begotten of fatigue, when his genius was off its guard. These evidences no one was so prompt as Root himself to point out and condemn. In the recent article on the architects of Chicago, statements were printed concerning Root similar to these; his friends were indignant until they found that it was written by Root himself. A recent minister to England cleverly said, in an after-dinner speech, "The man who does not make mistakes very seldom makes anything." But on the whole, Root's enjoyment of his work was so genuine, his resources of mind were so well ordered, his loyalty to his own ideals was so thorough, that he was enabled to keep his record incorrupted by vagaries or disloyalties. In the numerous dwelling-houses built by the firm we occasionally see excursions into free classic forms, into reminiscences of Flemish-Gothic or of the transitional era of Francis I., as illustrated in the royal châteaux of the Loire; in some of them we may discover faint reflections of the caprice of the hour, which, before the national architecture had been corrected and put in the line of national development by men of education, had tyrannized over the architectural expressions of the whole country. There is also evident in these minor buildings an occasional straining for novelty at the expense of that secure repose which is indicative of an art confirmed and established, as opposed to an art experimental and progressive. Nowhere, so far as I am aware, did Root give clear evidence of his love for the classic formulas, though the spirit of order and discipline, and the chastisement of refinement, which are the direct result of classic training, and which can scarcely be obtained by any other process, are patent in all his works.

Aberrations from purity of type, expressions of personal moods, occasional absence of discipline, experiments in form and in the sentiment and application of ornament, such as I have indicated, are in themselves unavoidable incidents of a condition of vigorous progress and signs of a living art. It advances by errors. If these errors are suffered to bear fruit and to multiply, if they are permitted to create side issues, and to encourage caprices of invention so that the fundamental architectural unit is at length masked by conceits, the art is not advancing, but groping in the dark, and there is no health in it; but if they are dropped as soon as they are found to be destructive or unessential and to interfere with the purity of type, they are a part of progress.

The series of important buildings executed by Burnham & Root from 1880 to 1891, from the Calumet Club to the Temple of the Women's Christian Union at Chicago, or the Mills Building of San Francisco, show a succession of experiments in form, mainly resting on a consistent Romanesque basis. It is easy to see which of these experiments were thrown aside in subsequent buildings as contributing no desirable element to the progressive power of the style, and which of them were retained and amalgamated, so that their accretions were gradually leading the style out of its condition of mere archæological correctness into one elastic to all the new and strange conditions of structure, material, and occupation. By reason of the very intelligent and spirited manner in which Root improved his vast opportunities, by reason of the serious way in which he attacked these more monumental problems, thoroughly realizing his responsibilities to art, it was his fortune to contribute to the development of this great Americo-Romanesque experiment nearly or quite as much as Richardson did. The latter introduced the revival, and, through the unexampled vigor of his personality, had already led it on to an interesting point of development, when his career was interrupted by death; the former carried it still further toward the point of its establishment as the characteristic architectural expression of American civilization. The latter conferred upon it power, the former, variety, and both, with their trained coadjutors in the profession, have already proved that the experiment is not merely a revival, barren of results, like the neo-Gothic, the free classic or Queen Anne, and other numerous English trials, but the introduction and probable acclimatization of a *basis of design*, established upon Romanesque round-arched elements, which elements had never been carried to perfection, and were, consequently, capable of progression. It seems to have been nearly proved that, in the hands of such men as Root, upon this basis can be built an elastic system, capable of expressing any degree of strength or lightness, simplicity or complexity, force or refinement. It has also been proved, largely by his efforts, that the maintenance of the essential principles of the style does not depend upon the preservation of its peculiar original archaic character in structure or ornament, but that it can amalgamate elements from classic, Gothic, Saracenic, or even Indian sources without being diverted from its strong natural growth, and that it is capable of a variety of expression and application which makes it adjustable to the most exacting requirements of that civilization which it is our duty to express.

A careful comparative analysis of the qualities exhibited in Root's first and last more important designs, with a glance at a few intermediate buildings, will serve to illustrate how a trained intelligence in active sympathy with the spirit of his times and loyal to a leading motive of composition, progresses with the progress of general civilization, and creates an art, which is not an exotic but ultimately a flower of our native fields. This analysis will further show that this flower is not an invention but a growth, having its roots in fundamental principles illustrated by historic forms, but varied in the process of development by new conditions of society, material and methods. To this process the persistence and force of one or two strong personalities seems to be absolutely essential. Such plants will become noxious weeds unless subjected to careful culture.

I think no such growth can be detected in any other modern phase of architectural thought either here or abroad. It is high time that it should be recognized, and that the man should be duly honored who, together with the lamented Richardson, availed himself of great opportunities to develop a definite architectural system by processes so logical and reasonable as to bring it within the range of public sympathy and appreciation. Indeed, it seems hardly too much to say that those two men have created a public for architecture.

Among the earliest important works of Burnham & Root, which attracted public attention, are the Grannis, Montauk, Calumet, and Insurance Exchange office buildings. In the last named, which of the four seems to have had the most extensive influence over architectural thought in the West, we have a composition of ten stories forced into five for the sake of establishing a harmonic proportion of horizontal divisions. Of these five architectural stories, the first is a basement of two floors with round arched windows; the second, of two floors, is a colonnade of pilasters; the third, of only one floor, is occupied by a row of low segmentally arched windows; the fourth and most important, inclosing four floors, is an arcade with long pilasters, and the fifth, of one story, is a frieze of closely grouped arched windows. The scheme of design is simple, effective, and easily understood, and the Romanesque element is plainly confessed. The distribution of ornament is temperate and its archaism is chastened with somewhat of Renaissance feeling. The skyline is accentuated with a round tourette at the two corners. The porch is composed of a low entrance arch, flanked by two round tourettes, corbelled out above the impost line, nearly detached from the wall, with conical finials, and connected by a corbelled balcony as a cornice, the whole inclosing two rows of windows continuous with the order of the second architectural story. This porch has been frequently imitated. The façades are of brick and terra-cotta construction; the spandrels of the basement story are decorated with quiet diapers of terra-cotta, and those of the upper arcade with marked horizontal lines composed of alternately recessed brick courses which are continued in the frieze above and assist the main cornice of brick corbels in adequately crowning the edifice. The vertical divisions by piers are distinctly subordinated to the horizontal divisions above described. These horizontal divisions are separated by four small string courses, which are carried around the façades continuously. The whole composition is distinguished by great reserve, and many of the experiments tried in it were repeated in subsequent buildings of the firm. To me its most pleasing feature is the interjection of the low story of single windows in the middle, by which there is obtained a strong harmonic or musical contrast with the lofty stories above and below. To the absence or presence of this agreeable feature of proportion by contrast in subsequent works is to be attributed not a little of their failure or success respectively.

The new Calumet Club House, which preceded this building, is less marked as an example of style and far more conventional in general character. We miss in it the simplicity of general outline and the reserved force which Root afterward obtained. The design is crowded and busy with detail, and the skyline is worried without obtaining a satisfactory result of picturesqueness. The building, of course, has some good detail, but it seems to have had no apparent influence over Root's subsequent work. It is a significant mile-stone in his career. [This building was destroyed by fire in 1894.]

The competitive design for the Cincinnati Chamber of Commerce and the executed design for the Art Institute of Chicago belong approximately to the same era as the Insurance Exchange. The former is an emphatic break from the Romanesque succession, and indicates a mood rather than a conviction. It presents a clever study, in the contemporary English manner, of a mediæval Flemish town hall, with a lofty hipped roof, corner towers with steep conical spires, dormers fantastically crowned with capricious, flamboyant open pediments; it has the carved balconies, the original canopies, and all the other picturesque features of the Low Countries in the fifteenth century, except their chimneys, which, strangely, are not apparent in this design. The design is interesting as an exotic. Many of its features made their appearance afterward in Root's domestic work, but it had no value whatever in the work of establishing the architectural system which was the greatest result of his more serious efforts. The Art Institute, however, takes up the thread of consistent progress much more effectively, and is one of the most successful works of this period of study.

In the Rialto Building, constructed in 1886, we have a design in which the vertical elements are much more strongly accentuated than in any previous trials. Very properly, most of its characteristic features were never repeated. It was a useful lesson. It has three architectural stories, of which the first and second inclose two floors each, and the third four floors. The pilasters or piers in the last story have the expression of buttresses, and their vertical lines are somewhat coarsely interrupted at the top by heavy balconies, which serve as the main cornice, above which is a final attic story through which the pier-lines break and form clumsy pinnacles against the sky.

The office building of the Central Safety Deposit Company, otherwise known as The Rookery, built about 1886, marks another step of progress, with far more adventurous detail. In this we feel the absence of subordination and repose. It was a large field for experiment in Romanesque detail used with an amount of intrepidity which commands respect. Horizontal and vertical divisions have nearly equal value — a fatal error in an architectural composition. There is an immense deal of successful and beautiful invention in these crowded façades, of which much found its way into Root's later, better, and more temperate work. The position of this building in the succession shows, I think, into what a state of feverish energy his powers were then stirred, and how large were his resources. Though perhaps the least successful of his more important works, it is one of the most interesting and suggestive.

By this time the organization and training of Burnham & Root's office force must have converted it into an orchestra controlled by a powerful but not tyrannical spirit. In no other way can we account for the immense amount of studious and thoughtful work accomplished at this period. "The Rookery" is not only a noted example of great fertility of design, but there is nothing bolder, more original, or more inspiring in modern civic architecture either here or elsewhere than its glass-covered court. Where the work has been committed to such a multitude of new devices in construction and to such a prodigality of invention in ornament, it is not strange that one may find reasonable objection to certain points of detail. One may admire the audacity of the double iron staircase which, supported by ingenious cantilevers, ramps with double curvature out into open space, meeting at a landing in the sky, as it were, from which the straight second run rises soberly backward to the stories above. One may admire this and wonder whether such an obvious *tour de force* is worth the study which must have been bestowed upon it. Even the imaginative prison visions in the famous etchings of Piranesi, with their aërial ladders and impossible galleries, present nothing more audacious.

The American Bank Building and the Exchange Building of Kansas City, which belonged to '87 and '88, fall into the line of steady and wholesome progress. Their fenestration is ample, but they have every desirable quality of refined repose. In these brick structures are emphasized several features which have had great influence over the style. Decorative terra-cotta is built into the brick surface, forming a part of it, with excellent and appropriate effect, and the rounding of the pier angles in brickwork is used with good judgment. The harmonious proportions of both buildings are masterly, and in the high stories the iron mullions, enveloped in brick fireproofing and forming slender colonettes, form a fine note of contrast with the corresponding massive brick pier-jambs. The flat segmental bays, which resulted from the experiment in "The Rookery" building at Chicago, are here used with infinitely greater elegance and success, and the scheme of ornament, largely infused with Saracenic spirit, shows how hospitably the growing style receives such accretions, which enlarge its resources without affecting its essential qualities of dignity and strength. These are beautiful buildings.

The Phœnix Building of Chicago strikes another note of variation. Its harmonic horizontal divisions would have been perfect but for the treatment of the attic story, which is placed above the balconied cornice, and overweights the building at the top. The experiment in oriels, of which the vertical members are heavy, round, decorated columns forming the angles, three to each bay, will never be tried again. There is also introduced into this building, with curious and not uninteresting effect, a certain amount of richly carved detail, which would never have been invented in America but for the copious suggestions in certain of the barbaric topes and Buddhist temples of India. The porch of this building is of noble and interesting design.

The current works of Root — momentarily interrupted by the inexplicable providence of his death, but sure to be fruitful in the future, through the spirit which he left behind him and which cannot die — show advances so distinct in all the elements of wholesome growth; they show a mind so capacious and so facile; a spirit which so happily combined conservatism with audacity, a power of progression so marked, that his sudden taking off becomes doubly pathetic, and almost assumes the proportions of a disaster to our beloved art. At all events, in him we have lost a Hotspur, whose gallant example kept the Lamp of Life blazing like a beacon.

The eighteen-storied tower of the Masonic Temple of Chicago, now erecting, is an extreme example of the daring quality of his genius; of his wise conservatism, the great structure now constructing under the auspices of the Woman's Christian Temperance Union of Chicago, and the Mills Building of San Francisco, may stand as final and triumphant witnesses. The former is a departure so fundamental from the traditions of decorative architecture that I hardly know how to characterize it. It is a building absolutely committed to what one may call a perpendicular tyranny of pilasters, resting upon an inadequate open stylobate, and supporting two severe gables, connected by a steep roof and broken by dormers. Thirteen stories of similar use and importance, typical of an industrial hive of democratic industry, find themselves expressed here externally in an absolutely monotonous and unmitigated system of fenestration, separated by vertical piers which rise from top to bottom without incident. It is perhaps the frankest admission of a structural and economical necessity ever expressed in architectural form. Between these pilasters, 160 feet high, rise several oriels equally vertical and equally monotonous. For the interruption of these vertical lines there would be of course only the excuse of design; none are supplied either by structure or use. It is probable that in this experiment, which looks like the apotheosis of the elevator in the modern social system, it was Root's desire to permit an exceptional character of structure to have the fullest and most honest architectural expression once for all. But, as Mr. Ferguson would say, one cannot but wonder why, under this conviction of duty, the stylobate was not made more massive and more evidently capable of the vast labor intrusted to it by the structural conditions above, and why, instead of connecting his pilasters together at the top by arches, he did not finish them with offsets like buttresses, treating the structure above like a group of lanterns recessed behind aërial galleries, the skyline being broken with pinnacles, dormers, gables, and chimneys, following the suggestions contained in such spires as Ulm and Freiburg. Doubtless Root could have defended this composition with eloquence which would fascinate, while it might not convince; we are sure that it was not a caprice, for this would be contrary to the serious habit of his mind when engaged with problems of such magnitude. But his lips are sealed, and we must await with curiosity such revelations and condonations as may be supplied by the total effect in execution.

As for the Temple erecting for the Woman's Christian Union, it is a design far more orderly and sane; a vast building in two lofty pavilions, with an open recessed court between, closed at the bottom by a curtain wall continuous with the two-storied stylobate, in which is the main entrance. Architecturally the building is committed to the style of the châteaux of the Loire before they had been greatly affected by the Renaissance. The group has twelve stories, two of which are in the stylobate, seven in the walls which arise thence to the machicolated cornice, and three in the battlements and dormers above.

The angles of the pavilions are mighty, round towers engaged in the corners, starting from corbels in the stylobate, finishing with an attic or battlement story above the cornice and crowned with conical roofs. Between are two-storied dormers with steep gables, grouped with noble effect, and the masses of the building behind are carried boldly to the sky with hipped roofs. There is a light and slender but adequate lantern in the centre. The skylines of this design are beyond all praise. The serious and noble quality of the building is due to the underlying Romanesque sentiment, which, though not expressed technically, has to my mind clearly served to eliminate the luxury and gayety which distinguished its prototypes, the royal châteaux of France. It is true that the Romanesque roof is nearly lost in the late Gothic expression into which it has flowered, while in the Masonic experiment it is much more frankly retained. Between the two one cannot but admit that the Gothic device is far more architectural as the crown for a building composed of the superimposition of numerous equal stories. I think it will be generally admitted that this last adaptation of architecture to structure, or, more properly, this growth of architecture from structure on a heroic scale, is, on the whole, the finest effort of Root's genius. As an expression of strength and dignity crowned worthily by beauty and grace, no nobler example has been given in modern times.

"Great men," said Longfellow, "stand like towers in the city of God." Perhaps the architectural treatment of these structures of unprecedented height, illustrating at once the loftiness of his aspirations, the delicate sensitiveness of his genius, and his high sense of professional duty in preserving for us to the last through many experiments a single consistent basis of design, may be accepted as a fitting expression of one who seems to me to have been one of the most interesting personalities in the history of modern architecture.

APPENDIX B

The following is an approximate list of buildings designed and erected by Burnham & Root from 1882 to the death of Root, arranged as closely as possible in the order of erection. Records of earlier works were burned in the destruction of the firm's offices in the Grannis Block. No attempt has been made to revise street addresses to modern usage. All addresses are listed in the same form as used at the time of construction of the buildings.

	Owner.	Location.
Residence	E. Morley	34th and Michigan Ave.
Fountain		Washington Park.
Water tower		Union Stock Yards.
Residence	John Whittaker	Garrison & Franklin, St. Louis, Mo.
Business building	Morley Bros.	East Saginaw, Michigan.
1st Regt. Armory		Lake Front.
Residence	Owen F. Aldis	Walton Pl., near Dearborn.
Montauk Block	P. C. Brooks	Monroe St., bet. Dearborn and Clark sts.
Residence	Augustus H. Byram	29th and Michigan Ave.
Residence	C. E. Baker	34th and Indiana Ave.
Residence	J. W. Brooks	293 Ontario St.
Residence	Arthur Bingham	Prairie Ave., near 29th St.
Business building	Chicago Provision and Stock Bd. Co.	Calhoun Pl., bet. LaSalle and 5th Ave.
Residence	W. F. Cobb	Rush St., near Huron.
Residence	Arthur I. Caton	Calumet Ave., near 20th St.
Residence	Thomas Dent	Prairie Ave., near 18th St.
Store	B. J. Ettelsohn	Franklin St. and Charles Pl.
Residence	S. E. Egan	Dearborn Ave., near North Ave.
Residence	N. B. Ream	Groveland Park.
Residence	W. D. Walker	Prairie Ave., near 29th St.
Residence	A. J. Kirkwood	LaSalle Ave., near Oak St.
Dancing academy	A. E. Bournique	23d St., near Calumet Ave.
Residence	J. C. Black	Walton Pl., near Dearborn.
Warehouse	Burdette, Smith & Co.	16th St., cor. Pierson.
Calumet Club		20th and Michigan Ave.
Office building	C., B. & Q. R. R.	Adams and Market sts.
Residence	James Charnley	Division St. and Lake Shore Drive.

	Owner.	Location.
Chicago Academy of Fine Arts		Van Buren, bet. Michigan and Wabash.
Casino		Garfield Park.
Residence	Chas. W. Clingman	Washington Boulevard.
Calumet Building		La Salle, near Adams St.
Residence	Sarah O. Egan	Dearborn Ave., near North Ave.
Flats	C. W. Fullerton	Walton Pl., near Dearborn Ave.
Residence	J. F. Goddard	Topeka, Kansas.
Residence	H. A. Huntington	Walton Pl., near Dearborn Ave.
Residences (2)	C. L. Hutchinson	Prairie Ave., near 29th St.
Residences (5)	Z. S. Holbrook	Evanston.
Residence	Geo. S. Lord	Evanston.
Residence	J. A. Mason	W. Monroe St.
Residences (2)	Matthews & Cornwell	West Side.
Residence	Frank C. Osborn	Woodlawn.
Residence	Jos. Sears	Prairie Ave., near 18th St.
Residence	H. H. Schufeldt	Dearborn and North aves.
Flats	W. D. Walker	63 18th St.
Residence	J. H. Wrenn	Prairie Ave., near 29th St.
Residences (5)	W. D. Walker	Indiana Ave. and 18th St.
Residence	Clara L. Woodyatt	Indiana Ave.
Residence	E. C. Waller	River Forest.
Residences (2)	R. Strahorn	47th St., near Woodlawn Ave.
Residence	Edw. Stickney	Huron St.
Office building	A. T. & S. F. R. R.	Topeka, Kansas.
Residences (2)	Thos. R. Burch	Prairie Ave. and 25th St.
Residence	Annie Barret	Prairie Ave., near 31st St.
Residence	Geo. D. Baldwin	Prairie Ave. and 29th St.
Office building	Chas. Counselman	238–240 LaSalle St.
Residence	H. A. Christy	Washington Boulevard.
Residence	Joseph Frank	Michigan Ave., near 24th St.
Residence	S. A. Kent	2944 Michigan Ave.
Residence	W. R. Linn	Michigan Ave., near 29th St.
Residence	John A. Lynch	560 North State St.
Residence	J. H. Pearson	West Adams St.
Residence	G. W. Spofford	End of Washington Boulevard.
Residence	A. A. Sprague	Prairie Ave., near 29th St.
Schools 61st St. Dist. No. 2	Towns of Lake and Hyde Park	43d St.
Skating rink	Willoughby, Hill & Co.	Washington Boulevard.
Residences (4)	Col. Watterman	Cornell Ave., 52d and 53d.
Residence	D. W. Mills	Lake Forest.
Stores and flats	J. W. Carpenter	Seeley Ave. and Van Buren St.
Chapel	Church of the Covenant	Halsted and Baldwin Ave.
Residence	Mrs. M. F. Crosby	Woodlawn Park, north side

	Owner.	Location.
Residence	A. Crossman	Woodlawn Park, north side.
Depots (3)		Union Stock Yards.
Residence	G. V. Hankins	Michigan Ave., 14th and 15th Sts.
Insurance Exchange	N. W. Safe & Trust Co.	La Salle and Adams sts.
Court house and Jail		Kenosha, Wisconsin.
Residence	Thos. Lord	Evanston.
Montezuma Hotel		Las Vegas, Hot Springs.
Residence	John McCully	Washington Boulevard.
Residence	Geo. E. Marshall	Lake View, Illinois.
Residence	Lot P. Smith	27 Bellevue Pl.
Flats	Mrs. E. E. Springer	La Salle Ave. and Division St.
Factory	I. K. W. Sherman	Charles St. and 5th Ave.
Residence	O. C. Thompson	3336 Michigan Ave.
Residence	A. L. Thomas	Woodlawn Park, north side.
Residence	G. H. Wheeler	Prairie Ave. and 18th St.
Residence	Mrs. J. W. Whittaker	Bar Harbor, Michigan.
Residence	J. R. True	Fullerton Ave. and Halsted.
Board of Trade		Kansas City.
Residences (3)	H. M. Kinsley	Prairie Avenue.
Armour Memorial	P. D. Armour	33d and Butterfield.
Residence	E. A. Burdette	49 Bellevue Pl.
Residences (3)	C. C. Collins	Prairie Ave. and 22d St.
Residences (2)	Clara L. Woodyatt	5131–5133 Cornell Ave.
Residence	W. E. Hale	49th and Drexel Boulevard.
Residence	Geo. Healy	Cedar St., near Lake Shore Drive.
Residence	Mrs. M. C. Jones	Woodlawn Park, north side.
Residence	J. W. Leidigh	335 Ashland Ave.
Residence	F. K. Morrill	Groveland Ave. and 29th St.
Traders Building	Traders' Safe and Trust Co.	Pacific Ave., near Jackson.
Residence	C. D. Wetherell	Calumet Ave., bet. 30th and 31st sts.
Warehouse	H. Du Pont	W. 22d St. and Union.
Art Inst. of Chicago		Michigan Ave. and Van Buren St.
Residence	Edw. E. Ayer	Cor. Banks and N. State sts.
Argyle Flats		Jackson St. and Michigan Ave.
Residence	J. Winterbotham	Woodlawn Park.
The Rialto	Chicago Dept. Vault Co.	Van Buren, bet. Sherman and Pacific.
Commerce Building	Com. Vault Co.	14 and 16 Pacific Ave.
Residence	D. K. Hill	Michigan Ave. and 26th St.
Pickwick Flats	Pickwick Associated Co.	Michigan Ave. and 20th St.

	Owner.	Location.
Monument	Mr. Ayer	Harvard, Illinois.
Dime Savings Bank		Peoria, Illinois.
Buena Park R. R. Station		Buena Park, Lake View.
Residence	Julian M. Case	Marquette, Michigan.
Flats	Geo. V. Hankins	29th, bet. Michigan and Wabash Aves.
Residence	Thos. Templeton	326 Ashland Avenue.
Residence	Rev. H. Willard	Woodlawn Ave. and 56th St.
Union Depot		Galesburg, Illinois.
Y. M. C. A. Building		Kansas City, Mo.
Amer. Bank Building		Kansas City, Mo.
Residence	Chas. Counselman	Greenwood Ave. and 51st St.
The Rookery	Cen. Saf. Dep. Co.	La Salle and Adams sts.
St. Gabriel's Church		45th and Wallace sts.
Phœnix Building	Phœnix Ins. Co.	Jackson and Clark sts.
School		Evanston, Illinois, Dist. 1.
1st Pres. Church		Buena, Lake View.
Residences (4)	J. L. Houghteling	Astor St., near Goethe.
Chamber of Commerce		Peoria, Illinois.
Church of the Covenant		N. Halsted and Belden Aves.
Warehouses No. 1 and 2	Davidson & Sons	Milwaukee, Wis.
1st National Bank		Peru, Indiana.
Residence	Chas. G. Fuller	Evanston.
Residence	J. L. Lombard	Kansas City, Mo.
Residence	J. S. Mitchell	2954 Prairie Ave.
Residence	C. W. Needham	Michigan Ave., bet. 36th and 37th sts.
Residence	J. H. Nolan	Drexel Boul., bet. 49th and 50th sts.
Residence	J. C. Pennoyer	Lake Park Ave., bet. 32d and 33d.
Residence	William Pretyman	Edgewater, Illinois.
Residence	P. W. Raber	Oakwood and Grand boulevards.
Residence	W. C. Scarritt	Kansas City, Mo.
Residence	Lot P. Smith	29 Bellevue Pl.
Office		Union Stock Yards.
Bank		Union Stock Yards.
Residences (2)	Hugh R. Wilson	Davis & Forest, Evanston.
Residence	W. T. Baker	Michigan Ave. and 23d St.
Union Depot		Burlington, Iowa.

	Owner.	Location.
School	Town of Lake	District No. 2.
Haymarket Monument		Desplaines and Randolph sts.
Residence	Reg. de Koven	65 Bellevue Pl.
Exchange Building		Kansas City, Mo.
Residence	J. W. Farlin	465 N. State St.
Old retail store alterations	Marshall Field & Co.	
Midland Hotel		Kansas City, Mo.
Sanitarium	Daily News	Lincoln Park.
Flats	J. McCarthy	State St., near Cloud Court.
Residence	Max A. Meyer	2009 Prairie Ave.
Residence	L. B. Mitchell	50 Astor St.
Flats	Arthur Orr	Dempster St., Evanston.
Flats	E. E. Springer	Division St., east of La Salle.
Sun & Dovers Journal		Union Stock Yards.
Residence	E. H. Valentine	Corner Goethe and N. State sts.
Residence	V. C. Turner	112 Lake Shore Drive.
Abstract Building	Ab. Saf. Vault Co.	83 Dearborn St.
Residence	A. L. Bell	5810 Washington Ave.
Chronicle Building		San Francisco, Cal.
Office	Fidelity Trust Co.	Tacoma, Washington.
Seed Houses	W. G. Metzger	Corner 18th and Rockwell sts.
Residence	J. J. Hoyt	Kenosha, Wis.
Residence	P. J. Kasper	Evanston.
Pacific Nat'l Bank		Tacoma, Washington.
Office building	Rand, McNally & Co.	Adams, bet. LaSalle and 5th Ave.
Residence	Geo. W. Scott	Lakeside, Illinois.
Society for Savings		Cleveland, Ohio.
Residence	I. N. W. Sherman	363 Oakwood Boulevard.
Store and Warehouse	T. P. Randall	5th Ave., near Jackson.
The Cuyahoga		Cleveland, Ohio.
Residence	Mrs. G. Adams	3350 South Park Ave.
Market	Central Market Co.	State and South Water sts.
Residence	A. H. Dainty	598 Dearborn Ave.
Argo Club		E. end I. C. Pier No. 3.
St. Gabriel's Convent		45th and Wallace sts.
1st Infantry Armory		16th and Michigan Ave.
Studio	J. Gelert	333 Oak St.
Residence	W. J. Goudy	Goethe and Astor sts.
Observatory	W. E. Hale	4545 Drexel Boulevard.
Emmanuel M. E. Church		Evanston, Ill.
Union Depot		Keokuk, Iowa.

	Owner.	Location.
Daily News Building	Daily News	175 to 181 Madison St.
Residence	Geo. W. Brandt	Michigan Ave., near 13th St.
Monadnock	P. C. Brooks	Dearborn and Jackson sts.
Kearsarge	P. C. Brooks	Dearborn and Jackson sts.
Herald Building	Chicago Herald	158 Washington St.
Masonic Temple		State and Randolph sts.
Mills Building	D. O. Mills	San Francisco, Cal.
Great Northern Hotel		Dearborn and Jackson sts.
Woman's Temple	W. C. T. U.	La Salle and Monroe sts.
Equitable Building		Atlanta, Ga.

INDEX